John Albert Broadus

Sermons and Addresses

John Albert Broadus

Sermons and Addresses

ISBN/EAN: 9783337159603

Printed in Europe, USA, Canada, Australia, Japan

Cover: Foto ©Lupo / pixelio.de

More available books at **www.hansebooks.com**

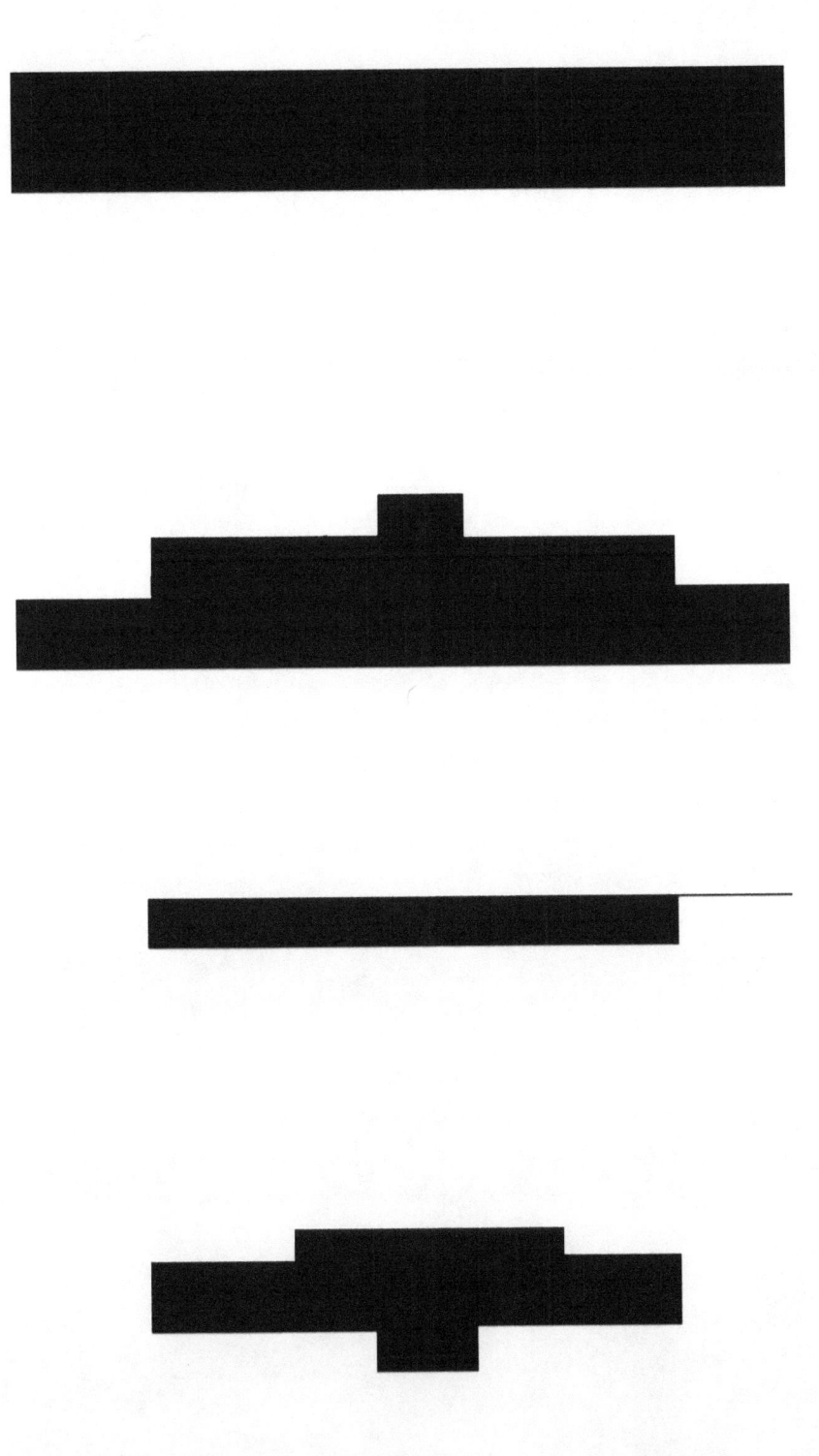

TO THE

Hon. J. L. M. CURRY, LL.D.,
UNITED STATES MINISTER TO SPAIN.

I send across the sea a slight token of our friendship. You have often shown that a man of the highest gifts as a public speaker may give to less favored men an interested and sympathetic attention. May you long live to serve your generation by the will of God.

With cordial affection,
J. A. B.

BY THE SAME AUTHOR:

A TREATISE ON THE PREPARATION AND DELIVERY OF SERMONS. New York: A. C. Armstrong & Son, 714 Broadway.

LECTURES ON THE HISTORY OF PREACHING. New York: Sheldon & Co., 724 Broadway.

A COMMENTARY ON MATTHEW. Philadelphia: American Baptist Publication Society, 1420 Chestnut St.

PREFACE.

Some of these sermons have been published in periodicals, or printed for private distribution; others are now for the first time in print. Nearly all were taken down by stenographers, whether for a periodical or for the preacher. In revising, it has not usually seemed best to remove the colloquial phrases, and the occasional breaks in construction, which naturally mark freely spoken discourse. Where necessary in order to account for illustrations or other allusions in a sermon or address, the occasion of its delivery has been stated in a note. Several of the sermons have been preached to a good many churches; and persons who remember well in that line may be interested in noticing differences, sometimes numerous and considerable, due to altered circumstances or the preacher's varying moods. Some of the addresses are quite familiar in tone; others were made on a dignified or solemn occasion.

Everything in the volume that is not of quite recent origin, has been carefully revised. The task has awakened a thousand precious memories of those among whom I have gone preaching the gospel. I pray God's blessing upon them all; and his blessing upon these printed discourses, that they may do some good.

VII.

HOW THE GOSPEL MAKES MEN HOLY.

O wretched man that I am! who shall deliver me out of the body of this death? I thank God through Jesus Christ our Lord.—Rom. vii. 24, 25 97

VIII.

INTENSE CONCERN FOR THE SALVATION OF OTHERS.

For I could wish that myself were accursed from Christ for my brethren.—Rom. ix. 3 110

IX.

THE MOTHER OF JESUS.

Mary, the mother of Jesus —Acts i. 14 124

X.

THE APOSTLE PAUL AS A PREACHER.

(Preached when chaplain to the University of Virginia.)

Unto me, who am less than the least of all saints, was this grace given, to preach unto the Gentiles the unsearchable riches of Christ.—Eph. iii. 8 . 139

XI.

THE HOLY SCRIPTURES.

And that from a child thou hast known the holy scriptures, which are able to make thee wise unto salvation through faith which is in Christ Jesus.—2 Tim. iii. 15. 155

XII.

ON READING THE BIBLE BY BOOKS.

Address before the International Convention of Young Men's Christian Associations at Cleveland, Ohio, 1881 167

XIII.

MINISTERIAL EDUCATION.

(Sermon before the Baptist Society for Ministerial Education in Missouri.)

Give diligence to present thyself approved unto God, a workman that needeth not to be ashamed, handling aright the word of truth.—2 Tim. ii. 15 . . 198

XIV.

AMERICAN BAPTIST MINISTRY IN A.D. 1774.

Address at the opening of a session of the Southern Baptist Theological Seminary 216

XV.

COLLEGE EDUCATION FOR MEN OF BUSINESS 248

XVI.

EDUCATION IN ATHENS.

Address before the Society of Alumni of the University of Virginia 268

XVII.

MEMORIAL OF GESSNER HARRISON.

Read before the Society of Alumni of the University of Virginia 303

XVIII.

AN EMINENT MAN OF SCIENCE AN EARNEST CHRISTIAN.

Address at a banquet in honor of Dr. J. Lawrence Smith, Louisville, Ky., 1879. 348

XIX.

FUNERAL SERMON FOR G. W. RIGGAN, D.D.

(*In the Broadway Baptist Church, Louisville, Ky.*, 1885.)

For none of us liveth to himself, and none dieth to himself. For whether we live, we live unto the Lord; or whether we die, we die unto the Lord; whether we live therefore, or die, we are the Lord's—ROM. xiv, 7, 8 . . . 352

XX.

THE CONFEDERATE DEAD.

At Cave Hill Cemetery, Louisville, 1886 368

XXI.

MEMORIAL OF A. M. POINDEXTER, D.D.

Read before the Virginia Baptist Historical Society, November, 1886 373

SERMONS AND ADDRESSES.

I.

WORSHIP.*

God is a Spirit, and they that worship him must worship him in spirit and in truth.—John iv. 24.

JESUS was tired. The little that we know of the history just before, yet enables us to see cause why He should have been tired.

He had been, for long months, engaged in active efforts to save men's souls—to lift men out of their sluggishness and worldliness toward God. That is hard work for mind and heart. And he had been at work among many who were hostile. The disciples of John were some of them envious that their master was decreasing and another was increasing, though John said it was right and good; and when the Pharisees heard that Jesus was now making and baptizing more disciples than John, they were jealous. They made it needful that he should withdraw from Judea, as so often during his brief ministry he had to withdraw from the jealousy of his enemies or the fanaticism of his friends, and seek a new field. Worn out and perhaps sad at heart, the Redeemer sat alone by Jacob's well.

* At the dedication of the Second Baptist Church in St. Louis, 1879.

Our artists owe us yet two companion pictures,—the one of Jesus, as the disciples saw him when they turned back to look, on their way to buy food, as he sat and rested, leaning with limbs relaxed, with face weary, yet gentle; and the other of Jesus as they found him when they came back, sitting up now with an animated look on his face, busily, eagerly talking.

Ah! there was an opening to do good, and he who "went about doing good" would give up even his needed rest, and often did, we know, to do good to the least and the lowest. The disciples wondered not that he was ready to do good; they had seen that often already. They wondered that he was talking with a woman, for that was contrary to the dignity of a man according to the ideas of that time and country,—to be seen talking with a woman in public. They wondered; they knew not yet what manner of spirit they were of,—that they had to deal with high saving truths that break through all weak conventionalities.

They would have wondered more if they had known what he knew full well,—that it was a woman of bad character; and yet he saw in her potencies for good, and he did win her that day to faith in the Messiah who had come, and sent her forth to tell others to come and see "a man who had told her all things whatsoever she did."

But she shrank in the process. Beautiful and wonderful it is to see how admirably our Lord led the casual conversation with a stranger so as to introduce the profoundest spiritual truths.

My Christian friends, let me not fail to point your

attention to this. I know no art of social life more needful to be cultivated in our time and country than the art of skilfully introducing religion into general conversation. It is a difficult task. It requires tact and skill to do this in such a way as to accomplish much good and no harm; but it is worth all your efforts. Old and young, men and women, yea—shall I say it?—especially young ladies, who are Christians, with that control which young ladies have in our American society, need to cultivate few things so much as just that power which the Saviour here showed. Oh! beautiful, blessed example of Jesus! How it shines more and more as we study and strive to imitate it! And not only did he lead on toward religious truth, but he knew how, in a quiet, skilful way, to awaken her consciousness to a realization of her sinfulness, so that she might come near to spiritual truth. She shrank from it, I said, as people will often shrink from us when we try to bring truth home to their souls. She shrank, and while not wishing to turn the conversation entirely away from religious things, she would turn it away to something not so uncomfortably close, and so she asked him about a great question much discussed.

"Sir, I perceive that thou art a prophet. Our fathers did worship in this mountain," and right up the steep slopes of Mount Gerizim she would point to the mount high above them, where were the ruins of the old temple of the Samaritans, destroyed a century and a half before. "Our fathers worshipped in this mountain; and ye say that in Jerusalem is the place where men ought to worship. O prophet, which is it?" Again the

Redeemer, while he answers her question, will turn it away from all matters of form and outward service, and strike deep by a blow into the spiritual heart of things. "Woman, believe me, the hour is coming, when neither in this mountain nor in Jerusalem shall ye worship the Father." He will not fail to imply in passing that Jerusalem had been the right place. "Ye worship that which ye know not. We worship that which we know, for salvation is from the Jews"—he only mentions that in passing—"but the hour cometh and now is, when the true worshippers shall worship the Father in spirit and truth, for such doth the Father seek to be his worshippers."

Only spiritual worship will be acceptable to God; this is what he seeks, and, more than that, this is what the very nature of the case requires. "For God is a spirit, and they that worship him must worship him in spirit and in truth."

I wish to speak of the worship of God, and I shall ask two very simple questions about it, and try to some little extent to answer each of them.

Why should we worship God? How should we worship God?

I. A man might well draw back and fear to say one word as to reasons why we should worship God. Oh! how high, and wide, and deep, that theme! And yet it may be useful just to remind you of some things included in these expressions. Why ought we to worship God? Because it is due to him; and because it is good for us.

(1.) That we should render to God worship is due

to him. My dear friends, if we were but unconcerned spectators of the glorious God and his wonderful works, it ought to draw out our hearts to admiration and adoration and loving worship. The German philosopher, Kant, probably the greatest philosopher of modern times, said: "There are two things that always awaken in me, when I contemplate them, the sentiment of the sublime. They are the starry heavens and the moral nature of man." Oh! God made them both, and all there is of the sublime in either or in both is but a dim, poor reflection of the glory of Him who made them. Whatever there is in this world that is suited to lift up men's souls at all ought to lift them towards God.

Robert Hall said that the idea of God subordinates to itself all that is great, borrows splendor from all that is fair, and sits enthroned on the riches of the universe. More than that is true. I repeat, all that exalts our souls ought to lift them up toward God. Especially ought we to adore the holiness of God.

O sinful human beings, still you know that holiness is the crown of existence. There is not a human heart that does not somehow, sometimes love goodness. Find me the most wicked man in all your great city, and there are times when that man admires goodness. Yea, I imagine there are times when he hopes that somehow or other he may yet be good himself. When a man we love has died, we are prone to exaggerate in our funeral discourse, in our inscriptions on tomb-stones and the like—to exaggerate what? We seldom exaggerate much in speaking of a man's talents, or learning, or possessions, or influence, but we are always ready to exaggerate his goodness. We want to make the best of the man in that solemn hour. We feel that goodness is the great thing for a human being when he has gone out of our view into the world unseen. And what is it that the Scriptures teach us is one of the great themes of the high worship of God, where worship is perfect? Long ago a prophet saw the Lord seated high on a throne in the temple, with flowing robes of majesty, and on either side adoring seraphs did bend and worship, and oh! what was it that was the theme of their worship? Was it God's power? Was it God's wisdom? You know what they said—"Holy, holy, holy, is the Lord of hosts. The whole earth is full of His glory." And there do come times, O my friends, to you and me, though we lift not holy hands, for we are sinful, though we dwell among a people of unclean lips, there come times to you and me when we want to adore the holiness of God.

And then think of his love and mercy! If you were only unconcerned spectators I said—think of his love and mercy!

He hates sin. We know not how to hate sin as the holy God must hate it. And yet how he loves the sinner! How he yearns over the sinful! How he longs to save him! Oh, heaven and earth, God so loved the world that he gave his only begotten Son, that whosoever will have it so, might through him be saved.

I know where that great provision, that mighty mercy is adored. I know from God's word that those high and glorious ones, who know far more than we do of the glorious attributes of the Creator and the wide wonders of his works, when they have sung their highest song of praise for God's character and for creation, will then strike a higher note as they sing the praises of redemption, for holiness and redemption are the great themes which the Scriptures make known to us of the worship in heaven. John saw in his vision how the four living creatures, representing the powers of nature, and the four and twenty elders, representing the saved of God, bowed in worship, and how a wide and encircling host of angels caught the sound, and how it spread wider still, till in all the universe it rolls, "Salvation and honor and glory and power be unto him that sitteth on the throne and unto the Lamb forever and ever."

Holiness and redemption! We ought to adore if we had nothing to do with it, for we have a moral nature to appreciate it. And oh! are we unconcerned spectators? That most wonderful manifestation of God's mercy and love has been made towards us. And, if the angels find their highest theme of praise in what the gracious God has done for us, how ought we to feel about it? Yea, there is a sense in which, amid the infirmities of earth, we can pay God a worship that the angels cannot themselves offer.

> "Earth has a joy unknown in heaven;
> The new-born bliss of sins forgiven."

And sinful beings here may strike, out of grateful hearts for sins forgiven, a note of praise to God that shall pierce through all the high anthems of the skies and enter into the ear of the Lord God of Hosts.

(2.) But I said we ought to worship God, not only

because it is due to Him, but because it is good for us. Only the worship of God can satisfy, O my friends, the highest and noblest aspirations of our natures.

When anything lifts us up, then we want God as the climax of our exalted thought, and our thought itself is imperfect without it. If you will look, as I looked this morning, in the early light, upon the glory of the autumn woods, faded now, yet still bright, and so beautiful; if you gaze upon the splendor, as you will do when this service is ended, of the nightly skies; if you stand in awe before the great mountains, snow-clad and towering, before Hermon, before the wonderful mountains of our own wonderful West; if you go and gaze in the silence of night upon the rush of your own imperial river, or stand by the sea-shore, and hear the mighty waters rolling evermore, there swells in the breast something that wants God for its crown and for its completeness. There are aspirations in these strange natures of ours that only God can satisfy. Our thinking is a mutilated fragment without God, and our hearts can never rest unless they rest in God.

And worship, oh, how it can soothe! Yea, sometimes worship alone can soothe our sorrows and our anxieties. There come times with all of us when everything else does fail us; there come times when we go to speak with sorrowing friends and feel that all other themes are weak and vain. You, wicked man yonder—you have gone sometimes to visit a friend that was in great distress, who had lost a dear child, it may be, or husband or wife; and as you have sat down by your friend and wanted to say something comforting, you have felt that everything else was vain but to point the poor sorrowing heart to God; and you felt ashamed of yourself that you did not dare to do that. How often have devout hearts found comfort in sorrow, found support in anxiety, by the worship of God; by the thought of submission to God and trust in God; a belief that God knows what he is doing; that God sees the end from the beginning; that God makes " all things work together for good to those that love him !"

And I add that the worship of God nourishes the deepest root of morality—individual and social. Morality cannot live upon mere ideas of expediency and utility. We have some philosophers in our day (and they show abilities and earnestness that command our respect, though they may seem to us to go so sadly and so far astray) who have persuaded themselves, alas! that Christianity must be flung aside; that belief in God even must be abandoned; but they are beginning to recognize the necessity for trying to tell the world what they are going to put in place of that, for the conservation of individual and social morality; and so the great English philosopher of the present time tells us in a recent work, and the gifted author of " Theophrastus Such," who is one of his followers, has told us, that natural sympathy will lead us to recognize that we owe duties to others as well as ourselves. Natural sympathy is going to do that. Ah, I trow not. Sometimes it will, if there be something mightier that can help. Often natural sympathy will fail. The root of morality is the sentiment of moral obligation. What does it mean when your little child first begins to say " I ought to do this " and

I ought not to do that?" What does it mean? "I ought." The beasts around us are some of them very intelligent. They seem to think in a crude fashion. They seem to reason in a rudimentary way. Our intellect is not peculiar to us. They have something of it, but they show no sign of having the rudiments of the notion that "I ought" and "I ought not." It is the glory of man. It marks him in the image of the spiritual one that made him. And what is to nourish and keep alive and make strong that sentiment of moral obligation in our souls, unless it be the recognition of the fact that there is a God who gave us this high, moral, spiritual being; who made us for himself; to whom we belong, because he made us, and because he made us to love him until the sentiment of obligation to him shall nourish in us the feeling of obligation to our fellow-men, who, like us, are made in his image.

But we are told that there is going to be a moral interregnum shortly; that so many cultivated men in England and in some parts of our country are rejecting all religion; that now there is danger that society will suffer until the new ideas can work themselves into popular favor. Yes, indeed, society would suffer but for one thing, and that is that still there are and still there will be not a few among the cultivated, and many, thank God! among those who are not blessed with cultivation, who hold fast their faith in the only true God and in Jesus Christ whom he has sent, and that will conserve society and hold up the very men who fancy they can do without Christianity.

For this reason, if there were no other, it would be

worth while to build great and noble churches in our great cities, as we build monuments for other things to remind men of grand events and heroic deeds; so that if churches were never entered, they would be worth building as memorials, as reminders of God and eternity. Amid the homes of wealth and luxury, amid the splendid centres of commerce, and amid, alas! the palaces of vice, our churches stand serene and still, pointing up, like the Christian's hope, toward heaven. The thoughtless, the wayward, worldly and wicked will sometimes look as they pass, and as from the monuments over some heroic dead man, they catch a moment's impression for good, so from the church edifice itself they will catch a momentary impression of higher things, and be at least a little restrained from what is wrong and a little incited towards what is right.

And that is but the least of it. The great nourisher of morality in the individual and the community is not the mere outward symbol; it is the worship that is paid within. But I shall say no more on this theme. All that I can say is weak, poor and vain. How can a man tell the reasons why we should worship God? They are as high as heaven, as wide as the world, as vast as the universe; all existence and all conception—everything is a reason why we should worship God; and I turn to the other question, to which the text especially points.

II. How should we worship God? I wish here to speak only of that line of thought which the text presents, How shall we worship God with spiritual worship?

The spiritual worship the text points out to us is

essentially independent of localities. Time was when it was not so: when the best worship that was to be expected in the world depended upon holy places and impressive rites. In the childhood of the race these ideas were necessary, but Christianity came as the maturity of revealed religion, and declared that those ideas should prevail no longer; that true Christian spiritual worship is essentially independent of localities.

My friends, under the Christian system you cannot make holy places; you cannot make a holy house. We speak very naturally and properly enough, if with due limitation, in the language of the Old Testament, about our places of worship, but we ought to remember constantly the limitations. You cannot consecrate a building in the light of Christianity. You can dedicate the building; you can set it apart to be used only for the worship of God; but you cannot make the house a holy house; it is an idea foreign to the intense spirituality which Jesus has taught us belongs to the Christian idea of worship. Why, then, one might say, why should we have houses of worship? not merely because if there is to be the worship of assemblies at all, with all the strange power that sympathy gives to aggregated worship, then there must be places of assembly; but because these soon become associated with the solemn worship we hold in them and sacred by their associations, and if we do not disturb those associations, if from the places where we are wont to hold solemn worship, we keep carefully away all that tends to violate those associations, they grow in power upon us; they do not make the place holy, but they make it easier by force of association and of beneficent habit for us to have holy thoughts and to pay holy worship in the place where we have often paid it before. So we can see why it is fit to set apart places of worship, houses of worship for God, though they be not in themselves holy, though spiritual worship is independent of locality.

Let us rise to a broader view of the matter. Spiritual worship must subordinate all these externals.

Can you listen a few minutes while I offer a plain, unadorned, unimpassioned statement about this really practical matter, surely suitable to our circumstances, worthy to be discussed; for there are many extremes about it among men, and though you may not go with my thought, it may help you to think the matter through for yourself. I say, then, on the one hand, spiritual worship must have its externals. For while we are spiritual, like God, we are something else also. We have a material nature, and we are all closely linked and inter-dependent and acting upon each other continually. It is idle, then, to think that our worship will be all that it is capable of becoming if we try to keep it exclusively spiritual and give it no outward expression at all. When you try to pray in private by your own bed-side, alone with your beating heart and your God, you mistake if you try to pray without couching your thought and feeling in words. We need the force of expression, though we utter not the words. We need to have the words in order to give clearness and form to our thought and our sentiment; and it is good, even when alone, in low, solemn tones to speak aloud one's private prayer, for that seems somehow, by a law of our nature, to make deeper the feeling which we thus outwardly express; and if we do so even in private prayer, how much more is it necessarily true in public worship!

We must have expression then for our worship, that there may be sympathy—expression that shall awaken and command sympathy. We must use the language of imagination and passion as in the Scriptures. The Scriptures are full of the language of imagination and passion—language that is meant to stir the souls of men. And when we sing—sing in the simplest and plainest way, if you please—we are yet striving to use that as one of the externals of spiritual worship. We need it. We must have externals. Why, then—a man might ask, and men often have asked—why not have anything and everything that will contribute at all to help the expression and cherish the devout feeling? Why not have everything in architecture, everything in painting and statuary, everything in special garments, in solemn processions, in significant posture? Why not anything and everything that may at all help as an external expression of devout feeling? Let us consider this, I pray you. I said spiritual worship must have its externals, and now I repeat that it must subordinate those externals; whatever externals it cannot subordinate it must discard, and the externals it does employ it must employ heedfully. There are some things that awaken in some men a sort of fictitious, quasi-devout feeling, which you never would think of recommending as aids to devotion. Some persons when they use opium have a dreamy sort of devoutness, and some persons, even when they become drunk, show a morbid sort of religion. Yet who would think of saying that these are acts that help to devotion? But there are feelings that are right in themselves and noble in their place that do in some cases help to promote devotional feeling. The husband and wife, when they bow down with their children by their sides to pray together, and then, rising up, look lovingly into each other's eyes, find their devout feeling towards God heightened by their love for each other and their children. I can fancy that the young man and maiden who both fear God and have learned to love each other may sometimes feel their devout sentiments truly heightened by this new, strange and beautiful affection which they have learned to feel for each other. That is so sometimes, and yet everybody sees that to recommend that as an avowed and systematic thing to be used as a help to devotion would be out of the question. Not everything, then, that may promote devotion is to be regularly used for this purpose.

There are some things that look as if they were necessary, are very often recommended as helpful, and often employed as helps, that turn out to be dangerous and erroneous. Why can't we use pictures and statuary as helps to devotion? Why can't we employ them as proper means of making the thought of our Saviour near and dear to us? Well, in all the ages of the world, the heathen have tried this. An educated young Hindoo, some years ago, educated in England, wrote an essay in which he complained bitterly that the Hindoos were accused of worshipping images, and quoted

Cowper's beautiful poem entitled, "My Mother's Picture:"

> "O, that those lips had language!
> Years have passed since thee I saw."

And he says, the picture of the poet's mother brought close and made real the thought of one long dead. That is the way, he said, that we use images. But that is not the way that the great mass of men use images in worship. They have often meant that at the outset; but how soon it degenerated and was degraded, and these things that were meant as helps to worship dragged down the aspirations of human hearts, instead of lifting them up! But, it seems to me, if I were to employ such helps in our time, persuading myself that they would be good, that I should feel it was wise to go back to the old ten commandments that we teach our children to repeat, and cut out the second commandment, that expressly forbids the use of graven images, because it necessarily leads to idolatry. I should cut that out. You can inquire, if you are curious to do so—and I say it in no unkindness—you can inquire whether those Christians in our own time and country who employ pictures and statuary to-day as helps to devotion have mutilated the ten commandments. They were obliged to leave out that which their little children would say was forbidding what they do.

Aye, the world has tried that experiment widely and in every way, and it is found that though you might think that pictures and statuary would be helps to devotion, they turn out to be hurtful. They may help a few; they harm many. They may do a little good; they do much evil.

But there are some of these things which we must have to some extent,—church buildings, architecture, music, cultivated eloquence. How about these? We are obliged to have these. We must have the rude and coarse, if we have not the refined and elegant; and just what we may have in this respect—why, it depends, of course, upon what we have been accustomed to in our homes, our places of public assembly, our halls of justice. That which is natural, needful and good for some would utterly distract the attention of others. Take a man from the most ignorant rural region, utterly unused to such things, and place him in this house next Sunday morning, and his attention would be utterly distracted by the architectural beauties of the place and the strange power of the music, and he would be scarcely able to have any other thought. These things would be hurtful to him; but to those who have been used to them and who, in their own houses, have been accustomed to elegance and beauty, or in the homes of others they sometimes enter, or in the great places of public assembly in the cities where they live, these things need not be hurtful to them. They may be helpful to them. Ah, my friends, they need to be used by us all with caution and with earnest efforts to make them helpful to devotion, or they will drag down our attention to themselves. Often it is so. You go home with your children, talking only about the beauty of your house of worship or the beauty of the music, and how soon your children will come to think and feel that that is all there is to come to church for, and how many there are who do thus think and feel.

It is easy to talk nonsense on the subject of church music. It is very difficult to talk wisely. But I think we sometimes forget in our time that there is a distinction between secular and sacred music. I have seen places where they did not seem to know there was such a distinction. They seem to have obliterated it by using so much purely secular music in sacred worship. It is a distinction not easy to define, I know, but easy enough to comprehend on the part of one who is cultivated and has an ear for music and a heart for devotion. It is a distinction that ought always to be heedfully regarded. Our beautiful church music I delight in. I have sat here this afternoon and evening, and it has done me good to listen to it; but we must learn to use it as a help to devotion, or else we are using it wrong, and it will do us harm. We must not only cultivate the use and enjoyment of artistic music for the sake of enjoyment, but what is far more than enjoyment, we must cultivate the power of making it a help to religious worship. We must learn to do that, or we must refuse to have it. There is danger here. My friends, you should rejoice in the high privileges of cultivated society and refined homes, beautiful places of worship, glorious sounds of music and a lofty style of eloquence; but there is danger for you. I have heard people say sometimes: "I don't believe in the religion of the negroes. I go to the place of worship of the negroes, and I find they work themselves into a mere animal excitement. They sway their bodies, and parade around the room, and shake hands, and shout, and embrace each other, and work up mere animal excitement;

but there is no religion in that." Oh, you child of culture! Go to your beautiful place of worship, with its dim, religious light, its pealing organ, its highly cultivated gentleman, trained in elegant literature to speak in a beautiful style, as he ought to do, and you may have excited in you a mere æsthetic sentiment which may have no more real worship in it than the poor negro's animal excitement. But, thank God! they sometimes really have a genuine religion about it, as genuine as yours.

There is danger there, but my friends there is always danger, and we must learn to discard that which we cannot subordinate to spiritual worship, learn to use heedfully, with constant effort for ourselves and for our families and for our friends to use that which it is right to use, that it may help and not hinder. I pray you, then, do not go to asking people to come just to see your beautiful house of worship or to listen to your noble music. Some will come for that reason alone, and you cannot help it. But do not encourage such a thought. Talk about worship. Talk about these externals as helps to the solemn worship of God. Try to take that view of it. Try to make other people take that view of it. Be afraid for yourselves, and try to speak of it for its own sake and not for the sake of the æsthetic gratification it may give.

And now, my brethren, can you listen a few moments longer to some closing words? Worship: spiritual worship. I think that in most of our churches—our churches that have no set ritual, no fixed form of worship—there is a disposition to underrate the importance of public worship; to think only of the preaching. I notice that in those churches, not only our own, but those like it that have no special form of worship, they always give notice for preaching and not for worship, they only talk about the preacher and not the worship. They seem to think it makes little difference if they are too late for worship, provided they are there in time for the sermon. I notice that many preachers seem to give their whole thought to their sermon, and think nothing of preparing themselves for that high task, that solemn, responsible undertaking, to try to lift up the hearts of a great assembly in prayer to God. What I wish to say is, wherever that may be true, let us consider whether we ought not to take more interest in our worship, in the reading of God's word for devotional impression, in solemn, sacred song and in humble prayer to God, in which we wish the hearts of the whole assembly to rise and melt together. It is true that we must have a care how we cultivate variety here, for the hearts of men seem to take delight in something of routine in their worship; they are rested if they know what comes next; they are harassed often if they are frequently disappointed and something quite unexpected comes in. We must keep our variety within limits, but within limits we must cultivate variety. I believe there should be more attention paid to making our worship varied in its interest than is usually the case; and then, oh, my brethren, something far more important for the preacher and people is this—we must put heart into our worship. We must not care merely to hear a man preach. I do not wish you to think less of preaching, but more of the other. We must put heart into our worship. Even the sermon is a two-sided thing—one side of it is part of our worship so far as it causes devotional feeling and lifts up the heart towards God, though on its other side of instruction and exhortation it is distinct from worship.

Now, I say we must put heart in our worship. Do not venture to come to this beautiful place of worship, or whatever place of worship you attend, and just sit languidly down to see if the choir can stir you or to see if the preacher can stir you. Oh! stir up your own souls. It is your solemn duty when you go to engage with others in the worship of God—it is your duty to yourself, it is your duty to others, it is your duty to the pastor who wishes to lead your worship, it is your duty to God, who wants the hearts of men, and who will have nothing but their hearts. I know how we feel. Worn by a week's toil, languid on the Lord's day through lack of our customary excitement, we go and take our places, jaded and dull, and we are tempted to think, "Now I will see whether the services can make any impression on me; whether the preacher can get hold of me—I hope they may," and we sit passive to wait and see. Oh, let us not dare thus to deal with the solemnity of the worship of God.

My brethren, if we learn to worship aright, there will be beautiful and blessed consequences. It will bring far more of good to our own souls. It will make worship far more impressive to our children. Haven't you observed that it is getting to be one of the questions of our day how the Sunday-school children are to be drawn to our public worship? We are often told that the preacher must try to make his sermon more attractive to children, and so he must. But let us also make our worship more impressive, and make our children feel that it is their duty to worship God, and try to bring them under the influence of this worship. I heard last week in Washington one of the foremost Sunday-school laborers of this country, a Methodist minister, make this statement in private. He said: "Of late I have been telling the people everywhere, if your children cannot do both, cannot go to Sunday-school and go to the public worship also, keep them away from the Sunday-school, for they must go to the public worship." You may call that an extravagant statement. I am not sure that it is extravagant, but I am sure of this, that we need not merely to try to make our preaching attract children, but to try to make the worship so solemn, so real, so genuine, so earnest, that those strange little earnest hearts of our children will feel that there is something there that strikes to their souls.

And if you have true, fervent worship of God, the stranger that comes into your place of worship will feel it too. Have you not noticed when you go into some houses how quickly you perceive that you are in an atmosphere of hospitality and genuine kindness? There may be no parade, no speech-making. Yet in some places you may feel it, you feel it in the atmosphere, you feel it at once in your soul; you see a place where they are kindly and loving. So it ought to be, that when a man comes into your place of worship he shall very soon feel a something that pervades the atmosphere he breathes, from the look of the people, from the solemn stillness, from the unaffected earnestness he shall feel that these people are genuine, solemn worshippers of God. When he feels that, he will conclude that God is with you of a truth and there will be power to move his soul in your solemn worship.

Now, my brethren, in this beautiful house which you have built for the worship of God, and are now dedicating to His worship, oh, may there be much of real spiritual worship. When your hearts are full sometimes and you come and try to throw your souls into God's worship, may you be moved and melted; when you are sorely tempted sometimes and, coming to the house of God, try to lift your heart to Him in prayer, may you get good from the wise and loving words of the man you love to see stand before you as your pastor.

As your children grow up by your side and learn to delight with you in coming to the house of God in company, oh, may you be permitted to see more and more of them gladly coming to tell what great things God has done for their souls, and gladly coming to put on Christ by baptism. And not only the children of your households, but strangers within your gates. How soon they will be pouring into this great city from the far East and the wonderful West, from all the North and all the South, and from beyond the sea! How they will, in these coming years, pour into this imperial, central city, with its vast possibilities that swell the souls of your business men, and that ought to swell the souls of your religious men. May the stranger within your gates learn here to love your Saviour and rejoice here to proclaim that love, and rise from the liquid grave to walk in newness of life. And again and again, as you gather for that simplest of all ceremonies, as it is the most solemn, which Jesus himself appointed, in all simplicity taking bread and wine in remembrance of him, may he who sees men's hearts, see always that your hearts are towards him in godly sincerity. And when offerings are asked here may they be offerings given as a part of the worship of God, offerings that come from your hearts, offerings that are accepted by him who wants the heart, offerings that are worthy of this beautiful home of your church life, and worthy to follow the gifts wherewith you have erected it. And time and again may there go forth those who have learned to worship here like successive swarms from fruitful hives to carry the same spirit of worship elsewhere, here and there, in great and growing and needy cities.

Yes, and when the young of your households begin to link those households more closely than ever together, and on the bright bridal day the brilliant procession comes sweeping up the aisle and all men's hearts are glad; may they always come reverently in the fear of the God they have here learned to worship. And O, mortal men and women, who have united to build high and glorious piles that will stand when you are gone, when in the hour of your departure from the works of your hands, and from the worship that you have loved on earth, and slow and solemn up the aisle they bear the casket that holds all that is left to earth of you, and behind come sad-faced men and sobbing women, and while the solemn music sounds through all these vaults and your pastor rises, struggling to control his own sorrow for the death of one he loved so well—O, may it be true, in that hour which is coming—may you begin from this night so to live that it shall then be true, that the mourners of that hour may sorrow here, not as those who have no hope, and that the men and women who honor you, and have gathered to pay honor to your memory, may feel like saying in simple sincerity as they look upon your coffin, "the memory of the just is blessed; let me die the death of the righteous and let my last end be like his." O begin to-day, God help you to begin from this hour of entrance into your new place of worship so to live that all this may be true when you pass away.

But one more thought. There will never be any perfect worship in this house. When was there ever any perfect worship? Once there was. There was a little obscure village; the military history of the country does not mention it; the older sacred writings do not. It was a despised village, and there was a lowly mechanic, who spent his early life in that village quietly, unpretending and unnoticed, and who used to go on the Sabbath day to the synagogue. He paid perfect worship. Oh, glorious, beautiful spectacle! He paid perfect worship, but since his day there has never been any perfect worship in this world. Shall there be any perfect worship for us then, dear hearers, who sometimes aspire towards God and long to worship him in true spirituality, but never find the full attainment? God be thanked, we have hope of that higher and better life where we shall worship without effort and without imperfection. And God help us that we may strive to worship here with all our hearts, in the hope that at last we shall worship perfectly there.

II.

SOME LAWS OF SPIRITUAL WORK.*

But he said unto them, I have meat to eat that ye know not. The disciples therefore said one to another, Hath any man brought him aught to eat? Jesus saith unto them, My meat is to do the will of him that sent me, and to accomplish his work. Say not ye, There are yet four months, and then cometh the harvest? Behold, I say unto you, Lift up your eyes and look on the fields, that they are white already unto harvest. He that reapeth receiveth wages, and gathereth fruit unto life eternal; that he that soweth and he that reapeth may rejoice together. For herein is the saying true, One soweth, and another reapeth. I sent you to reap that whereon ye have not labored: others have labored, and ye are entered into their labor.—John iv. 32-38.

THE disciples must have been very much astonished at the change which they observed in the Master's appearance. They left him, when they went away to a neighboring city to buy food, reclining beside Jacob's well, quite worn out with the fatigue of their journey, following upon the fatigues of long spiritual labors. And here now he is sitting up, his face is animated, his eyes kindled. He has been at work again. Presently they ask him to partake of the food which they had brought, and his answer surprised them: "I have food to eat that ye know not." They looked around, and saw nobody; the woman to whom he had been speaking was gone, and they said: "Has any one brought him something to eat?" Jesus answered: "My food is to do the will of him that sent me, and

* Washington Avenue Baptist Church, Brooklyn, 1884.

to accomplish his work." And then, with this thought of work, he changes the image to sowing and reaping, and bids them go forth to the harvest.

Now, from this passage with its images, I have wished to discourse upon *some laws of spiritual work,* as here set forth. For we are beginning to see, in our time, that there are laws in the spiritual sphere as truly as in the mental and in the physical spheres. What are the laws of spiritual work which the Saviour here indicates? I name four:

I. Spiritual work is *refreshing* to soul and body. "My food is," said the tired, hungry one, who had aroused himself, "to do the will of him that sent me, and to accomplish his work." We all know the power of the body over the mind, and we all know, I trust, the power of the mind over the body; how any animating theme can kindle the mind until the wearied body will be stirred to new activities; until the man will forget that he was tired, because of that in which he is interested. But it must be something that does deeply interest the mind. And so there is suggested to us the thought that we ought to learn to love spiritual work. If we love spiritual work it will kindle our souls; it will even give health and vigor to our bodies. There are some well-meaning, but good-for-nothing, professed Christians in our time, who would have better health of mind and even better health of body, if they would do more religious work and be good for something in their day and generation.

How shall we learn to love religious work so that it may kindle and refresh us? Old Daniel Sharp, who was a famous Baptist minister in Boston years ago, used to be very fond of repeating, "The only way to learn to preach is to preach." Certainly, the only way to learn to do anything is to *do* the thing. The only way to learn to do spiritual work is to *do* spiritual work, the only way to learn to love spiritual work is to keep doing it until we gain pleasure from the doing; until we discern rewards in connection with the doing; and to cherish all the sentiments which will awaken in us that "enthusiasm of humanity" which it was Jesus that introduced among men; and to love the souls of our fellow-men, to love the wandering, misguided lives, to love the suffering and sinning all around us with such an impassioned love that it shall be a delight to us to do them good and to try to save them from death. Then that will refresh both mind and body.

II. There are *seasons* in the spiritual sphere—sowing seasons and reaping seasons, just as there are in farming. "Say not ye," said Jesus, "there are yet four months and then cometh the harvest?"—that is to say, it was four months from that time till the harvest. They sowed their wheat in December; they began to reap it in April. "Say not ye, there are four months, and then cometh the harvest? behold, I say unto you, lift up your eyes and look on the fields; for they are white already to harvest." In the spiritual sphere it was a harvest time then, and they were bidden to go forth and reap the harvest that waved white and perishing. We can see, as we look back, that the ends of all the ages had now come to that time; that the long course of providential preparation, dimly outlined in the Old

Testament, had led to the state of things that then prevailed; that the fulness of the times had come, when God sent forth his Son to teach men and to atone for men, and to rise again and come forth as their Saviour, and that his servants should go forth in his name. And the like has been true in many other seasons of Christianity; there have been great reaping times, when men have harvested the fruits which come from the seed scattered by others long before.

I persuade myself that such a time will be seen ere long in the world again. I think that the young who are here present to-day—though they may forget the preacher and his prediction—will live to see the time when there will be a great season of harvest that will astonish mankind. In the great heathen world I think it will be true that the labors of our missionaries are preparing the way, and that in the course of divine providence—the same providence that overruled the history of Egypt and Assyria and Greece and Rome—the greatest nations of Asia are now becoming rapidly prepared to receive a new faith. They say, who live there and ought to know, that there is a wonderful breaking up of religious opinion in all Hindostan, with its two hundred and fifty millions of people—five times as many, almost, as in our great country—that they are learning to let go their old faiths, and that the time must soon come when, in sheer bewilderment and blindness, as it were, men will search round for something else to look upon, something else to lay hold upon. It is a sad thing to see great nations of mankind surrendered to utter unbelief, but it has often proven the preparation for their accepting a true and mighty and blessed faith. I think one can see, in the marvellous changes which are going on in Japan, a preparation for like effects there; and as Japan is, for the civilized world, the gateway into China, and our missionaries are already at work there and great changes are taking place there, so it is quite possible that even in one or two generations there will be a wide spread of Christianity in that wonderful nation of mankind. God grant that it may be so!

I think the same thing is going to happen in our own country. We have been living in a time of eclipse, so to speak, of late years, but I think another reaction will come. Some of us can remember that thirty or forty years ago there was almost no avowed infidelity in this country. There was not a publisher in New York, who had any respect for himself and any large hope of success, that would have had a book with one page of avowed unbelief in it on his shelves. How different it is now!

We have been passing, as I said, through a reaction. In the early part of this century our whole country was honeycombed with infidelity. It was ten times worse than it is to-day. But in 1825, 1830, 1840, 1850, there were wide spread changes, revivals; and a great many men were brought into our churches who had not the root of the matter in them, and a lax discipline and a low state of religious living became, alas! too common, and we have been reaping the bitter fruits. Alas! how often it has happened that some man has become notorious in the newspapers as a defaulter, or a criminal in some other way, and we have been compelled to read the added statement, that he was a member of such and such a church, was a Sunday-school superintendent, teacher, or what not. How often it has happened! This has been one of many causes—I cannot stop now to analyze and point out, but they can be analyzed and pointed out—of such widespread unbelief of late years. But it cannot last. There never was such activity in the Christian world; and if our earnest Christian people stand firm, if they practice in all directions that earnestness of Christian purpose, if they try to maintain the truth of the gospel and live up to it in their own lives, and lift up their prayer to God for his blessing, there will come another great sweeping reaction. It is as sure to come as there is logic in history or in human nature. It is as sure to come as there is truth in the promises of God's word. O, may many of you live to see that day and rejoice at its coming!

The same thing is true in individual churches, that there are seasons of sowing and reaping. It has to be so. We sometimes say we do not believe in the revival idea; we think there ought to be revival in the church all the time. If you mean that we ought always to be seeking for spiritual fruits, always aiming at spiritual advancement, it is true. But if you mean that you expect that piety will go on with even current in the church, that there will be just as much sowing and reaping at any one time as at any other, then you will certainly be disappointed. That is not the law of human nature. That is not posssible in the world. Periodicity pervades the universe. Periodicity controls the life of all individuals, shows itself in the operations of our minds. Periodicity necessarily appears in the spiritual sphere also. People have their ups and downs. They ought to strive against falling low. They ought not to be content with growing cold. They ought to seek to maintain good health of body all the while, but it will not be always equally good; and good health of mind and soul all the time, but it will not be always equally good. They ought to be seeking to reap a harvest of spiritual good among those around them all the while; but they will have seasons which are rather of sowing, and other seasons which will be rather of reaping. O! do you want to see a great season of harvest among your own congregation? And do you not know, brethren, as well as the preacher can tell you, what is necessary in order that you may see it? What are the conditions but deepened spiritual life in your own individual souls, stronger spiritual examples set forth in your lives, more earnest spirituality in your homes, a truer standard in your business and social relations to mankind, more of heartfelt prayer for God's blessing, and more untiring and patient and persevering effort, in season and out of season, to bring others to seek their salvation?

III. Spiritual work *links the workers in unity.* "Herein is the saying true," said Jesus; "one soweth, and another reapeth. Other men have labored, and ye are entered into their labors." The prophets, centuries before, had been preparing for that day, and the forerunner had been preparing for that day, and the labors of Jesus himself in his early ministry had been preparing the way, and now the disciples could look around them upon fields where, from the sowing of others, there were opportunities for them to reap. "Other men have labored, and ye are entered into their labors. One soweth, and another reapeth." That is the law everywhere; it is true of all the higher work of humanity,—"One soweth, and another reapeth;" and our labors link us into unity. It is true of human knowledge. How little has any one individual of mankind been able to find out beyond what the world has known before! Even the great minds that stand like mountain peaks as we look back over the history of human thought, when we come to look into it, do really but uplift the thought that is all around them; else they themselves could not have risen. It is true in practical inventions. We pride ourselves on the fact that ours is an age of such wonderful practical inventions; we sometimes persuade ourselves that we must be the most intelligent generation of mankind that ever lived, past all comparison; that no other race, no other century, has such wonderful things to boast of. How much of it do we owe to the men of the past! Every practical invention of to-day has been rendered possible by what seemed to us the feeble attainments of other centuries, by the patient investigation of the men who, in many cases, have passed away and been forgotten. We stand upon the shoulders of the past, and rejoice in our possessions, and boast; and when we grow conceited and proud of it, we are like a little boy lifted by his father's supporting arms, and standing on his father's shoulders, and clapping his hands above his father's head, and saying, in childish glee, "I am taller than papa!" A childish conclusion, to be sure. We stand upon the shoulders of the past, and thereby we are lifted up in all the higher work of mankind; and we ought to be grateful to the past, and mindful of our duty to the future; for the time will come when men will look back upon our inventions, our slow travel, our wonderful ignorance of the power of physical forces and the adaptations of them to physical advancement, and smile at the childishness with which, in the fag end of the nineteenth century, we boasted of ourselves and our time.

And now it is not strange that this same thing should be true of spiritual work. When you undertake to do some good in a great city like this, you might sit down and say, "What can I do with all this mass of vice and sin?" But you do not have to work alone. You can associate yourselves with other workers, in a church, with various organizations of workers, and thereby re-enforce your own exertions; you can feel that you are a working force, and you can feel that you are a part of a mighty force of workers, of your own name and other Christian names. Grace be with all them that love our Lord Jesus Christ in sincerity, and are trying to do good in his name! And it will cheer our hearts to remember that wide over the land and over the world are unnumbered millions of workers of the army to which we belong. They tell us that the International Sunday-school lessons which most of us study every Sunday, are actually studied now every Lord's day by at least ten millions of people, all studying on the same day the same portion of the Bible. That is but one fact to remind us that we are members of a great spiritual host, doing a great work in the world.

And not merely are there many cotemporaries with whom we are linked in unity, but we are in unity with the past; other men have labored and we have entered into their labors. All the good that all the devout women and all the zealous men of past ages have been doing has come down to us, opening the way for us to do good. And not merely with the past, but we are linked with the laborers of the future. They may hear our names or they may hear them not. We may perish from all memory of mankind, but our work will not perish, for he that doeth the will of God abideth forever, and if we are engaged in his work, we link ourselves to his permanency and his almightiness, and our work will go down to help the men who are to come after.

The same thing is true here, also, in the individual church; one soweth and another reapeth. A pastor seldom gathers half as much fruit from the seed of his own sowing as he gathers from the seed that others have sown. And there will come some man here—God grant it may be soon, and wisely, and well—who will gather seed from the sowing of the venerable pastor so well and worthily beloved in years ago, seed from the sowing of the energetic pastor of recent years, and O my soul, he may gather some harvest, even from the seed scattered in the brief fleeting interim of this summer. We put all our work together. We sink our work in the one great common work. We scatter seed for God and for souls, and we leave it to God's own care and blessing. One soweth, and another reapeth.

My brethren, there is nothing like Christianity to individualize mankind. It was Christianity that taught us to appreciate the individuality of men: "Every man must give account of himself unto God." Men were no longer to lose themselves in the state, as classical antiquity taught them to do, but to stand out in their separate personality and individual responsibility and individual rights and duties. But at the same time much of what we can do that is best in the world we must do by close connection and interaction one with another. Let us rejoice to act through others. Priscilla and Aquila! what a power they were for early Christianity when they took that eloquent young Alexandrian Apollos and taught him in private the way of God more perfectly! Priscilla, that devout woman, stood, in fact, before delighted assemblies in Corinth and spoke to them the perfect way of God through the eloquent man whom she had taught. And how often does the Sunday-school teacher, who labored long and, as the world might have thought, fruitlessly, with her little naughty boys and girls, become in future times a great power for good in the world through one or other of them! The teacher has to sink himself in his pupils: never mind if he sinks all out of the world's sight, provided he can make his mark upon *them* and prepare them for greater usefulness, can put into them some good spirit, and send them forth to do the work which to him personally is denied. Here lies the great power of Christian women. There is much they can do personally, with their own voice and their own action, but there is more they can do by that wondrous influence which men vainly strive to depict, that influence over son and brother and husband and friend whereby all the strength and power of the man is softened and guided and sobered and made wiser through the blessed influence of the woman. God be thanked that we can not only do good in our individual efforts, but we can do good through others! Let us cultivate this, let us delight in this, that we can labor through others. Whenever your pastor may stand before the gathered assembly he can speak with more power because of you, if you do your duty to him and through him.

May I mention some of the ways in which we may help our pastor? I speak as one who at home sits for the most part, a private member of the church in the pew, toiling all the week, and often unable to preach on Sunday, and yet as one whose heart is all in sympathy with the pastor's heart, and perhaps a little better able than common to sympathize with both sides. We can help him to draw a congregation. You know we always say now-a-days, that it is very important to get a man who can draw a congregation. So it is, though it is very important to consider what he draws them there for, and what he does with them after he gets them there; and sometimes it does seem to me that it would be better for some people to remain not drawn than to be drawn merely to hear and to witness that which does them harm rather than good. But we do want a man who can draw a congregation; and we can help our pastor to draw a congregation. How? Well, by taking care that we are always drawn ourselves, by occupying our own place, sometimes when we do not feel like it, on Sunday evening; because it is our duty to our pastor, our duty to the congregation, and our duty to the world. And we can do something to bring others. I recall a story, that a few years after the war (which is the great chronological epoch in a large part of our country), at the White Sulphur Springs, in Virginia, was a venerable man at whom all the people looked with profound admiration, whose name was Robert E. Lee. He was a devout Episcopalian. One day a Presbyterian minister came to preach in the ball-room, according to custom, and he told me this story. He noticed that General Lee, who was a very particular man about all the proprieties of life, came in late, and he thought it was rather strange. He learned afterwards that the General had waited until all the people who were likely to attend the service had entered the room, and then he walked very quietly around in the corridors and parlors, and out under the trees, and wherever he saw a man or two standing he would go up and say gently: "We are going to have divine service this morning in the ball-room; won't you come?" And they all went. To me it was very touching that that grand old man, whose name was known all over the world and before whom all the people wanted to bow, should so quietly go around, and for a minister of another denomination also, and persuade them to go. Should not we take means to help our pastor to draw a congregation? And when he begins to preach, cannot we help him to preach? Demosthenes is reported to have said (and he ought to have known something about it), that eloquence lies as much in the ear as in the tongue. Everybody who can speak effectively knows that the power of speaking depends very largely upon the way it is heard, upon the sympathy which one succeeds in gaining from those he addresses. If I were asked what is the first thing in effective preaching, I should say, sympathy; and what is the second thing, I should say, sympathy; and what is the third thing, sympathy. We should give our pastor *sympathy* when he preaches. Sometimes one good listener can make a good sermon; but ah! sometimes one listener who does not care much about the gospel can put the sermon all out of harmony. The soul of a man who can speak effectively is a very sensitive soul, easily repelled and chilled by what is unfavorable, and easily helped by the manifestation of simple and unpretentious sympathy.

How can we help our pastor? We can help him by talking about what he says; not talking about the performance and about the performer, and all that, which, if it is appropriate anywhere, is surely all inappropriate when we turn away from the solemn worship of God, and from listening to sermons intended to do us good— but talking about the thoughts that he has given us, recalling them sometimes to one who has heard them like ourselves, repeating them sometimes to some one who has not had the opportunity of hearing them. Thus may we multiply whatever good thoughts the preacher is able to present, and keep them alive in our own minds and the minds of fellow-Christians. Will you pardon an illustration here, even if it be a personal one? Last year in a city in Texas, I was told of the desire on the part of a lady for conversation, and when we met by arrangement she came in widow's weeds, with a little boy of ten or twelve years old, and began to tell this story: Her husband was once a student at the University of Virginia, when the person she was talking to was the chaplain there, more than twenty-five years ago. He was of a Presbyterian family from Alabama, and said he never got acquainted with the chaplain, for the students were numerous, but that he heard the preaching a great deal, and in consequence of it, by God's blessing upon it, he was led to take hold as a Christian, and went home and joined the church of his parents. After the war he married this lady, and a few years ago he passed away. She said he was in the habit, before she knew him, she learned, of talking often in the family about things he used to hear the preacher say; the preacher's words had gotten to be household words in the family. And then when they were married he taught some of them to her, and was often repeating things he used to hear the preacher say. Since he died she had been teaching them to the little boy—the preacher's words. The heart of the preacher might well melt in his bosom at the story. To think that your poor words, which you yourself had wholly forgotten, which you could never have imagined had vitality enough for that, had been repeated among strangers, had been repeated by the young man to his mother, repeated by the young widow to the child—your poor words, thus mighty because they were God's truth you were trying to speak and because you had humbly sought God's blessing! And through all the years it went on, and the man knew not, for more than a quarter of a century, of all that story. Ah, we never know when we are doing good. Sometimes we may think we are going to do great things, and so far as can ever be ascertained, we do nothing; and sometimes when we think we have done nothing, yet, by the blessing of God, some truth has been lodged in a mind here and there, to bear fruit after many days.

How can we help our pastor? We can furnish him illustrations. Mr. Spurgeon tells us that he requests his teachers, and his wife, and various other friends to hunt up illustrations for him. He asks them, whenever they have come across anything in reading or in conversation that strikes them as good, to write it down and let him have it, and whenever he sees a fit opportunity he makes a point of it. We can all furnish our pastors with illustrations. In that very way, perhaps, we might give a preacher many things that would be useful to him. In other ways we can all do so. Ah, when the preacher tells how it ought to be, if you can sometimes humbly testify, in the next meeting on Tuesday or Friday evening, how it has been in your experience, you are illustrating for the preacher. When the preacher tells what Christianity can do for people, if your life illustrates it for all around, there is a power that no speech can ever have. There remains a fourth law of spiritual work.

IV. Spiritual work has rich rewards: "And he that reapeth receiveth wages," saith Jesus, "and gathereth fruit unto life eternal." Spiritual work has rich rewards. It has the reward of success. It is not in vain to try to do good to the souls of men through the truth of God and seeking his grace. Sometimes you may feel as if you were standing at the foot of a precipice a thousand feet high and trying to spring to its summit, and were all powerless. Sometimes you may feel as if you had flung your words against a stone wall and made no impression at all. Sometimes you may go away all ashamed of what you have said in public or in private. But there was never a word spoken that uttered God's truth and sought God's blessing, that was spoken in vain. Somehow it does good to somebody, it does good at some time or other; it shall be known in earth or in heaven that it did do good. Comfort your hearts with these words: It is not in vain to try to do good. You may say, "I have not the lips of the eloquent, the tongue of the learned, how can I talk?" There is many a minister who is eloquent and has preached to gathered congregations, who could tell you that he knows of many more instances in which his private words have been blest to individuals than he knows of in his public discourses. I knew of a girl who had been so afflicted that she could not leave her couch for years, who had to be lifted constantly—poor, helpless creature!—but who would talk to those who came into her room about her joy in God, and would persuade them to seek the consolations of the gospel, and many were benefited and would bring their friends to her, till after a while they brought them from adjoining counties, that she, the poor, helpless girl, might influence them; at length she even began to write letters to people far away, and that girl's sick-bed became a centre of blessing to people throughout a whole region. We talk about doing nothing in the world. Ah, if our hearts were in it! we do not know what we can do. That tiger in the cage has been there since he was a baby tiger, and does not know that he could burst those bars if he were but to exert his strength. O the untried strength in all our churches, and the good that the people could do if we would only try, and keep trying, and pray for God's blessing. My friends, you cannot save your soul as a solitary, and you ought not to be content to go alone into the paradise of God. We shall best promote our own piety when we are trying to save others. We shall be most helpful to ourselves when we are most helpful to those around us. Many of you have found it so; and all of you may find it so, again and again, with repetitions that shall pass all human telling. "For he that watereth shall be watered also again."

Spiritual work shall also be rewarded in the Lord of the harvest's commendation and welcome. Ah, he will know which was the sowing and which was the reaping. The world may not know; *we* may never hear; but *he* will know which was the sowing and which was the reaping, and who tried to do good and thought he had not done it, and who was sad and bowed down with the thought of being utterly unable to be useful, and yet *was* useful. He will know, he will reward even the desire of the heart, which there was no opportunity to carry out. He will reward the emotion that trembled on the lip and could find no utterance. He will reward David for wanting to build the temple as well as Solomon for building it. He will reward all that we do, and all that we try to do, and all that we wish to do. O blessed God! he will be your reward and mine, forever and forever.

III.

THE HABIT OF THANKFULNESS.

In everything give thanks.—1 Thess. 5: 18.

WE hear a great deal said about habits. But it nearly always means bad habits. Why should we not think and speak much about good habits? They are as real, and almost as great, a power for good as bad habits are for evil. We do our work largely by the aid of habit. How much this helps one in playing on an instrument, or writing on a type-writer. Through many a familiar conjunction of notes or of letters the fingers fly with the very smallest amount of attention and exertion. Many a man who is growing old will every day get through an amount of work that surprises his friends, and it is possible because he works in the lines of lifelong habit. Besides, the only possible way to keep out bad habits is to form good habits. By a necessity of our nature, whatever is frequently and at all regularly done becomes habitual. If a man has been the slave of evil habits, and wishes to be permanently free, he must proceed by systematic and persevering effort to establish corresponding good habits. The education of our children, both at school and at home, the self-education of our own early life, consists mainly in the formation of intellectual and moral habits. I think we ought to talk more upon this subject, in public and in private—upon the power and blessing of good habits. And the theme of this discourse will be, the habit of thankfulness to God.

I. Consider the value of the habit of thankfulness.

It tends to quell repining. We are all prone, especially in certain moods, to complain of our lot. Every one of us has at some time or other imagined, and perhaps declared, that he has a particularly hard time in this world. It is to be hoped that in other moods we are heartily ashamed of ourselves for such repining. But how prevent its recurrence? A most valuable help will be the habit of thankfulness to God. Then if a fretful, repining spirit begins to arise, just in the middle, perhaps, of some complaining sentence, we shall suddenly change to an expression of thankfulness—and perhaps end with laughing at ourselves for the folly of such repining.

It tends to enhance enjoyment. We all know that when we receive a gift, with any true sentiment and any suitable expression of thankfulness, the reaction of gratitude augments our gratification.

It serves to soothe distress. Persons who are greatly afflicted, and not wont to be thankful, sometimes find the memory of past joys only an aggravation of present sorrow. Far otherwise with one who has learned to be habitually thankful. For him the recollection of happier hours is still a comfort.

It helps to allay anxiety. Did you ever notice what the apostle says to the Philippians? "In nothing be anxious; but in everything by prayer and supplication *with thanksgiving* let your requests be made known unto God. And the peace of God, which passeth all understanding, shall guard your hearts and your thoughts in Christ Jesus." Notice carefully that we are to prevent anxiety by prayer as to the future with thanksgiving for the past.

It cannot fail to deepen penitence. "The goodness of God leadeth thee to repentance." When we are fully in the habit of thankfully observing and recalling the loving kindnesses and tender mercies of our heavenly Father, this will make us perceive more clearly, and lament more earnestly, the evil of sin against him; and what is more, this will strengthen us to turn from our sins to his blessed service.

It has as one necessary effect to brighten hope. "I love to think on mercies past, And future good implore," is a very natural conjunction of ideas. If we have been wont to set up Ebenezers upon our path of life, then every glance backward along these mile-stones of God's mercy will help us to look forward with more of humble hope.

It serves to strengthen for endurance and exertion. We all know how much more easily and effectively they work who work cheerfully; and the very nutriment of cheerfulness is found in thankfulness as to the past and hope as to the future.

If this habit of thankfulness to God is so valuable, it is certainly worth our while to consider,

II. Occasions of habitual thankfulness. It is obvious that these are numerous and various beyond description. But we may find profit in summing them all up under two heads.

1. We should be thankful to God for everything

that is pleasant. No one will dispute that proposition in theory, whatever may be our practice. The apostle James tells us that "every good gift and every perfect boon is from above, coming down from the Father of lights." We have so much occasion to speak about the religious benefits of affliction, to dwell on the blessed consolations of Christian piety amid the sorrows of life, that we are in danger of overlooking the other side. It is a religious duty to enjoy to the utmost every rightful pleasure of earthly existence. He who gave us these bodies, so "fearfully and wonderfully made," who created us in his own image, with spirits of such keen appetency and longing aspiration, desires that we should find life a pleasure. As already intimated, we work best at what we enjoy. It is highly important that the young should enjoy what they are studying; and while this may, to some extent, be accomplished by giving them studies they fancy, it is also possible that by well guided efforts they should learn to relish studies to which they were at first disinclined. I sometimes hear young married people say, "We are going to housekeeping, and then we can have what we like." I sometimes feel at liberty to reply, "Yes, to a certain extent you may; but what is far more important and interesting, you will be apt to like what you have." To have what we like is for the most part an impossible dream of human life; to like what we have is a possibility, and not only a duty, but a high privilege.

2. We should be thankful to God for everything that is painful. Well, that may seem to be stating the matter too strongly. We can help ourselves by noticing

that whatever may be possible in that direction, the apostle has not in the text enjoined quite so much as the phrase just used would propose. He does not say, "for everything give thanks," though that might be enjoined; he says, "in everything give thanks." Now that, surely, need not seem impossible.

We may always be thankful that the situation is no worse. The old negro's philosophy was wise and good: "Bress de Lord, 'taint no wuss." We always deserve that it should be worse, no matter how sorrowful may be the actual situation. We can never allow ourselves to question that with some persons it has been worse. Let us always bless the Lord, that but for his special mercies it would be worse with us to-day. I recall an unpublished anecdote of President Madison, told to me in the region where he lived and died. It may be mentioned, by the way, that Mr. Madison was a rarely excellent and blameless man. His biographer told me that, notwithstanding all the political conflicts of a life so long and so distinguished, he found no indication that Mr. Madison's private character had ever been in the slightest degree assailed—an example which it would perhaps be difficult to parallel. In his old age the venerable ex-President suffered from many diseases, took a variety of medicines and contrived to live notwithstanding. An old friend from the adjoining county of Albemarle sent him a box of vegetable pills of his own production, and begged to be informed whether they did not help him. In due time came back one of those carefully-written and often felicitous notes for which Mr. Madison and Mr. Jefferson were both famous, to somewhat the following effect: "My dear friend. I thank you very much for the box of pills. I have taken them all; and while I cannot say that I am better since taking them, it is quite possible that I might have been worse if I had not taken them, and so I beg you to accept my sincere acknowledgments." Really, my friends, this is not a mere pleasantry. There is always something, known or unknown, but for which our condition might have been worse, and at the very least, that something constitutes an occasion for gratitude. Whatever we may have lost, there is always something left.

As already observed, our present sufferings may well set in brighter relief the remembered happiness of other days. And though men are prone to make this an occasion of repining, yet it ought to be an occasion of thankfulness. Not long ago a young husband spoke to me, with bitter sorrow, about the death of his wife. I suggested that he might well be thankful for having lived several happy years in the most intimate companionship with one so lovely; and that in coming years, when the blessed alchemy of memory should make her character seem all-perfect in his eyes, he might well find pathetic and ineffable pleasure in the memory of that early time. We all know how to repeat, amid sorrowful recollections, those words of Tennyson, "O, death in life, the days that are no more!" But it is surely possible so to cherish blessed and inspiring memories as to invert the line, and say, "O, life in death, the days that are no more!"

There is a still more important view of this matter.

It has become a blessed commonplace of Christian philosophy that our sufferings may, through the grace of God, be the means of improving our character. Such a result is by no means a matter of course. Sufferings may be so borne, with such bitter repining and selfish brooding, as greatly to damage character. But the Scriptures assure us that devout souls may regard affliction as but a loving Father's chastisement, meant for their highest good. In all the ages there has never been a pious life that did not share this experience. To be exempt from it would, as the Bible expressly declares, give clear proof that we are not children of God at all. Many of us could testify to-day, if it were appropriate, that the sorrows of life have by God's blessing done us good. All of us have occasion to lay more thoroughly to heart the lessons of affliction. And oh! if we do ever climb the shining hills of glory, and look back with clearer vision upon the strangely mingled joys and sorrows of this earthly life, then how deeply grateful we shall be for those very afflictions, which at the time we find it so hard to endure. If we believe this to be true, and it is a belief clearly founded on Scripture, then can we not contrive, even amid the severest sufferings, to be thankful for the lessons of sorrow, for the benefits of affliction?

Remember, too, how our seasons of affliction make real to us the blessed thought of Divine compassion and sympathy. When you look with parental anguish upon your own suffering child, then you know, as never before, the meaning of those words, "Like as a father pitieth his children, so the Lord pitieth them that fear him." When you find the trials of life hard to bear, then it becomes unspeakably sweet to remember that our high priest can be touched with the feeling of our infirmities, having been " in all points tempted like as we are, yet without sin." Thus affliction brings to the devout mind blessed views of the Divine character, which otherwise we should never fully gain.

> "Then sorrow, touched by thee, grows bright
> With more than rapture's ray;
> As darkness shows us worlds of light
> We never saw by day."

Besides all this, remember that the sufferings of this present life will but enhance, by their contrast, the blessed exemptions of the life to come. A thousand times have I remembered the text of my first funeral sermon, "And there shall be no more death, neither sorrow nor crying; neither shall there be any more pain: for the former things are passed away." These are the present things now—all around us and within us; but the time is coming when they will be the former things, quite passed away. You know the use which skilful composers make of discords in music. The free use of them is among the characteristics of Wagner; but they are often found in our simplest tunes for public worship. The jarring discord is solved, and makes more sweet the harmony into which it passes. And oh! the time is coming when all the pains and pangs of this present life will seem to have been only " a brief discordant prelude to an everlasting harmony."

My friends, are you optimists or pessimists? Let me

explain to the children what those words mean. The Latin word *optimus* means best, and *pessimus* means worst. So an Optimist is one who maintains that this is the best possible world; and a Pessimist, that it is the worst possible world. Now which are you, an optimist or a pessimist? For my part, I am neither. Surely no man can really imagine that this is the best possible world, save in some brief moment of dreamy forgetfulness. And as to thinking it the worst possible world, —well, a person would have to be uncommonly well off who could afford to think that. I read, some time ago, a biography of Arthur Schopenhauer, the celebrated German pessimist. I was not surprised to find that his father left him an independent fortune, and he had no painful bodily diseases. He could afford to spend his time in trying to persuade everybody to be miserable, in building pessimistic theories. But most of us have so many real toils and troubles that we are instinctively driven to search for the bright side of life, to seek all possible consolation and cheer. Agassiz had "no time to make money;" and few of us will ever have time to be pessimists. No, we cannot begin to say with Pope, "Whatever is, is right;" nor yet to reverse it, "Whatever is, is wrong." But whether poetical or not, it will be a very true and valuable saying if we read, "Whatever is, you must make the best of it." And just in proportion as we strive to make the best of everything, we shall find it practicable to carry out the apostle's injunction, "In everything give thanks."

The greatest of early Christian preachers, perhaps the greatest in all Christian history, was Chrysostom. His motto was, "Glory to God for all things." He probably derived it from the story of Job, which was his favorite subject of devout meditation, and is mentioned in a large proportion of his eloquent sermons. You might fancy that it was easy for the young man to say, "Glory to God for all things," when he was growing up in Antioch, the idol of his widowed mother, with ample means, and the finest instructors of the age. You might think it easy to say this when he was a famous preacher, in Antioch, and afterwards in Constantinople, when ten thousand people crowded the great churches to hear him; though such a preacher could not fail to suffer profoundly through compassion for the perishing, and anxious effort to reclaim the wandering, and sympathy for all the distressed, as well as with many a pang of grief and shame that he did not preach better. But Chrysostom continued to say this, when the Court at Constantinople turned against him, when the wicked Empress became his enemy, and compassed his banishment again and again. When his friends would go to far Armenia and visit him in exile, he would say to them, "Glory to God for all things." When he was sent to more distant and inhospitable regions, so as to be out of reach of such pious visiting, his letters were apt to end, "Glory to God for all things." And when the soldiers were dragging him through winter snows, and, utterly worn out, he begged to be taken into a little way-side church that he might die, his last words, as he lay on the cold stone floor, were, "Glory to God for all things."

III. How may the habit of thankfulness be formed and maintained? Well, how do we form other habits?

If you wish to establish the habit of doing a certain thing, you take pains to do that thing, upon every possible occasion, and to avoid everything inconsistent therewith. Now, then, if you wish to form the habit of thankfulness, just begin by being thankful—not next year, but to-night; not for some great event or experience, but for whatever has just occurred, whatever has been pleasant, yes, and we did say, for whatever has been painful. You certainly can find some special occasion for thanksgiving this very night. And then go on searching for matter of gratitude, and just continuing to be thankful, hour by hour, day by day. Thus the habit will be formed, by a very law of our nature.

But remember that good habits cannot be maintained without attention. They require a certain self-control, a studious self-constraint. Is not the habit of thankfulness worth taking pains to maintain? The older persons present remember Ole Bull, the celebrated violinist. I once dined in company with him, and in an hour's conversation across the table found him a man of generous soul, full of noble impulses and beautiful enthusiasms, and rich with the experience of wide travel. And I was greatly interested in a remark of his which is recorded in the recent biography: "When I stop practicing one day, I see the difference; when I stop two days, my friends see the difference; when I stop a week, everybody sees the difference." Here was a man who had cultivated a wonderful natural gift, by lifelong labor, until, as a performer upon the finest of instruments, he was probably the foremost man of his time; and yet he could not afford to stop practicing for a single week, or even for a single day. "They do it for an earthly crown; but we for a heavenly." Christian brethren, shall we shrink from incessant vigilance and perpetual effort to keep up the habit of thankfulness to God?

I see many young persons present this evening. Will not some of you at once begin the thoughtful exercise of continual thankfulness? Will you not think over it, pray over it, labor to establish and maintain so beautiful and blessed a habit? Ah, what a help it will be to you amid all the struggles of youth and all the sorrows of age! And in far-coming years, when you are gray, when the preacher of this hour has long been forgotten, let us hope that you will still be gladly recommending to the young around you the Habit of Thankfulness.

IV.

ASK AND IT SHALL BE GIVEN YOU.

Ask and it shall be given you.—Matthew vii. 7.

ONE thing is certain, the Lord Jesus Christ believed in prayer. It is no new thing to find some persons who question the reality of prayer. There have always been such persons; but the Lord Jesus Christ believed in it. He showed his belief by often teaching us that we ought to pray, by assuring us that prayer will be heard, and by praying much himself. When a person, profoundly sincere and highly intelligent, frequently urges others to do a certain thing, and frequently does it himself, we are sure that he believes in it; so, whenever a man undertakes to say that prayer is not a reality, it ought to be distinctly borne in mind that he flings away the authority of Jesus Christ; that he arrays himself openly and hopelessly against the whole genius of the Christian religion, against the plainest teachings and constant practice of its founder. We ought always to see where we are and to see what is the meaning of this or that position.

I do not know whether it is worth while, in passing, even for a moment, to recall the sensation of a few years ago on this subject, and remark upon it. I suppose that the idea of what they used to call a prayer-test in the newspapers is plainly enough a thing improper and impossible. It is improper, because to ask Christians to confine their prayers to one side of a hospital, and pray not at all for the unhappy sufferers on the other side, is to ask a thing out of the question— a refined species of cruelty to be practiced by those who believe in prayer. It is improper, too, because it proposes that we should try experiments upon God. They did sometimes try that sort of thing upon Jesus Christ, and he invariably refused to submit to it. He wrought wonders and signs beyond number when he thought proper; but when they demanded a sign according to what they thought proper, he never granted it. For us to do this that is proposed would be just that which they did. And besides being improper, it is also impossible. We do not believe that prayer now works miracles. It is not the idea at all that prayer operates with respect to physical fixed forces otherwise than in accordance with physical laws. And so if you suppose prayer to be answered in such a case, it could only be in concurrence with proper physical conditions. Then the unbeliever would say at once that this is not a result of prayer. Such a test is impossible unless prayer works miracles, and no one who understands the matter would suppose that to be the idea. Is it not true, then—plain enough now as we look back upon it—that the great newspaper sensation of a few years since was a thing improper and a thing impossible?

But for us who believe in the Lord Jesus Christ, it comes back to this, that our yearning after God and that disposition to cry out to him for mercy and help, which is no invention of theological thinkers, which is the natural product of the human heart and the natural expression of human need and dependence, has the high sanction of the Founder of Christianity. He believed in prayer; he taught us to pray; he said: "Ask, and it shall be given."

And notice how often he has repeated it. One might say that that one word was enough; one might say that all human hearts ought to fasten on that one utterance, and feed themselves on it, and rejoice in its assurances. But he said it three times: "Ask, and it shall be given you; seek, and ye shall find; knock, and it shall be opened unto you." As if not content with that, he repeats it three times again, in the form of an assurance that so it always is. "For every one that asketh receiveth, and he that seeketh findeth, and to him that knocketh it is opened." And even after that he goes on to argue it by a most cogent argument and affecting appeal. Why this multiplied repetition and assurance? Ah! my friends and brethren, he knew very well how imperfectly we believe in prayer; how difficult it is for us to treat prayer as a reality, and he wanted to help us. He condescends to our infirmity, and again and again, in multiplied forms of expression, he would assure us that if we ask, we shall receive. You know how prone we are to make prayer degenerate into an outward thing. A little child needs to be constantly reminded by its mother that it must not just *say* prayers, but must mean what it is saying. And we, with all our intelligence and culture, are apt to make our public and private prayer a mere outward thing.

How hard it is for us also, when we try to pray, to *realize* what we are doing! I remember being once deeply impressed with this thought when present at an institution for the deaf and dumb. After some teaching had been done, one of the principal instructors proceeded to give them a little address on religion, we were told, and then he called upon them to pray. The whole room was still. He stood with reverent face and slowly moved his hands and arms in the signs which they understood, and they sat before him with distended, gazing eyes, and the room grew still as with the stillness of death. I said to myself—I could hear my heart beat—I said *"This is praying."* Not a word spoken, but this was praying, praying without any of the forms to which we are accustomed. The eyes were wide open, not a sound was heard, and yet human souls were entering into communion with the Father of all spirits. I went away with a profounder sense than ever before of the distinction between the mere outward form and means of prayer, and the inner spirit which *is* prayer. Now, our Saviour knows that it is hard for us to realize what we do when we are trying to pray.

He also knows how prone we are to be discouraged in our attempts to pray; when we try experiments upon prayer, and get out of heart, and quit. As a man who is endeavoring to effect some invention, and has given all his labor and used all his materials, hoping that he will get the result, when he fails, gives over the experiment, so, how often do we make a mere half-hearted experiment of praying for a certain blessing upon ourselves and others, and when it does not come, we are tempted to give it up as a failure! The Saviour knows how impatient we are that the blessing shall come quickly, and therefore cautions us not to faint when we do not receive it on the instant. We may not receive it in the form we looked for. It may come in a form so different that we shall scarcely recognize it as what we asked for; and so he gives us his assurance and seeks to build up confidence in our hearts that praying is a reality, that prayer is a power.

And now notice the affecting appeal our Lord proceeds to make—an appeal which those of us who are parents will feel in all its fullness, but which all of us can feel more or less because all of us know something of the affection of our own parents. "What man is there of you—a mere man—who, if his son ask for bread, will he give him a stone?" Will he give him something that looks like bread, but which is worthless? "Or if he ask a fish, will he give him a serpent?"—something that looks like a fish but which is poisonous and deadly? Will he mock his child's petition by giving him something like what he asked for, but that would be useless and harmful? And if ye who are evil, with all the imperfections of your sinful humanity, if ye know how to give good gifts to your children, how much more will your Heavenly Father give good things to them that ask him. It is not an argument merely, as I used to think it was—it is not an argument merely as to willingness to give. It is an argument as to wisdom in giving. If ye then, being evil, *know how* to give good gifts to your children. The parent might make a mistake himself and give a stone for bread, or a serpent for a fish; as a rule, parents do not do this; and if even ye, in your ignorance, know how to give good gifts to your children, how much more will your Heavenly Father give good gifts to those who ask him! It does at times happen that when our children ask for bread we do give them a stone; sometimes, alas! when they ask for a fish we give them a serpent. We do this because we make sad mistakes. How many parents think they are giving their children something good when they are giving them that which is useless or hurtful, as if they should give them a poisonous serpent that would sting them to death, though they do not know it! Often, too, we are ignorant, slothful or even selfish, and when the child asks, we won't take the pains to judge carefully, and when the child entreats again and again, we weakly yield. But if even we who are ignorant, heedless, selfish, know how to give good gifts, how much more will our Heavenly Father give good gifts to them that ask him, for he never makes mistakes and never neglects! How beautiful that old saying, "He is too wise to err, and too good to be unkind!" He never makes mistakes in listening to our requests. He is never too busy to attend to our wishes. And the very thought of his being unkind is intolerable.

So, then, our Father is not only willing to give, he is *wise* in giving. That is the point, and just there lies one of the greatest privileges the Scriptures open up to us, in the assurance that God will give wisely, and this involves withholding where he shall see that withholding is better. That is the sweetest privilege of prayer. For if God should give to you and me an unlimited promise of earthly good for the asking, the more we know ourselves and the more we understand human nature and human life, the more afraid we should be that we might ask for things which would be harmful. Have you not often asked God for something which you have lived to find out would have been a curse to you? Have you not often entreated God to spare you something which it turned out to be a blessing to you that he did not spare? Have you not learned more and more how little you could rely upon your judgment as to what was really best? So I say in that case the wisest and best people would be the slowest to ask, and people would pray less in proportion as they are better fitted to receive. But, as God is wise in giving, we may ask without fear. If we ask for something that we think is good and he sees it is evil, we may be sure that he will not grant it. If we ask for what is really good,—he will do for us either what we ask or something which he sees to be better than what we asked. And so I repeat that this is a part of the privilege of prayer.

One Sunday afternoon, now many years ago, I remember to have been sitting in a darkened room with the body of a little child; and in the room was a little boy ten or twelve years of age, one of those strange, thoughtful children that startle us so by asking questions that sink down deep into the mysteries of human life. After a long silence the boy spoke, and said, "Uncle, I should like to ask you something." "Well." "Does not the Bible say that whatever we ask God, he will do for us?" "Yes." "Well, I did ask him to spare my little cousin's life—I did ask him and he did not do it. I asked him and I don't know what to think about it." Ah! I thought, as we sat in the darkened room, how far down the child is going already into the sorrowful depths of the human heart! The answer I made was something like this: "You know that if your father should send you off to boarding-school, and were to tell you in parting that whatever you wanted you must write to him and you should have it; and if you were to write to your father, on the strength of that promise, for something that was not right for him to give, or was not really best for you, your father would be very sure not to give it to you, and if he did not give it to you, would you think he had broken his promise?" The child heaved a sigh and said, "Yes; I think I see how it is." And my friends, the more you reflect upon it, the more comfort there is in that thought, that, in answering our prayer for temporal good, our Heavenly Father will give wisely, and so will even refuse our prayer when He sees that something else is better.

This remarkable encouragement to prayer occurs towards the close of the Sermon on the Mount. Some of the commentators think there is no connection between it and the discourse that precedes; but it seems to me that the connection is plain. "Ask, and ye shall receive," explains what he had been saying a little before. He said: "Judge not, that you be not judged;" and what good man ever heard that read, or read it himself, without smitings of heart? It is one of the commonest things, this business of harsh judgment of others, and it is very difficult for us to avoid it. We are so ready, the most thoughtful and purest of us, so ready to be hard upon others and easy upon ourselves, when we ought to reverse that proceeding. "Judge not, that ye be not judged." Then, as you read along, behold you find something that seems to present a new and opposite difficulty. "Give not that which is holy to the dogs, neither cast ye your pearls before swine, lest they trample them under their feet, and turn again and rend you." The purport of this is somewhat obscure; but one thing is clearly involved. We must know the character of those with whom we have intercourse, and deal with them accordingly; and yet we must not judge harshly. We must refrain from judgment, and at the same time must keep our own eyes open and know men. Now, when you put those things together, you say, Ah! who is sufficient for these things? Who can go through life, knowing the folly of men, understanding their wiles and their weaknesses, and yet not judging his fellow-men in an unkindly spirit? But he who enjoins these two difficult and seemingly antagonistic precepts immediately afterwards says: "Ask, and it shall be given you." Hard it is for us to do such things as these; but "ask, and it shall be given you."

Again, if you go a little further back in the discourse, you will find he urges upon us not to be anxious about temporal good, not to be anxious about food and raiment, not to be anxious about to-morrow; and those who most earnestly try to follow that know best how hard it is to obey the command. Ah, as the responsibilities of life thicken around us, and there come to be others concerned in our action, it grows all the harder to restrain ourselves from anxiety about human affairs. In fact, we are obliged to look sharply to the future and plan for it, even for the far distant future. And yet here is Jesus Christ telling us not to be anxious about temporal good, not to be anxious about the future, but to put our trust in God's providence and to seek God's righteousness, and then there shall come a blessing upon our planning and exertion, and we need not be anxious. It is so hard, you say, for a man to go on amid grave responsibilities, and yet to restrain himself from this anxiety, so hard; but he who urged this upon us did not cease speaking before he said: "Ask, and it shall be given you."

Yet again, going further back in the discourse, you find that we must seek ever, and not be content without, a higher spiritual morality than that of the Scribes and Pharisees. Now, the Scribes and Pharisees, so far as outward proprieties of life are concerned, were eminently good men; and yet he tells us we must be better than they were. We must not only be outwardly good, but within we must be pure from sin. We must not only have the outward appearance of chastity, but he tells us that there may be in a lustful look the essential element, and therefore the guilt, of unchastity. We are not only to restrain ourselves from external wrong-doing, but govern our thoughts and desires, and control our whole inner being, and make the world within us conform to the spirit of the teachings of Christ. And you say: "O, how difficult, how difficult!" Yes, difficult; but he who enjoined this upon us did not cease to speak on that same occasion till he had said: "Ask, and it shall be given you."

So, then, my hearers, let us learn to put the precepts

of Christ along with Christ's invitation to seek help from on high. He who gave these stringent commands gave us encouragement to come and ask for help, the help of his grace, the help of his Holy Spirit. "How much more," as our Lord expressed it on another occasion, "will your Heavenly Father give the Holy Spirit to them that ask him."

My friends, why do you not pray? Are you ashamed to pray? There are people not ashamed to be practicing vice, not ashamed to be heard speaking blasphemy, but ashamed to have it known that they pray. There are people that are too proud to bow their knees before the Lord God. There are people that think somehow it is beneath their dignity to pray. Are you ashamed to pray? The poet Coleridge wrote something in his youth which made light of prayer; but, in his later years, he called a friend to him one day and referred to what he had written and published, and said, "It was all folly," and then he said in earnest tones, "The very noblest possible exercise of the human mind is prayer." Is it not so? When men in all the loftiness of intellect look deepest into the spaces of the universe and widest into its wonders; when men, in the might of administrative talent, make it their ruling thought to control whole nations and the age they live in; when men govern great assemblies and sway them as the wind sways the harvest grain, even then it is all a little thing compared to the nobleness of the exercise of the human mind in prayer, wherein a human being, high or low, rich or poor, elevates his thought into communion with the thought of God, lifts up his spirit into fellowship with the Father of Spirits.

There was a man that trod the earth once who was superior to all men in holiness and wisdom, who lived all his life on earth without sin. He so wise and good, loved to pray, and are you ashamed to pray?

My hearers, why do you not all pray? God knows whether you do or not, and you know. Are you afraid to pray? Well a man might be, when he thinks of all his sinfulness, when he remembers all the wicked things that he has done that men know of, and all the wicked things he has thought that men know not of, but God must know; when he sees he has not half confidence in the God he thinks of praying to. But there is a name we may plead; there is an intercessor we may lean on; there is a Holy Spirit to help our infirmities in praying. O! sinful and troubled soul of man, you need not be afraid to pray! If you come in the name of Jesus Christ, you may come boldly to the throne of grace. If you come leaning on the Spirit's help, you may come assured that your request will be granted.

My hearers, why do you not pray? Have you no need to pray? Is there no good thing that God can give, and that you need? No earthly good for yourself or others, about which you had better be asking the Giver of every good and perfect gift? No spiritual good? Have you no sins to be forgiven? Have you no weakness to be helped, no temptations to struggle against? Have you no troubles? O child of man, child of sin and sorrow, living in the strange world we are called to inhabit, have you no need to pray to your Father and your God? Why do you not pray?

My friends, let us make it a practical lesson for us all.

Christian people, begin to pray more. Fathers of families, if you have neglected to pray with your families, begin now at once. If you have been negligent in public or private prayer, renew your petitions with earnestness. O, troubled one, shrinking away from the Saviour, remember that he said, " Ask and it shall be given you." And, if there is somebody here this evening that has not prayed for months, that has not prayed for years; if there is some man that has not prayed since the time long ago when he prayed by his mother's knee, and who all these years has been slighting God's word and rejecting God's invitation; O soul, O fellow-sinner, will you not to-night take Jesus' word home to your heart, and begin to find in your experience what some like you have found, that you have but to ask and it shall be given?

V.

HE EVER LIVETH TO INTERCEDE.

Wherefore also he is able to save to the uttermost them that draw near unto God through him, seeing he ever liveth to make intercession for them.—Heb. 7: 25.

YEARS ago, in the city of Philadelphia, I went to hear an eminent musician. He played with genius and skill some magnificent music, but the pieces were nearly all new to me, and, as often happens in such cases, it required so much effort to comprehend the idea of the piece, that I could but partially enjoy its beauty. At length, upon being loudly applauded, the musician returned, and seating himself at the instrument, struck out in full tones the opening notes of "Home, Sweet Home." I shall never forget while I live the thrill that passed through the audience. I seemed to feel that it was approaching me, seemed to feel when it reached and embraced me. That was a theme that all could comprehend, and rich for us all in a thousand delightful suggestions and associations; and, strangers as we were, the hearts of the vast assembly seemed melted into one as we listened to those swelling tones. My brethren, I wish it might always be so with us when one begins to speak to us of Jesus. There is many a subject of public discourse that well deserves our attention. Especially the topics drawn from the Bible and usually presented from the pulpit are all important and should all be interesting. Whatever pertains to God and his providence, to his gracious dealings with man in the past, and his purposes of mercy for the future, whatever to the condition and wants of our race as sinful and immortal, should awaken our minds and impress our hearts. Difficult and mysterious as some of these topics are, they are useful; and if we resist the temptation to wander into speculation or descend into secularity, they will give us pleasure and do us good. But Jesus—it is a theme which all alike can understand, in which all alike are profoundly concerned, a theme associated with all the sweetest recollections of our spiritual life, with all the brightest hopes of our immortal future. Ah! we are perishing and helpless sinners, and it ought to thrill through our very hearts, to link us in living sympathy, and kindle our souls into a glow of love and joy to hear of Jesus, our divine, our loving, our precious Saviour. It ought to be not mere poetry, but the true expression of genuine feeling, when we sing,—

> "Jesus, I love thy charming name;
> 'Tis music to mine ear;
> Fain would I sound it out so loud
> That earth and heaven might hear."

And my text to-day treats of Jesus.

The Jewish Christians to whom this Epistle was addressed were strongly urged, both in the way of persecution and persuasion, to apostatize from Christianity, and return to Judaism. Among the arguments employed for this purpose, it was urged that Christianity had no priesthood, no sacrifice or temple, and so was really no religion at all. The inspired writer of this Epistle meets these arguments, and, in fact, turns them into proofs of the superiority of Christianity. Thus, in regard to the priesthood, he shows that Christianity has a priest, a great High-Priest, immensely superior to the Levitical priesthood. His office is held forever. He has offered, once for all, the wonderful sacrifice of himself, which is forever sufficient. He has passed through the heavens into the true sanctuary, bearing his own precious, atoning blood. Then Christianity is superior in this, as in other respects, to Judaism, that is, to the Mosaic dispensation if regarded as complete in itself, and designed to be permanent; and so the sacred writer urges his brethren not to apostatize, interspersing everywhere throughout his arguments the most earnest exhortations to hold fast their profession, the most solemn warnings of the guilt and ruin of apostasy. And for us as well as for them, grievous is the guilt and hopeless the ruin of abandoning the gospel of Christ, our sole hope of salvation.

One of the points he makes to prove this superiority of Christ and Christianity, is that from which the text is an inference. The Levitical priesthood was held by many persons in succession, "because that by death they were hindered from continuing;" but Jesus, "because he abideth forever, hath his priesthood unchangeable. Wherefore he is able to save to the uttermost them that draw near unto God through him, seeing he ever liveth to make intercession for them." The phrase translated "to the uttermost" signifies "perfectly," "completely;" he can save completely, can complete the salvation of them that come unto God through him. And the thought of the text is that he is able to complete their salvation, because he ever lives to intercede for them.

Perhaps we are accustomed to look too exclusively to the Saviour's atoning death, not dwelling as we should upon the idea of his interceding life. See how the apostle speaks in Romans: "For if, while we were enemies, we were reconciled to God through the death of his Son, much more, being reconciled, we shall be saved by his life." And again: "Christ Jesus that died, yea rather that was raised from the dead, who is at the right hand of God, who also maketh intercession for us." He who loved us and gave himself for us ever liveth to accomplish the objects for which he died; as the mediatorial priest, he is ever interceding for the salvation of them that come unto God through him; as the mediatorial king, having all authority given unto him in heaven and earth, he controls all things so as to carry forward to completion the work of their salvation.

My brethren, it is just such a Saviour that we need. From the first moment when we approach God through him, onward through life, and in a certain just sense onward without end, we continually need God's mercy and grace for the Saviour's sake. If we dwell on this, we shall be better prepared to rejoice that our great High Priest ever lives to intercede for us, and thus can complete our salvation.

1. We are tempted. And what hope have we of conquering temptation, save "through him that loved us?" Remember what our Lord said to his disciples, with

regard to the sore temptations that would soon befall them: "Simon, Simon, behold, Satan asked to have you, that he might sift you as wheat; but I made supplication for thee, that thy faith fail not." As Satan is described as seeking permission from that Sovereign Ruler, without whose permission all his might and his malice are powerless, to tempt Job with peculiar trials, in the hope that he could bring him to renounce the Lord, so here as to the disciples. "Satan asked to have you"—and the term, as well as the connection, shows that he was permitted to have them, "that he might sift you as wheat." Jesus himself is represented by John the Baptist as engaged in a similar process: "Whose fan is in his hand, and he will thoroughly cleanse his threshing-floor, and gather his wheat into the garner; but he will burn up the chaff with unquenchable fire." But how different is the object in the two cases! Satan sifts with the hope of showing that all is really worthless, fit only for destruction. Jesus sifts in order to separate the precious from the vile, and preserve the pure wheat for the garner of heaven. And often what Satan meant as a sifting for evil is overruled by the stronger power so as to be for good.

How was it with Peter? The Saviour said: "But I made supplication for thee, that thy faith fail not;" and though his faith mournfully gave way, it did not utterly give out. I am not excusing Peter at all. We may be sure he never forgave himself. It was a sad and shameful fall; but Jesus had made supplication for him; and how different the result in his case from that of Judas. He, too, was one of those whom Satan obtained to sift them, and the result proved him to be all that Satan could wish. When he saw the consequences of his horrid crime, and had time to reflect upon it, he was sorry; but it was not the tender grief of a truly penitent heart which would have brought him back with humble submission—it was the sorrow of the world that worketh death—it was remorse that drove him headlong into self-destruction. But Peter—when the cock crowed after his third denial of his Lord and that injured one turned and looked upon him—Peter went out and wept bitterly, with the sorrow "that worketh repentance unto salvation," the sorrow of a deeply humble and really loving heart. There was a great change from that time in Peter, for the Lord had prayed for him, and Divine grace not only preserved him from utter spiritual ruin, but overruled his own dreadful wickedness to his spiritual good.

Observe with what special emphasis the Saviour's intercession for the tempted is spoken of in this Epistle. The persons therein addressed were, as we have seen, peculiarly and sorely tempted—tempted even to forsake Christianity, through which alone they could find salvation; apart from which "there remaineth no more sacrifice for sins, but a certain fearful expectation of judgment and a fierceness of fire which shall devour the adversary." The Jewish high priest, being taken from among men, "could bear gently with the ignorant and erring, for that he himself also was compassed with infirmity." So our great High Priest took upon him human nature partly for this very reason, that he might sympathize with the tempted, and that we might feel sure he does sympathize. "Wherefore in all things it behooved him to be made like unto his brethren, that he might be a merciful and faithful High Priest in things pertaining to God, to make propitiation for the sins of the people. For in that he himself hath suffered, being tempted, he is able to succor them that are tempted." And it is because of his atoning sacrifice and sympathizing intercession that we are urged to hold fast our profession as Christians, and encouraged to come to God with entire confidence. This is done in words that have been very dear to tempted hearts in every age since the holy man of God spake them as he was moved by the Holy Ghost. "Having, then, a great High Priest who hath passed through the heavens, Jesus, the Son of God, let us hold fast our confession. For we have not a high priest that cannot be touched with the feeling of our infirmities; but one that hath been in all points tempted like as we are, yet without sin. Let us THEREFORE draw near with boldness unto the throne of grace that we may receive mercy, and may find grace to help us in time of need."

Ah! mighty, to the most favored, are the temptations of life. Many belong to all periods; others mark some special season. Many are "common to man;" others belong to some particular condition or calling. "The heart knoweth its own bitterness;" yea, and its own trials, and its own weakness. Be this our support—our Saviour lives, he sympathizes with us, he intercedes for us; let us draw near unto God through him, unto God who has said, "As thy days, so shall thy strength be."

> "The soul that on Jesus hath leaned for repose,
> I will not, I will not desert to its foes;
> That soul, though all hell should endeavor to shake,
> I'll never, no never, no never forsake."

2. But many times, sad as is the confession, we yield to temptation, we sin; and "the soul that sinneth, it shall die." Must we then despair? Must the hopes we had cherished be abandoned, and this new sin be the terror of our souls? Listen! The apostle John wrote an Epistle for the express purpose of restraining his brethren from sin; yet he does not cut off those who are conscious they have sinned from the hope of forgiveness and salvation. He says: "My little children, these things write I unto you, that ye may not sin. And if any man sin, we have an Advocate with the Father, Jesus Christ, the righteous; and he is the propitiation for our sins; and not for ours only, but also for the whole world." Now we know what an advocate was, according to the usages of the Roman law, and is among ourselves, viz.: one who undertakes the management of another's case in court, and pleads his cause. So Jesus is our Advocate with the Father. But, as in other cases where spiritual things are illustrated by temporal, the analogy is not perfect; there are differences. Our advocate does not argue that we are innocent, but confessing our guilt, pleads for mercy to us; and he does not present *our* merits as a reason why mercy should be shown us, but *his* merits. "He is the propitiation for our sins." His atoning death does, as it were, render God propitious, or favorable to sinners. Not that God is unwilling to show favor to poor sinners, and only prevailed on to do so by

the death and intercession of his Son. Oh no! far from it. "Herein is love," says John in the same Epistle, "not that we loved God, but that he loved us, and sent his Son to be the propitiation for our sins." It was because God loved us, and wanted us to be saved, that he devised this way of saving us. And God is made propitious, favorable to us, not when he is made willing to save, but when it is made right that he should save us, and therefore we need not die, but may have everlasting life. When a sinner is pardoned, simply for the sake of the atoning and interceding Saviour, there is in that no encouragement to God's creatures to sin, as if it were a little thing and could be readily passed over, but a most solemn and impressive exhibition of the dreadful evil of sin, since it was only through the atonement and intercession of the only-begotten Son of God that any sinner could be forgiven—an exhibition at once of God's love to the perishing, and of his justice, that "will by no means clear the guilty."

Bearing in mind the difference between the pleading of our great Advocate and any parallel which human affairs presents, we may look at a story of Grecian history, which has been often used to illustrate the Saviour's intercession. The poet Æschylus had incurred the displeasure of the Athenians. He was on trial before the great popular tribunal, consisting of many hundreds of citizens, and was about to be condemned. But Æschylus had a brother, who had lost an arm in battle—in the great battle of Salamis, where the Greeks fought for their existence against the Persian aggressors. This brother came into the court, and did not speak words of entreaty, but letting fall his mantle, he showed the stump of his arm, lost in his country's defense, and there stood until the Athenians relented, and Æschylus was suffered to go free. So, my brethren, imperfect and unworthy as is the illustration, so we may conceive that when we are about to be condemned, and justly condemned for our sins, our glorious Brother stands up in our behalf, and does not need to speak a word, but only to show where he was wounded on the cross—

> "Five bleeding wounds he bears,
>   Received on Calvary;
> They pour effectual prayers,
>   They strongly speak for me;
> 'Forgive him, O forgive,' they cry,
> 'Nor let that ransomed sinner die!'"

Here, then, is hope for us. "If any man sin," much as he ought to deplore it, he need not despair. Our Advocate with the Father ever liveth to make intercession for them that come unto God through him, and through him we may find mercy. And here is no encouragement to sin, but the very contrary. If we truly trust in, truly love our interceding Lord, we shall be supremely anxious for his dear sake to turn from sin, to live for him who died for us; yea, who ever lives as our Saviour.

3. This suggests another respect in which is seen our need of our Lord's perpetual intercession. We make such slow progress in attaining holiness—holiness, which is the noblest thing men can aspire to—holiness, "without which no man shall see the Lord." Many a Christian, as he sorrowfully sees how often he yields to

temptation, how his character breaks down afresh where he thought it had grown most firm, is at times inclined to think it impossible that he should ever become really holy. But remember how Jesus prayed the night before his atoning death, "Sanctify them in the truth; thy word is truth." "I pray not that thou shouldest take them out of the world, but that thou shouldest keep them from the evil." Think you that he, who ever lives to intercede for his people, does not still pray this prayer, that they may be sanctified and kept from the evil? Do you doubt that he prays for them still, as he did when on earth? His people's wants have not changed, and as for him, he is "the same yesterday and to-day and forever." Find me a young man far from his home whose mother used to pray for him when they were together, and try to make him believe that she does not pray for him still. "No, no," he would say, "if she is living, she prays for me." Brethren, he who prays for us "ever lives." When the Jews gathered at the temple on the great day of atonement, and the high priest went into the holy of holies to pray for the people and himself, did the people doubt whether he was praying? Why, for that very purpose he had withdrawn from their view. So for that very purpose our High Priest has entered "not into a holy place made with hands, like in pattern to the true, but into heaven itself, now to appear before the face of God for us." And do not say that the Jewish high priest was absent but a few minutes, while it is long since Jesus went away. On the scale of the ages it is but a little while since he entered the heavenly sanctuary, having "been once offered to bear the sins of many," and any moment he may "appear a second time apart from sin unto salvation." Let us be sure that while absent he perpetually carries on his work of intercession.

Think of him, then, as still praying, "Sanctify them in the truth. Keep them from the evil." In all our disheartening failures to keep good resolutions, even when we may be tempted to think it scarce worth while for us to try to be holy, let us remember that Jesus prays for us, and, "forgetting the things which are behind, and reaching forth unto those things which are before, let us press toward the mark." Ah! brethren, though it might often seem to us the bitterest irony now for a man to call you and me the saints of the Lord, yet, if indeed we are in Christ, and thus are new creatures, we have but to trust in his intercession for the sanctifying Spirit, and earnestly strive to "grow in grace," and we shall make progress; yea, sadly imperfect as is now our conformity to the Saviour's beautiful image, "we know that when he shall appear we shall be like him, for we shall see him as he is." O burdened spirit, crying, "Wretched man that I am, who shall deliver me from the body of this death?" be sure to add, "I thank God, through Jesus Christ our Lord." The Saviour will continue to intercede, the Spirit will help your infirmities, and you shall at last be pure from sin, and safe from temptation to sin, a saint of the Lord forever.

4. When we are in sorrow it is a blessed thing that Jesus ever lives to pray for us. He was himself while on earth, "a man of sorrows, and acquainted with grief."

And he showed the truest, tenderest sympathy with the sorrows of others. Who does not think at once of that touching scene at Bethany? "Jesus wept," in affection for the departed, in sympathy with the bereaved. And presently, standing by the tomb, he said, "Father, I thank thee that thou hast heard me." Then he had been praying, asking that he might be able to raise Lazarus from the dead. We do not expect him now to pray that miracles may be wrought in behalf of the bereaved. We do not expect him now to give back the buried brother to his sisters, or to the widowed mother her only son. But shall it not be a consolation to us all in our afflictions, to feel assured that he now intercedes for us; that now, too, the Father hears him, and that by the gracious influences of the Holy Ghost, the Comforter, this affliction shall work for us glory? And though we cannot now see his tears, nor hear his loving voice, as did the mourners at Bethany, neither do we need to send a messenger many miles, and wait, day after day, and go forth into the suburbs to meet him; he is everywhere alike near, and ever ready to pray for us to his Father and our Father, to his God and our God.

5. When we come to die—he is "alive forevermore." One of his servants, when near to death, saw "heaven opened, and the Son of Man standing on the right hand of God," where he represents and intercedes for his people. And so in departing he committed his spirit to him, as now exalted and glorious, and ready to receive it. And so, amid all the cruel injustice and suffering, he was calm and forgiving. And so, though they were stoning him to death, "he fell asleep." O, whenever

you are called to die, brother, and however, whether among loving friends in your pleasant home, or far away in loneliness and want, whether with ample forewarning or in the suddenness of a moment, think of your interceding Saviour standing on the right hand of God, and say, "Lord Jesus, receive my spirit," and you too shall fall asleep.

6. Even this is not the end of his work for his people. There shall be a "redemption of the body." Many have been sad in the last twenty years, because the bodies of their loved ones lie so far away, lie perhaps undistinguished among the huge masses of the unnamed dead. But he who receives the departing spirit to himself will also care for the mouldering body. His resurrection is a pledge of the glorious resurrection of his people. "If we believe that Jesus died and rose again, even so them also who through Jesus have fallen asleep, will God bring with him." "Who shall fashion anew the body of our humiliation, that it may be conformed to the body of his glory." Then, the spirit reunited with the risen and glorified body, "so shall we ever be with the Lord."

And he who saved them will be ever living to keep them safe, unto all eternity.

My friends, how shall we think of Jesus? What conception shall we cherish of him whom, "having not seen, we love," who ever liveth to intercede for us? Many centuries ago, on the eastern slope of Mount Olivet, towards Bethany, twelve men stood together, one talking to the others. Presently he lifted up his hands and blessed them; and with hands still uplifted, and words of blessing still lingering on his lips, he was parted from them and rose toward heaven, till a cloud received him out of their sight. Years passed, and one of the eleven was an exile on a lonely island. It was the Lord's day, and he was in the Spirit. Hearing behind him a mighty voice that seemed to call him, he turned, and lo! one like unto the Son of Man—it was the Saviour who had been parted from him long years before. He was arrayed in robes of majesty, and girt about with a golden girdle; his whole head shone white as snow with celestial glory; his eyes were as a flame of fire; and his feet like unto burnished brass, as if it had been refined in a furnace; and his voice as the voice of many waters; and his countenance as the sun shineth in his strength. Yes, the feet that once wearily trod the dusty roads of Judea now shone like molten brass. The eyes that were full of tears as he gazed upon doomed Jerusalem now gleamed as a flame of fire. The countenance that writhed in agony as he lay prostrate on his face in the garden, that was streaked with the blood that fell from his thorn-pierced brow, was now as the sun shineth in his strength. And the voice as the voice of many waters—it was the same voice that in gentleness and love had so often encouraged the sinful and sorrowing to draw near—it is the same voice that now calls us to come unto God through him, and declares that he is able to save us completely, since he ever lives to intercede for us. O, my hearer, slight all the sounds of earth, all the voices of the universe; be deaf to the thunder's mighty tones, and stand careless amid "the wreck of matter and the crush of worlds"— but O, slight not the loving voice of Jesus.

VI.

LET US HAVE PEACE WITH GOD.

Therefore being justified by faith, let us have peace with God, through our Lord Jesus Christ.—Romans 5: 1.

IT is nearly four centuries ago now, that a young professor from the north of Germany went to Rome. He was a man of considerable learning and versatile mind. Yet he did not go to Rome to survey the remains of antiquity or the treasures of modern art. He went to Rome because he was in trouble about his sins and could find no peace. Having been educated to regard Rome as the centre of the Christian world, he thought he would go to the heart of things and see what he could there find. He had reflected somewhat at home, and had talked with other men more advanced than himself, on the thought that the just shall live by faith; but still that thought had never taken hold of him. We read—some of you remember the story quite well—how one day, according to the strange ideas that prevailed and still prevail at Rome, he went climbing up a stairway on his knees, pausing to pray on every step, to see if that would not help him about his sins. Then, as he climbed slowly up, he seemed to hear a voice echoing down the stairway, "The just shall live by faith; the just shall live by faith." And so he left alone his dead works, he arose from his knees and went down the stairway to his home to think about that great saying: "The just shall live by faith."

It is no wonder that with such an experience, and such a nature, Martin Luther should have lived to shake the Christian world with the thought that justification by faith is the great doctrine of Christianity, "the article of a standing or a falling church." It is no wonder that John Wesley, rising up with living earnestness, when England was covered with a pall of spiritual death, should have revived the same thought—justification by faith.

Yet it is not true that the doctrine of justification by faith is all of the Gospel. It is true that the doctrine of justification by faith is simply one of the several ways by which the Gospel takes hold of men. You do not hear anything of that doctrine in the Epistles of John. He has another way of presenting the Gospel salvation, namely, that we must love Christ, and be like him, and obey him. I think sometimes that Martin Luther made the world somewhat one-sided by his doctrine of justification by faith; that the great mass of the Protestant world are inclined to suppose there is no other way of looking on the Gospel. There are very likely some here to-day who would be more impressed by John's way of presenting the matter; but probably the majority would be more impressed by Paul's way, and it is our business to present now this and now that, to present first one side and then the other. So we have here before us to-day Paul's great doctrine of justification by faith, in perhaps one of his most striking statements, "Therefore, being justified by faith, let us have peace with God through our Lord Jesus Christ."

My friends, we talk and hear about these Gospel truths, and repeat these Scripture words, and never stop to ask ourselves whether we have a clear idea of what is meant. What does Paul mean, when he talks about being justified? There has been a great deal of misapprehension as to his meaning. Martin Luther was all wrong in his early life, because he had been reared up in the idea that a justified man means simply a just man, a good man, and that he could not account himself justified or hope for salvation until he was a thoroughly good man. Now, the Latin word from which we borrow our word "justified" does mean *to make just,* and as the Romanists use the Latin, their error is natural. But Paul's Greek word means not to *make* just, but to *regard* as just, to treat as just. That is a very important difference,— not to make just, but to regard and treat as just. How would God treat you, if you were a righteous man; if you had, through all your life, faithfully performed all your duties, conforming to all your relations to your fellow-beings,—how would he regard you and treat you? He would look upon you with complacency. He would smile on you as one that was in his sight pleasing. He would bless you as long as you lived in this world, and, when you were done with this world, he would delight to take you home to his bosom, in another world, because you would deserve it. And now as God would treat a man who was just because he deserved it, so the Gospel proposes to treat men who are not just and who do not deserve it, if they believe in the Lord Jesus Christ. He will treat them as just, though they are not just, if they believe in Christ; that is to say, he will look upon them with his favor; he will smile upon them in his love; he will bless them with every good as long as they live, and when they die he will delight to take them home to his own bosom, though they never deserved it, through his Son, Jesus Christ. That is what Paul means by justification. And when Martin Luther found that out he found peace. This Epistle to the Romans had always stopped his progress when reading the New Testament. He would read, in the Latin version, "For therein is revealed the justice of God," and he felt in his heart that God's justice must condemn him. But now he came to see what was really meant by the righteousness of God, the righteousness which God provides and bestows on the believer in Jesus. A sinful man, an undeserving man, may get God Almighty's forgiveness and favor and love, may be regarded with complacency and delight, though he does not deserve it, if he believes in the Lord Jesus Christ. That is justification by faith.

It is one thing to take hold of this matter in the way of doctrinal conception and expression, and of course, God be thanked! it is another thing to receive it in the heart. There are many people who get hold of it all in the heart with trust and peace that never have a correct conception of it as a doctrine. Yet I suppose it is worth while that we should endeavor to see these things clearly. Other things being equal, they will be the holiest and most useful Christians who have the clearest perception of the great facts and truths of the Gospel. So I recommend to you that whenever any one tries to explain to you one of these great doctrinal truths, you shall listen with fixed attention and see if you cannot get a clearer view of the Gospel teachings on that subject, for it will do you good.

Now let us come to the second thought here, viz.: being justified *by faith*. A man might say, if God proposes to deal with those who are not just, as if they were, why does he condition it upon their believing the Gospel of Jesus Christ? Why cannot God proclaim a universal amnesty at once, and be done with it, to all his sinful, weak children, and treat them all as if they were just, without their believing? I don't think this is hard to see. God does not merely propose to deal with us for the time being as if we were just, but he proposes in the end to make us actually just. It would be an unsatisfactory salvation to a right-minded man if God proposed merely to exempt us from the consequences of our sins and not to deliver us from our sins. You do not want merely to escape punishment for sin without ever becoming good; you want to be righteous and holy; you want to be delivered from sin itself as well as from the consequences of sin. And this Gospel, which begins by its proclamation that God is willing to treat men as just, although they are not just, does not stop there. It proposes to be the means by which God will take hold of men's characters and make them just, make them holy. You may, for the moment, conceive of such a thing as that God should make a proclamation of universal amnesty, and treat all men as if they were just; but that would not make them any better. The Gospel is not merely to deliver us from the consequences of sin, but to deliver us from the power of sin. You can conceive of an amnesty as to the consequences of sin, which should extend to persons that will not even believe there is such an amnesty; but you cannot see how the Gospel is to have any power in delivering us from the *dominion* of sin, unless we *believe* the Gospel. It can do so only through belief. Therefore it is not possible that a man should be justified without belief. I think it is useful that we should thus try to see that this is not a matter of mere arbitrary appointment on the part of the Sovereign Power of the Universe, but that the condition is necessary—that it cannot be otherwise. "Being justified by faith," it reads; and we cannot be justified without faith, because the same Gospel is also to take hold of us and make us just.

And now, some one who feels a little freshened interest in this subject, some man who has never got hold of the Gospel faith says to himself: "I wonder if the preacher is going to explain to me what believing is, what faith is. I never heard any one succeed in explaining faith." Well, if you will pardon me, the best explanation of faith I ever heard was given by a negro preacher in Virginia. As the story was told me, one Sunday afternoon, a few years ago, some of them were lying on the ground together, and one of them spoke and said, "Uncle Reuben, can you explain this: Faith in de Lord, and faith in de debbil." "To be sure I can. There is two things: in de fust place, faith in de Lord, and then faith in de debbil. Now, in the fust place, fustly, there is faith. What is faith? What is faith? Why, faith is jes faith. Faith ain't nothing less than faith. Faith ain't nothing more than faith. Faith is jes faith—now

I done splain it." Really, that man was right, there is nothing to explain. Faith is as simple a conception as the human mind can have. How, then, can you explain faith? You are neither able to analyze it into parts, nor can you find anything simpler with which to compare it. So also as to some other things, that are perfectly easy and natural in practical exercise, and cannot be explained. What is love? Well, I won't go into an elaborate metaphysical definition of love, but if I wanted a child to love me, I should try to exhibit myself in such a character to him and act in such ways that the little child would see in me something to love, and would feel like loving. There would then be no need of an explanation of what love is Did you ever hear a satisfactory definition of laughter? If you wanted to make a man laugh, would you attempt to define laughter to him? You might possibly succeed in making a laughable definition; but otherwise definitions won't make a man laugh. You would simply say or do something ludicrous, and he would laugh readily enough if he was so disposed; and if the man be not in a mood for laughing, all your explanations are utterly useless. And so what is faith? There is nothing to explain. Everybody knows what faith is. If you want to induce a man to believe in the Lord Jesus Christ, you must hold up the Lord to him in his true character, and then, if he is in a mood to believe, he will believe, and if he is disinclined to belief, all your explanations will be fruitless. The practical result may even be obstructed by attempts to explain. What is faith? You know what faith is. Every one knows.

Well, then, a man might say, "If you mean by faith in the Lord, the simple idea of believing what the Scripture says concerning him, the idea of believing its teachings about the Lord Jesus Christ to be true, if that is what faith means, then all of us are believers, all have faith." I am afraid not. I am afraid there are some here who have not faith. Has a man faith in the Lord Jesus Christ who simply does not disbelieve in him? I may not deny that what the Gospel says is true, but is that believing? Yonder sits a gentleman; suppose some one should come hastily up the aisle, calling his name, and say, "Your house is afire." The gentleman sits perfectly quiet and looks unconcerned, as people so often do when listening to preaching. The man repeats it: "I say your house is afire." But still he sits in his place. Some one near him says, "You hear what that man says. Do you believe it?" "Yes, I believe it," he carelessly replies, and does not stir. You would all say, "The man is insane, or certainly he does not believe it; for if he did, he would not sit perfectly still and remain perfectly unconcerned." Even so when the preacher speaks of sin and guilt and ruin, of God's wrath and the fire that is not quenched; or when he stands with joyful face and proclaims to his hearers that for their sin and ruin there is a Saviour; and they say they believe, and yet look as if it were of no concern to them at all, at all; then I say they do not believe it—the thing is not possible. They may not disbelieve it; they may not care to make an attempt to overturn it; they may be in a sort of negative mood; but they do not believe it. With that statement I suppose there are a great many of us who concur and who will at once say, "Often I fear that I do not really believe it. If I did believe it, the Gospel would have more power over my heart and more power over my life than it does have. And what, oh, what shall I do?" The preacher has to remind you of that father to whom the Saviour came when the disciples had tried in vain to heal his suffering child. Jesus said to him: "All things are possible to him that believeth;" and he replied: "I believe; help thou my unbelief." That should be your cry: "I believe; help thou my unbelief." The man would not deny that he believed, and yet felt bound to add that he knew he did not believe as he ought to. Now the comfort is, that he who sees all hearts accepted that man's confessedly imperfect faith, and granted his request. That has often been the preacher's comfort as he uttered the same cry, "I believe; help thou my unbelief;" and God give it as a comfort to you! But do not content yourself with such a state of things, with any such feeble, half-way believing. Nay, let us cherish all that tends to strengthen our faith in the Gospel; let us read the Word of God, praying that we may be able to believe; let us say from day to day, as the disciples said: "Lord, increase our faith."

The text proceeds: "Therefore, being justified by faith, let us have peace with God." Instead of the declaration, "We have peace with God," the best authorities for the text make it an exhortation, "Let us have peace with God;" and so the Revised Version reads. Some critics admit that the documents require us so to read, but say that they can see no propriety in an exhortation at this point—that it seems much more appropriate to understand the apostle as asserting a fact. Yet I think we can see meaning and fitness in the text as corrected: "Being justified by faith, let us have peace with God."

Let us have peace with God, notwithstanding our unworthiness. My friends, we cannot have peace with God so long as we cling to the notion that we are going to deserve it. Just there is the difficulty with many of those who are trying to be at peace with God. They have been clinging to the thought that they must first become worthy, and then become reconciled to God; and they will have to see more clearly that they must come to Christ in order that, being reconciled, they may be made good, may become worthy. We may say there are two conceivable ways to have peace with God. It is conceivable to have peace with God through our worthiness, and it is conceivable and also practicable to have peace with God through our Lord Jesus Christ, though we be unworthy. Then let us have peace with him, although so unworthy, through our Lord Jesus Christ.

Again, let us have peace with God, though we are still sinful and unholy, though we know we come far short in character and in life of what God's children ought to be. We must be, ought to be, intensely dissatisfied with ourselves; but let us be satisfied with our Saviour, and have peace with God through him; not content with the idea of remaining such as we are, but, seeing that the same Gospel which offers us forgiveness and acceptance offers us also a genuine renewal through our Lord Jesus Christ, and promises that finally we shall be made holy, as God is holy, shall indeed be perfect, as our Father in heaven is perfect. Let us rejoice in the gracious promise of that perfect life, and, while seeking to be what we ought to be, let us have peace with God. Our *sanctification* is still sadly imperfect—the best of us well know that, and probably the best of us feel it most deeply; but, if we believe in the Lord Jesus Christ, our *justification* is perfect. We can never be more justified than we are now justified, though we shall be more and more made holy as long as we live, and at last made perfectly holy as we pass into the perfect world. My brethren, do think more and talk more of that. It is an intensely practical matter, not only for your comfort but for the strength of your life. If we believe in the Lord Jesus Christ, although we are painfully conscious that we are far from being in character and life what we ought to be, yet, through the perfect justification which we have at once, we shall in the end by his grace be made perfectly holy.

Let us have peace with God, though we have perpetual conflict with sin. What a singular idea! Peace with God, and yet conflict, yes, perpetual conflict, with a thousand forms of temptation to sin, temptations springing from our fellow-men, and temptations springing from spiritual tempters—perpetual conflict, and yet peace with God. Is not that conceivable? Is not that possible? In this conflict we are on the Lord's side; in this conflict the Lord is on our side; and so, though the battle must be waged against every form of sin, we may have peace with God.

And finally, let us have peace with God though he leaves us to suffer a thousand forms of distress and trial. "Let us have peace with God through our Lord Jesus Christ, by whom also we have had our access by faith into this grace wherein we stand: and let us rejoice in hope of the glory of God. And not only so, but let us also rejoice in our tribulations; knowing that tribulation worketh patience; and patience, proving; and proving, hope; and hope maketh not ashamed, because the love of God hath been shed abroad in our hearts through the Holy Ghost which was given unto us." Surely man may have peace with God, though he be left to suffer. For none of these things can separate us from God's love. Who shall separate us from Christ's love? "For I am persuaded that neither death nor life, neither angels nor principalities nor powers, neither things present nor things to come, neither height nor depth, nor any other creature, shall be able to separate us from the love of God which is in Christ Jesus our Lord." When we are in trouble, let us take fast hold upon that great thought, that trouble does not divide us from the love of God. Yea, God's peace can conquer trouble, and guard us, as in a fortress, against its assaults. "In nothing be anxious; but in everything, by prayer and supplication, with thanksgiving, let your requests be made known unto God. And the peace of God, which passeth all understanding, shall guard your hearts and your thoughts in Christ Jesus."

VII.

HOW THE GOSPEL MAKES MEN HOLY.

O wretched man that I am! who shall deliver me out of the body of this death? I thank God through Jesus Christ our Lord.—Rom. 7 : 24, 25.

THE language is intensely passionate,—" O wretched man that I am! who shall deliver me out of the body of this death?" Then with the sudden transition of passion, " I thank God through Jesus Christ our Lord."

"How shall I be good?" is a question that used sometimes to rise in your mind when you were a child, sometimes when nobody would imagine you were thinking of such things as that. "How shall I get to be good." And it is a question which, amid all the commotion of this runaway life of ours, comes back to us very often, comes back even to people whom you would not suppose to be thinking of such things at all. The grossly wicked men, the men who are the slaves of vice, many of them, perhaps all of them, have their moments when there is a sort of longing that rises in their souls to be good, and when the hope returns, indestructible, that somehow or other they will get to be good after all. It became a sort of jest a few years ago, I know, to speak of "the wickedest man in New York," but I wonder sometimes if the wickedest man —whoever he might happen to be, considered as God considers—does not sometimes want to be good.

For many of us it has been much more than a vague longing that comes back again and again. It has been an earnest effort, sometimes a fearful struggle, when we have been trying to be good, and we have wondered whether something would not come in the course of the varied experiences of life, that would render it easier for us to conquer in this struggle, easier to become good. As a man lives on, he cannot help thinking—it is so hard now—he cannot help thinking it will become easier to be good. And when changes occur in his outward life he hopes now to find it easier. He sets up a new home, it may be, and has a vague feeling that there he will be able to be good. He marries a pious woman, may be, and although he may not say a word about it, he has a sort of notion that perhaps that will be blessed to him, and he will become pious too. He loses a parent whom he leaned on, maybe he loses a little child that lay in his bosom, and amid the strange feelings that rise up then, and which he would not tell any one about, he thinks, "Now surely I shall become good." And so, as the experiences of life come and go, men still hope to be good. Who is there here to-day that does not hope to be good? Who is there here to-day that at this solemn moment, when we are thinking about the soul and its immortality, does not feel that to be good is the loftiest human aspiration and the best earthly attainment? O tell me, do *you* not feel it?

Now I have something to say about this great question; not to cite my own experience nor to give my own ideas, but I want to get your attention fixed on the apostle Paul's account of this matter, including some details of his own experience about it. Let us see how he treats the question. Here, in the Epistle to the Romans, the early chapters of the Epistle are occupied with what we call justification by faith, telling how, by believing in Jesus Christ, a man may be justified—that is, may be regarded and treated in the sight of God's law as if he were a just man. And then the next question that will arise to any reflecting mind, and which the apostle at once thought of, is, Ah! but how does this bear on the matter of making a man good, in his real personal character? It looks at first like a sort of legal fiction, the idea of considering a man as just in the sight of God's law, though he is not just, because of Jesus Christ in whom he believes. And then remains the question how a man is to be made righteous in his own character, how he is to be made holy. Many persons say that this is the weak point of the Gospel, that the Gospel tends to lessen the inducements to seek personal holiness, by undertaking to make a man just simply upon believing, by offering him amnesty. They talk as if the Gospel offer of free pardon for somebody else's sake, yea, and of title to everlasting life for somebody else's sake, were an encouragement to do wrong. There are many men holding the subject at arm's length who maintain that the Gospel tends to prevent us from trying to do right by thus offering salvation gratuitously.

Now the apostle Paul goes on to show in the first place the absurdity of such an idea; to show that when men talk as if it were a small thing to believe in Jesus Christ the Lord, they don't understand what they are talking about. He shows by several different illustrative arguments that if a man believes in Jesus Christ, that means something; that it means a power in his life, that it involves a change in his inner character. He says first that if we are believers, we are dead to sin and have risen to a new life. He reminds his readers that this great thought was symbolized by that affecting ceremony in which they entered upon the professed life of a Christian. "Know ye not that so many of us as were baptized unto Jesus Christ were baptized unto his death?" Our baptism referred to Jesus Christ, and don't you know that it referred especially to his death and resurrection? "That like as Christ was raised from the dead by the glory of the Father, even so we also should walk in newness of life." Do you not know that your baptism, at the outset of your Christian life, meant that you had died to sin and risen up from a grave like the symbolic grave in the waters, and that you were henceforth to walk in newness of life?

Then he takes a second illustration. We were slaves to sin; but now, by believing in Jesus Christ, we have changed masters; we have become, so to speak, the slaves of holiness, the slaves, as it were, of God. We have a new Master, and we shall render service to him. If a man is a *believer*, it means something. It means that he has changed masters. And yet again he says the case is like that of a woman whose husband died, and who is now married to a new husband; the children she now bears are no longer the children of the old husband, but of the new. If we are believers, we are indeed dead to the law; but we are married to Christ, and the fruit of our life is to be borne to him.

So, then, if anybody ever tells you that this Gospel of free grace is an encouragement to men to do wrong, tell him it cannot be so for a man who *believes* this Gospel, for that means something.

But the apostle by no means stops at that. Not only is it absurd to say that salvation by grace will encourage a man to do wrong, but justification by faith, salvation by grace, furnishes the only way in which a man can really become holy. The apostle shows this negatively and then positively. In this remarkable passage in the seventh chapter of Romans, over which so many religious controversies have been waged, and over which—what is ten thousand times better than religious controversies—have bent many troubled, yet trusting hearts as they found themselves exactly portrayed—in this passage the apostle first points out what is the best that the law can do to make a man holy. What is the best that a man can do in the way of becoming holy, by just trying to do right, simply trying, in his own strength, to do what he learns from God's law to be right? There are people who are trying to do that, some of them honest in it, some of them very earnest. They have got their notion as to what is right, and are trying to do right. Some of them look in the word of God; they push aside what they call its mysteries and all matters pertaining to doctrine, and take out of it only its rules of right, and they say: "Now I am trying to live according to these rules of right." What is the best they can do? Here is the apostle's answer.

In the first place, he says, God's law, which **is holy**

and just and good, will make a man see how bad he is. The child yonder will perhaps know what is meant by a plummet, and may have seen a man building on a wall and hanging down his plummet to see if his wall was perpendicular. "And judgment I have set to the line, and righteousness to the plummet." God's word applied to a man's life will help him to see whether he has been upright. Or the law of God is like a carpenter's straight edge, and, laid on his character, will enable him to see where his character deviates from rectitude. Ah, me! whosoever will honestly apply this test, the result will be a deep and painful consciousness that he does not come up to it.

But more than that happens. By the strange perversity of human nature, through the terrible sinfulness of sin, God's law not only makes us see how bad we are, but actually makes us worse. This is the thought that startles us here. God's law makes us worse instead of making us better. It stimulates sinfulness by restraint. Have you not often observed how restraint stimulates men to act contrary to it? Not long ago a lad of my acquaintance was talked to by his father about smoking, with an earnest request that he would not form the habit. Afterwards he said to his mother, "I am so glad that papa did not say I must not smoke, for if he had said I must not smoke, I could not have kept from it, but he simply said he wished I would not; I am so glad." There was a great deal of human nature in that.

There is a story of an old woman in one of the German towns who had lived to be seventy years old without going outside the ancient wall of the city. The fact was told to the Grand Duke, who sent the old lady word that he wished the fact to go down to history and begged she would be sure and not go out during the rest of her life. You may know what would happen. She got to thinking about it, and in a short time she went out. But, alas! not merely in ludicrous ways does this propensity of ours show itself, but in terrible earnest. The more a man knows something is wrong, sometimes the more it seems he cannot help doing it. If you should go into a darkened room, that had long been shut up, and with a broom should begin to clean it out, there might be a nest of vipers in one corner lying still in the darkness, but when you disturbed them they would thrust out their forked tongues and hiss and threaten to destroy you. So when God's law comes with its demand upon us to clean out the sin from our souls, how our sinful propensities, that were asleep maybe, will wake up and threaten us! The apostle says, "I was alive without the law once—I thought I was leading a true spiritual life and that I was a good man—but when the commandment came to me, sin revived (came to life again), and I died. I saw that all my spirituality was nothing, I was not a good man at all."

Is this the fault of the law of God? Paul says, No; the law of God is all right; the commandment of God is holy and just and good—the law is just as good as it can be, it is God's own law. It is not the fault of the law, it is the fault of sin. And this shows what a terrible thing sin is, that it takes the very rule of God that is given to direct our life, and perverts it into the occasion of doing worse—"that sin by the commandment might become exceeding sinful." Ah, when God has reached down to this sin-ruined world of ours and given his own rule of what is right, men take that and pervert it and become worse than they would have been without it. Does not sin thus show itself to be exceeding sinful? So the result is that man finds in himself a struggle which the apostle himself describes; there rise up desires to do right, and then there arise sinful dispositions, contrary to God's law; and these stimulate one another until sometimes his whole bosom is a battle-field.

Ah! the battle-fields in human bosoms! Do you know what it means? Don't you know? That is what the apostle proceeds to describe. "What I want to do," he says, "I do not do, and what I don't want to do I keep doing. I am fighting against myself; there are good tendencies in me, but there are evil tendencies in me, and I war, and I struggle, and I wrestle—O wretched man that I am! who shall deliver me from the body of this death?" That is the climax; that is the highest that ever soul of man reached on earth in trying to be good in his own strength—to come up to such an intensity of fearful, painful struggle that he would cry out in the agony of utmost desperation, "O wretched, wretched man that I am! who shall deliver me?" Does any one sit coolly here to-day and say there is a touch of extravagance there? Well, it is the apostle's extravagance. And oh, the more a man strives to be what he ought to be, while losing sight of the gospel of Jesus Christ, the more he will find himself in sympathy with that wild, passionate cry of a struggling, tortured soul.

There has been a good deal of controversy between what are called Calvinists and what are called Arminians, as to whether this passage I have just been speaking of gives the experience of a renewed man or of an unrenewed man. I think the truth is, as some recent writers have been showing, that it does not really give either, but gives the experience of any man, either renewed or unrenewed, who is looking to the law to make him holy. Renewed men often fall back upon that. They lose the firm hold on justification by faith, and they get to thinking to save themselves, to make themselves holy by their own merit. Then no wonder they fall down in despondency and almost in despair. Unrenewed men, on the other hand, are often trying to do right according to what they see to be right—according to their own knowledge of God's word. And *any* man who tries to be holy in his own strength, this is his experience. Such a conflict there is in the bosoms of men, and of the best men, yea, a battle-field in every bosom here on earth. Nowhere is sin completely triumphant, and nowhere, yet, has holiness completely triumphed. But, oh! the difference between those beaten back on the field of battle, beaten back and ever back, who can see no hope of aught but destruction, unless something strange they cannot anticipate should occur, and those who triumphantly rely on the help of God, and are certain of success. O the difference! And so Paul breaks forth, "I thank God through Jesus Christ our Lord."

Let us then turn to the other thought of the apostle,

as to what the gospel can do towards making a man holy. He makes three points about this.

First, the gospel sets a man free from condemnation, because of his past sin. "There is therefore now no condemnation to them that are in Christ Jesus." The first thought of a man who begins to think of leading a new life is, "What am I to do with all these sins I have already committed?" But the gospel of Jesus Christ frees us from the guilt of sin, from condemnation because of our sin. There is now no condemnation. The gospel comes to the ruined debtor to pay all his debts in a moment; it comes to the prisoner to break the bonds that bound him and to open the doors of his prison and set him free.

And then, in the next place, the gospel comes with a new moral power. The apostle speaks of a third law that comes in like a reinforcement: "But the law of the spirit of life in Christ Jesus hath emancipated me from the law of sin and death." This new reinforcing power is the Spirit of God. He calls it the law of the Spirit. The law of God and the law in our members are in fierce conflict, and there comes a new moral power to give us the victory. My brethren, we do not preach as much as we ought, nor think half as much as we ought, about the Spirit of God. I do not want you to talk less or think less of the atoning death, or the interceding life, or the tender sympathy, or the beautiful example, or the divine power of the divine Redeemer; not less of that, but more of the Spirit of God. Why, Jesus himself said a very remarkable thing about the Holy Spirit when he was just taking leave of the disciples. On that night he said: "Nevertheless, I tell you the truth." Now, when a dignified, self-respecting person condescends to say: "I am telling you the truth," there must be some very special occasion for it. He knew he was about to say something hard for them to believe: "Nevertheless, I tell you the truth; it is expedient for you that I go away; for if I go not away, the Comforter will not come to you." He himself says you are better off as it is with the Holy Spirit, the great Counsellor and Guide and Comforter, in his special mission, than if he had not come, and Jesus himself were still on earth. Think of that; cherish the Spirit's mission; pray, above all things, when you pray, that your Heavenly Father will give the Holy Spirit to you, that you may be strengthened. I say again, we think too little about that great idea and element of the gospel. We go struggling on, forgetting that mighty reinforcement that our gracious God offers us in our life's battle, "the law of the Spirit of life in Christ Jesus." The next time you are specially tempted cry out mightily for the help of the Spirit of God. And when you are despondent, and fancy you can never get to be what your soul longs for, remember what the Spirit of God can make out of even such materials as your character and your life.

One more point. The apostle mentions a new and mighty incentive which the Gospel presents, when he says, a little further on: "For as many as are led by the Spirit of God, they are the sons of God." My friends, there are four ways in which it is conceivable that a man should serve God. One of them is practically impossible, that you should serve God with fear and trembling as a subject serves a tyrant. There are people who look upon God in the light of a despot; but they cannot really serve him thus. Again, are we to serve God as a poor, cowering slave serves a hard master, from fear of punishment? Nay, no man would truly serve God, simply from fear that God would punish him if he did not. The third way a man may conceivably serve God is in the hope that he will reward him. But nobody would ever truly serve God, if it were simply and alone from a desire of reward, not even from a desire to reach the blessed heaven. The other way to serve God, of which the apostle speaks, is to serve him out of filial love; to serve him, not as the subject serves a tyrant, not as the servant his master, not as a hireling for pay, but to serve him as a loving son serves a kind father, out of filial love. That is the great idea which Christianity brought into the world on this subject. That is the new motive which Jesus Christ brings to bear on the souls of men, to try to do right out of filial love to their Father. And so Paul proceeds to speak of the " Spirit of adoption, whereby we cry, Abba, Father."

The apostle's heart is very tender here. He has been depicting those terrible struggles which he himself had had in other days with his own sinful propensities; his heart is now very tender, and so he falls back upon his mother tongue. He is writing in Greek; but he uses the Aramaic word, *Abba*. If you were talking French or German, and were beginning to speak of things that very much touched your heart; if you began, for instance, to speak of your dead mother, whose very name makes you quiver, you would not then speak in French or German; you would not say mother in French or German; you would use the word you used when a child. So the apostle here uses the Aramaic language he had spoken in childhood: "the Spirit of adoption, whereby we cry, Abba." This is what he used to say when he was a boy, and he translates it afterwards,— "*Abba*, Father."

I met a young man not long ago, a friend of mine, who told me his father had recently died, and a little after his wife's father. My young friend was talking about it until he could not talk. He broke down with emotion as he told me how lonely he felt now that both were gone and he had no one to lean on, no one to look up to. Even some old men, when they get into trouble, think about the father they used to go to, and say, "I wish I could ask him what he thinks about the matter." The Scriptures take hold of that thought and tell us we are not to look to God simply as a master who will punish, not merely as one who will reward, but to look to God as our Father, Father, Father in heaven.

So, then, if a man looks to the law to make him holy, the highest result will be a cry of anguish, "Wretched man that I am, who shall deliver me?" But turning to the gospel, he sees hope of being delivered and becoming holy, and may say, "I thank God, through Jesus Christ our Lord."

VIII.

INTENSE CONCERN FOR THE SALVATION OF OTHERS.

For I could wish that myself were accursed from Christ for my brethren.—Romans ix: 3.

THIS is known to students of the Scriptures as one of the passages which are commonly accounted difficult,—one of the hard places. A preacher would not be likely to take such a passage as his text, unless he supposed it possible to present a simple and natural explanation of it, and to draw from it as thus explained some useful, practical lessons. Before I try to do this, it may be allowable to offer two or three hints as to the course we ought to pursue in studying the difficult passages of Scripture,—hints that would, indeed, apply to all our Scriptural studies.

My first hint would be this: Be willing to let the Scripture mean what it wants to mean. You may say, "that, of course," but it is very far from being a matter of course. Be willing to let the Scripture mean what it wants to mean. We come to it knowing beforehand what things we like and what things we dislike, and if we find in the passage something not in accordance with the ideas we have been reared in, or that now have possession of our minds, we say, "Well, of course it can't mean that," and then we begin to search for some other meaning. The plainer the passage, the harder to find anything else than what is plainly meant, and so we go off and say, " What a difficult passage of Scripture!" Has not that often happened to you? It has happened to me. I have waked up to find, after long years of study, that something I always thought was a very hard passage was plain enough, only I had never been willing to allow it to mean what it wished to mean.

My second hint would be: Take good account of the connection. We are peculiarly prone to neglect the connection in dealing with Scripture, because we have the Bible printed—most unfortunately, I think—in little scraps of broken sentences, set before us as if they were separate paragraphs—which is not done in any other book in the world—and broken up also in larger portions which are called chapters, where the connection is often completely severed, and yet we cannot help imagining there must be a new subject at the beginning of a new chapter. Moreover, we are accustomed to hear short passages taken as texts, and too often interpreted without regard to the connection. The connection is sometimes the entire book. I doubt if there is one sentence in the epistle to the Hebrews, and there are very few in the epistle to the Romans, which can be really understood without taking account of the whole epistle. But often the connection is only some sentences before and after. Now, if you consider the connection, it is wonderful how it will help you to understand a difficult passage. You go above the difficult place; you launch on the stream above, and come floating down, and your boat is borne over the rocks. If you cannot determine the precise meaning of the words, you will see what is the general thought of the passage as a whole, and that is the main consideration.

The last hint I shall mention is, that we must take good account of the state of the writer's mind, when he says these things. What is he thinking about? What is he aiming at? How is he feeling, when he uses this language? I am sure, if any of you have tried it, you will find that the more care you exercise, when reading the Scriptures, in trying to enter into sympathy with the thought and feeling of the sacred writer, the better you will be prepared to see what he really means.

Now, all these hints I have ventured to offer are of importance to us in studying the text: "I could wish that myself were accursed from Christ for my brethren." Observe he does not say "I wish." Not he. He could not say that. But he almost says it. The original could not be better translated in any other words than those used in our version. The apostle seems to be like one who is on the point of saying something wrong. He rushes, as it were, towards the brink of saying that he wishes to be accursed for his brethren, only he does not say it—stopping on the brink because it would be wrong, because his devout heart would shrink back from the idea of being accursed from Christ, even for his brethren. Now, why does the inspired apostle use this strange language? Why does Paul almost say a terrible thing, so terrible that many people, as they come upon it, and begin to inquire into the meaning, all out of sympathy with the passion of the writer, imagine that they must explain it away—that it must be impossible for him to approach even to the brink of saying what would be so dreadful.

The epistle to the Romans is taken up in its doctrinal portion with the great thought of justification by faith: that men are justified simply by believing in Jesus. The apostle discusses that in the first five chapters. We had a text from that portion some Sundays ago. Then, in the next three chapters he discusses the bearing of this justification by faith upon the matter of sanctification, showing how it works in helping us to be good. We had a text from that portion not long ago. In three more chapters he now discusses the bearing of justification by faith upon the privileges of the Jews. The Jews considered themselves far superior, in point of religion, to any nation in the world, and they would begin to see at once that if the apostle's doctrine be true, and a man is accepted through simple faith in Jesus Christ, then a Gentile might exercise that as well as a Jew, and so a Gentile would be as good as a Jew. We cannot imagine how they would shrink back from any doctrine with such a conclusion, that a Gentile is as good as a Jew. We do not know of any national or race prejudices in our time that are so strong as the prejudices then existing between Jew and Gentile. They would especially dislike such teaching from Paul the apostle. They would say he is a renegade himself to the religion of his fathers. He is a traitor to his people. They were indignant at the idea of his saying that a Gentile could be saved as well as a Jew. When Paul said, the following spring, in his address at Jerusalem, that Jesus had told him to go to the Gentiles, they broke out in rage, and he had to be saved by the Roman garrison. The apostle knew how intensely they would dislike this idea, and so he wanted to assure them in entering upon this topic—the bearing of justification by faith upon the privileges of the Jews—he wanted to assure them that he loved his own people, and although he is bound to acknowledge, as he is going to acknowledge, that the great mass of his people are rejecting the Messiah, while Gentiles all around are believing unto salvation, yet he acknowledges this with inexpressible pain and grief. That is the way he feels. That is what he wants to impress upon them. He sees what is coming for his nation. This epistle was written twelve years before the destruction of Jerusalem, and only eight years before the war that led to that destruction. The apostle saw that soon their hot fanaticism would break out in desperate rebellion against the Roman authority, and sooner or later they must be crushed out and ground to atoms. Here was a man who saw that his own nation, his own race, bound to him not merely by nationality in the ordinary sense, but by ties of blood through long and pure descent, was going to ruin. His race alone of all the great races of the earth can trace their history back to a historic ancestor; for all the other peoples find their ancestry lost in darkness, but the Jews could go back in history to their common father. His race had great and glorious deeds connected with its history in the past, and had yet more glorious promises for the future in connection with the Messiah. And this man, who loved his people, who loved them so intensely that when the Lord appeared to him in a vision, and said, "Go preach to the heathen," he remonstrated and did not want to obey, and had to be driven by persecution, clearly sees that the Jewish nation is about to perish. Not only does he see that national destruction awaits them, but he sees that the great mass of them are slighting their own Messiah, now that he is come, are rejecting the salvation that is in him alone, and plunging madly into the darkness of eternity. He feels all that. And listen how he speaks, in introducing this subject, " I say the truth in Christ—I lie not." A man of self-respect never condescends to assure people that he is telling the truth and not lying, unless there is some extraordinary reason for it. "I say the truth in Christ—I lie not, my conscience also bearing me witness in the Holy Ghost, that I have great heaviness and continual sorrow in my heart. For I could wish that myself were accursed from Christ for my brethren, my kinsmen according to the flesh ; who are Israelites ; to whom pertaineth the adoption, and the glory, and the covenants, and the giving of the law, and the service of God, and the promises ; whose are the fathers, and of whom as concerning the flesh the Messiah came, who is over all, God blessed forever." You see that ordinary language does not suffice to express his emotion. In his swelling passion of soul he rushes to the very brink of saying what would be wrong to say, and shrinks back from saying it. That seems to me to be the plain meaning of the passage, and all that is necessary to understand it is sympathy with the sacred writer's state of mind.

Now, as thus explained, the passage is rich in instruction. I shall only gather out three or four of its lessons, all of which connect themselves with one thought: intense concern for the salvation of others.

1. And first. Concern for the salvation of others is naturally enhanced by patriotism. If a man feels at all as a Christian ought to feel in the way of desire for the salvation of all his fellow-men, through common human sympathies and common wants and destinies, then he will naturally feel more of such concern for those who are allied to him by ties of nationality; dear to him through feelings of patriotism—his own people. And all the more if they are also dear to him by ties of personal affection—if they live in his own locality, if they share all his peculiar interests, his difficulties, his joys. Still more if they are his friends, and most of all if they are his kindred. All the reasons we have for desiring the salvation of mankind at large exist in such cases, and then all these additional reasons enhance the concern we naturally feel for their salvation. My friends, not only Paul felt thus, but he who stood on Olivet and looked out on the splendid capital of his country, which he knew was doomed to destruction, shall we not suppose that he felt some peculiar interest in his own people? Why not?

2. Again. Concern for the salvation of others is not prevented by a belief in what we call the doctrines of grace; is not prevented by believing in divine sovereignty, and predestination and election. Many persons intensely dislike the ideas which are expressed by these phrases. Many persons shrink away from ever accepting them, because those ideas are in their minds asso-

ciated with the notion of stolid indifference. They say if predestination be true, then it follows that a man cannot do anything for his own salvation; that if he is to be saved he will be saved, and he has nothing to do with it, and need not care, nor need any one else care. Now, this does not at all follow, and I will prove that it does not follow, by the fact that Paul himself, the great oracle of this doctrine in the Scripture, has uttered these words of burning passionate concern for the salvation of others, so close by the passages in which he has taught the doctrines in question. Look back from the text, run back a few sentences and you will find the very passage upon which many stumble: "Moreover, whom he did predestinate"—there are people who shudder at the very words—" them he also called, and whom he called, them he also justified; and whom he justified, them he also glorified." Just a little while after he uttered those words from which men want to infer that the man who believes it need not feel concerned for his salvation or the salvation of others, just a little after, came the passionate words of the text. Nor is that all, for you will find just following the text, where he speaks of Esau and Jacob, that God made a difference between them before they were born, and where he says of Pharaoh that God raised him up that he might show his power in him, and that God's name might be declared throughout all the earth. "Therefore he hath mercy on whom he will, and whom he will he hardeneth." Some good people fairly shiver at the inference, which seems to them to be inevitable from such language as that. But I say the inference must be wrong, for the inspired man who uttered this language, only a few moments before had uttered these words of the text. And whenever you find your heart or the heart of your friend inclined to shrink away from these great teachings of divine Scripture concerning sovereignty and predestination, then I pray you make no argument about it, but turn to this language of concern for the salvation of others, so intensely passionate that men wonder and think surely it cannot mean what it says. The trouble is in this and many cases that we draw unwarranted inferences from the teachings of the Bible, and then cast all the odium of those inferences upon the truths from which we draw them. Now, I say that whatever be true, for or against the apostle's doctrines of predestination and divine sovereignty in salvation, it is not true that they will make a man careless as to his own salvation or that of others; seeing that they had no such effect on Paul himself, but right in between these two great passages come the wonderful words of the text.

3. The third lesson is, that concern for the salvation of others will sometimes rise to intense passion. The Apostle Paul is not always saying, "Woe is me if I preach not the gospel." He said that under certain circumstances. Nor does he anywhere else use such an expression as this of the text. So, as I said, concern for the salvation of others will sometimes rise to intense passion.

And more generally, let us say, piety has elements of passionate feeling. I suppose that piety is threefold: there is thought, and feeling, and action. Different persons are inclined to prefer one or the other of these three, according to their own natural constitution, their education, prejudices, etc.; but all three are necessary to a symmetrical Christian character and Christian life. Some persons will say, if you talk with them, "O, I do love Christian thought—I love to hear a preacher who presents to me inspiring thoughts, especially if there is some new thought." And then some of them are carried away with the idea that they want modern thought, as they call it, instead of Scripture. But meantime it is true that we also need feeling. A man who finds himself inclined to prefer what he calls thought in connection with Christianity, and to neglect Christian feeling and Christian action, ought to see to it lest his character be deformed because wanting in essential elements, and ought to cultivate in himself a regard for feeling and for action. Many cultivated people in our time, as they look with ill-concealed disgust upon the poor negroes, with their wild passionate way of expressing religious feeling, had better see to it lest they themselves be ruinously lacking in the element which appears in the blacks to be too exclusive. Then there are those who care nothing about anything but feeling. They say, "I love to hear a man that makes me feel." Their danger is that they will not know what they are feeling about, because it is not Scripture truths that make them feel, and such feeling will not lead to pious action. Emotion in religion is proper and necessary, and I do not condemn those who value it highly; but such persons must see to it that they have truth, which is the circulating life-blood of piety, and that their feelings shall lead to corresponding earnest and intense activity; for emotion about religion, as in anything else, if it does not express itself in activity, will not only be worthless, but will injure the character. Others there are who talk of nothing but action, work, work. Now, work is a noble word, but the danger of these persons is, that they will forget to love Christian truth and to cultivate Christian feeling.

The same thing is true as to bodies of men. You can easily think of a great religious denomination in our country, who care mainly for thought, instruction, knowledge. A noble idea it is, but possibly their danger may be that they will underrate Christian feeling. You can very easily think of another powerful and useful denomination of Christians whose great idea is feeling. Everything is made to contribute to working up emotion, and their danger is that they will neglect the importance of holding truth, even if they do not neglect the importance of activity.

The same thing is also true about certain periods of Christian history. You can find periods when all the Christian world seemed devoted to the idea of doctrine, when men disputed through a lifetime about the doctrines of Christianity, when all the great divisions of the time centred themselves upon the difference between two words of Scripture. You can find other periods where Christianity seemed to run altogether into mystical feeling; when good people gave themselves up to solitary lives, or retired to the privacy of their homes, and thought that all that could be done was to try to cultivate Christian sentiment in private. And ours is an age which runs towards activity. The Christian idea now is work. I thank God that we live in such an age. It is good to live in a time when the idea is to work. It is a noble privilege to live in such a period. But our danger is that we shall not care for Christian truth, and that in our fancied superiority to all mere emotion we shall shrink away from those great sentiments, that passionate Christian feeling, which alone will stir us up to intense, loving and persevering Christian activity.

4. One more lesson. Concern for the salvation of others, such as Paul here expresses, must have had some good ground in the nature of things. Ah! my friends, you cannot tell me that the man who wrote those words thought that everybody was going to be saved at last. If *he* did not believe in divine mercy and divine love; if he did not believe in the salvation that is in Jesus Christ—in the glory and the power of his grace, and his everlasting intercession—then who ever did? He did believe in these. And yet do you think a man could have felt that passionate distress to which he here gives such strong utterance, if he had thought, as so many well-meaning people think now-a-days, that God is so good and merciful, that somehow or other, may be not at first when they die, but sometime or other, it will be well with everybody at last? Paul did not think so. He could not have thought so. And I venture to say Jesus Christ did not think so. If we are determined that we will cling to certain ideas, because they suit our natural feeling, then I am persuaded we must turn our back upon the authority of the word of God. There must be some ground for such concern as Paul felt. I shrink from telling what it is. I think of the awful

terms which the Scriptures themselves sometimes employ,—the images of horror, the words of everlasting fire—and I do not wish here and now to speak of them. But there must be some ground for this passionate concern for men's salvation which Paul expresses. And if men ought to feel so, and if devout people do feel so with reference to others, then tell me how those others ought to feel as regards themselves? My friends, who do not care anything about your souls, you must be madmen and irresponsible, or else you ought to care.

I humbly confess to-day, in behalf of my Christian hearers, that we do not feel on this subject as we ought to feel. It is only now and then that we catch glimpses of the reality. "Life is oft so like a dream, we know not where we are," and we do not realize things, and so we do not feel the concern we ought to feel. We are wanting in our duty to you in this respect. And yet you do not know how much concern we do feel. Many and many a time have persons who are here to-day, when they found themselves in the presence of those they loved, wanted to say something, their very life has trembled with the desire to say something, and they have shrunk back. May be they were afraid they would meet no sympathy. This may have been true in some cases. And yet, my brethren, I suspect it has sometimes happened that you shrank from speaking when that very one you loved was secretly wishing that you would speak, but from a like shrinking to yours, perhaps from a fear that you would suppose he cared more than he did, or from a strange sensitiveness with regard to the feelings that lie deepest in our hearts, would offer you no encouragement. But I venture to say to such as are not Christians, there are those that do feel a deep yearning, an unutterable concern sometimes for your salvation, and O, my friends, you ought to feel concern for yourselves.

IX.

THE MOTHER OF JESUS.

Mary, the mother of Jesus.—Acts i : 14.

THERE is a well-known tendency of human thought to oscillate from one extreme to another. I think this tendency was exhibited in several points of what we call the Protestant Reformation. In certain important respects, we are all agreed that there was a real and thorough reformation. In certain other respects most of us think it was a very partial reformation. And there are yet several other respects in which it was a violent reaction from one extreme to the opposite extreme. It appears to me that this has been the case as regards the position of Protestants toward the mother of Jesus. The Romanists, we may say without uncharitableness, have come very near making her an object of worship. Their theologians make nice distinctions on the subject, but practically, for the ignorant mass, she is really an object of worship, a sort of goddess. The Protestant mind, starting back in horror from that terrible idolatry, has seemed to shrink sensitively away from ever saying a word or ever thinking for a moment about the mother of Jesus.

It is all natural enough, the growth of what we consider to be the grave Romanist error about Mary. The associations connected with all those who followed Jesus would naturally have caused the early Christians to feel a peculiar interest in her, as they ought to have done. And then the feeling which rapidly grew up, of a desire for human mediation between us and God—between us and the Saviour himself—and which led, in the course of the centuries, to praying to the saints for their mediation, would naturally cause the mother of Jesus to be regarded as the most influential of all these interceding saints. Moreover, the Roman Church, with that talent for governing which has characterized the Roman people through all their history, readily adapted itself to the tastes of mankind, to the tendencies of human nature in general, and to the special usages of the old Pagan Romans, introducing, for example, a number of festivals, so that there would be something corresponding to the ancient festivals to please the people. And as all Pagan nations had their female deities, there naturally arose a feeling which made the mother of Jesus a sort of female divinity. Then, when art came into use in the churches, when they introduced image worship, there was nothing more natural than that the mother and the babe in her arms should be the chosen subject of artistic representation in places of worship; that the great artists of Italy should not only find this most popular and remunerative for their pencil, but most pleasing for themselves. So galleries were filled with many charming delineations of the Virgin and child. I suppose, also, that the spirit of chivalry in the Middle Ages may have had something to do with this. There was then a high, romantic sentiment towards woman as such, and this may have caused Mary to be regarded as the representative woman, so that romance added itself to devotion. For these and other causes it has come to pass that not only in the Roman Church, but in the Greek and Armenian and Coptic Churches, and all through the East, they talk a great deal more about Mary than about her son. I have at home a great collection of Latin hymns of the Middle Ages, made by a German scholar, in which there are three times as many about Mary as about Jesus and the apostles all put together.

Now, I say the Protestant mind has violently reacted from all this, and it is not strange that we should shrink shuddering from what is practical idolatry, no matter how skillfully explained away. But isn't it a pity that we should go to the opposite extreme as regards the mother of our Lord? Let us look, then, at what the Scriptures teach. It was said to her by the angel, "Blessed art thou among women," and she said, "Henceforth all generations shall call me blessed." There is no ground there for worship. "Blessed among women," Elizabeth was called, and Jael, who killed Sisera. The meaning of Mary's own saying is, all generations shall call me happy, shall felicitate me, shall recognize that my position is a happy one. There is no foundation for calling her "the Blessed Virgin Mary," as an act of worship, but there is a foundation for taking peculiar interest in what the Scriptures teach concerning her. It is not much that they do teach, and doubtless that is well, for otherwise it would have been perverted in the interest of that semi-idolatry we have been speaking about; but from what they do teach we may draw some useful lessons, and may, at the same time, get some interesting views of her son, who is, O wonder of wonders! our Divine Redeemer.

1. First recall Mary's early life. Now, I could bring you some so-called manuals about the Blessed Virgin Mary, which would give you a great mass of detail about her early life, but unfortunately they are all late tradition; in fact, they are all pure fiction, and without the advantage of being well invented. They are commonly dull and stupid. But when we look to the Scriptures themselves, some things we do know about her early life. We know that instead of being at a convent at Jerusalem, as the silly traditions say, she lived at the little town of Nazareth.

This village, nestling down in its deep and retired valley, is never mentioned in the Old Testament, and even Josephus, who writes about a dozen places within a few miles of it, never speaks of Nazareth. It was an insignificant and quite out of the way place, far from the bustling, noisy world. Yet here Mary was to rear the appointed Saviour of men. Out of silence and obscurity was to come in the appointed time the Saviour of mankind.

Nor must you suppose it was a desirable community to live in. Those who wrestle with the giant vices that gather in great cities often dream that in a quiet little retired village it would be easy to do right, but Arcadian simplicity and purity is seldom anything more than a dream. Those people of Nazareth were singularly bad.

They showed towards Jesus himself a rudeness and ferocity to which we know of no parallel in his ministry. They rejected him rudely. They tried to take his life. And one of whom Jesus said that he was an Israelite in whom there was no guile, and who lived in a neighboring village, asked in astonishment, "Can anything good come out of Nazareth?" It was a bad place. And Mary lived among those rude people of Nazareth.

Besides knowing the place of her abode, we know of Mary that she was familiar with Scripture. For when the great time in her life came, and, inspired, she burst out into praise, almost every expression she uses is from the Old Testament. Her whole mind and heart were full of the sacred writings, so that their language came spontaneously to her lips. That is an important point; she was familiar with the Scriptures.

2. In the next place, think of Mary's belief and rejoicing. There came to her the most wonderful promise that ever was made on earth, and the most incredible. It seemed at first blush to be impossible, and the question she asked concerning it touched that very point. She said : "How can these things be?" It is in that respect we see an instructive difference between Mary and Zachariah. Zachariah said : "How shall I know this, seeing I am an old man and my wife is old?" He speaks as a man not disposed to believe and who insists upon having better proof. But Mary speaks as one who is disposed to believe, and asks only to have an apparent impossibility removed, that she may believe. You see here two types of character, two states of mind, such as often exist with us in relation to the Scriptures. There are people that present their difficulties in such a way as to show plainly that they are like Zachariah ; they

don't much want to believe, and they insist on their difficulties and cherish them, and are not anxious you should remove them. There are others who have sore difficulty in the way of believing, so that we owe them our tender respect and sympathy, who are asking only that they may get rid of what seems to them to stand in the way, so that they may believe. God be gracious to all such! God help them out of their trouble! Mary believed, not "because it was impossible," as a Latin Father once rhetorically said; she believed notwithstanding it seemed impossible, because it was expressly ascribed to the power of God. "The Holy Ghost shall come upon thee, and the power of the Highest shall overshadow thee." And Mary said: "Behold the hand-maid of the Lord; be it unto me according to thy word." We do not want to believe a thing that is impossible, but, like Mary, we have to believe what includes many elements that are incomprehensible. In the nature of things it must be so. There was much that Mary could not understand, and as the years came and went she did not understand them still.

When the shepherds came after the babe had been actually born, and reported what the angels had said, we are told that Mary "kept all these things and pondered them in her heart." She could not know the meaning. When Simeon, in the Temple, said such wonderful things about the child, we read that Mary and Joseph wondered about all these things that were told concerning him; and when the child showed such extraordinary knowledge at twelve years of age, we are told that Mary and Joseph were amazed. It was necessary that they should not understand it. If the reality as to what it was had forced itself upon them, it would have been impossible that they should have lived under the same roof. So Mrs. Browning makes her say:

> " Bright angels,—move not!—lest ye stir the cloud
>   Betwixt my soul and his futurity!
> I must not die, with mother's work to do,
>   And could not live—and see."

In the very idea of an incarnation there are necessarily many things incomprehensible. My friends, if you take this Bible, which comes so strangely home to all our spiritual wants, which, in all seasons of conscious spiritual weakness, offers the very strength we need, which affords us that help against sin which is not found anywhere else in this world—this Bible, which the more progress we make in trying to do right, seems the more sweetly adapted to all our spiritual wants—if you take this Bible, you find that it reveals an incarnation, and that this, from the necessity of the case, involves many things that seem almost impossible. There must be ever so many allusions to things in which we can make no progress at all, as to comprehending their nature. We are in Mary's position. We are not expected to believe an impossibility, but warranted and bound to believe an assured fact, notwithstanding there be many things about it whose nature we cannot possibly comprehend. It seems that this distinction might have value to any one troubled about these problems, and anxious to receive the truth.

Notice, further, that Mary, in believing, rejoices. She

said: "My soul doth magnify the Lord; from henceforth all generations shall call me happy." It was a wonderful thing, that young girl, the child of poverty, in that little out of the way village, daring to say that all coming generations should know of her and call her happy; but she said it, because God had promised. She said it with no idea of personal merit, with no thought of personal pride, but because God had promised. If one of you should stand here by my side, and we two should, with the most genuine humility in our power, say we think we are children of God, we hope we shall be blessed forever in Heaven, we are confident we shall dwell amid the purity and glory of the better world, there are some people ready enough—I know not that there are such here present, but you find cases of that sort everywhere—there are some people ready enough to say: "You think a great deal of yourselves; you count yourselves favorites of heaven," and all that. Yet, in fact, the profession would be made not in self-complacency, but in simple, humble reliance on a divine promise. And why should not a human heart trust a divine promise, as then, so now and henceforward and for ever more, and trusting a divine promise, rejoice in a divine hope?

3. In the third place, think of Mary training her child. We know something of the nature of that training. We have read of young Timothy, that from a child he knew the Holy Scripture that his mother and grandmother had taught him, and had learned to share the faith that was in them. That is a picture we may transfer to the humble home of the carpenter in Nazareth. That child

needed to be trained. Do we not read that he grew in wisdom and stature? If he increased in wisdom, there was need of education. We find that the mother trusted him almost without bound. And we know that he was really what children so often imagine themselves to be, wiser than his parents. Yet, he went down with them and was subject to them. The human mind has to grow. If there was a real incarnation, the human mind had to grow. It needed to be developed. There was room for education. There was demand for it. Yea, and he himself, toward the close of his ministry, must have meant the same thing as to the capacity of the human mind to contain knowledge, when he said: "Of that day and hour knoweth no man, not even the angels in heaven, nor even the Son, but the Father only." The human mind cannot know all things. And our Lord's human mind could not hold all knowledge. Such is the declaration of the record, that his mind grew in wisdom as his body grew in stature, and Mary was the mother that trained him. It seems idle sometimes for a poor toiling mother to indulge in the romantic ideas which poets and novelists write about a mother's high mission; and yet it is good for such a one, amid trial and sacrifice and suffering and struggles, to remember, and comfort herself in remembering, that hers is a high mission. After all, the noblest thing that is done in this world is when a mother does in truth and wisdom and fear of God train up a child. Let us all stand back in her presence. Let us call upon all men whose aspirations are the highest, whose work is the noblest, to stand aside and acknowledge cheerfully, " Hers is the best work, hers is the noblest work done in the world." And if that be the case, it must be a work of sacrifice and suffering, for there is nothing good ever done on earth save with sacrifice. Let the toiling mother solace herself with the thought that all motherhood has been dignified and made sublime by the young mother in the little town of Galilee, who was training in an humble home that child that was to be the Saviour of the world and the glory of the universe. It was a unique task no doubt, and yet I say it has ennobled all motherhood, and any struggling, sorrowing mother may take comfort in the thought that she is engaged in a like good work. Blessed be God! what mother here knows of the high possibilities that are before her child? What Christian mother can fail to know of that supreme possibility, that blessed certainty, that she trains up a spirit immortal when she brings up a child in the fear of the Lord.

But, now, please observe that Mary must have trained this child in the knowledge of God's word. My friends who are parents, we abuse everything; and so we abuse the benefits of the Sunday-school. There is grievous danger that we parents shall turn over to the Sunday-school our parental duty of training our children in God's word. It is one of the perils of our time. Though we have those in the Sunday-school to help us in the task, and ought to be heartily thankful for their help, yet the work is ours none the less, and the work will, for the most part, remain undone unless we do it—the work of training our children in the knowledge of God's word. Let us train them to look at God's word as the guide of their life. I read somewhere of a mother whose husband was a grossly wicked man, who used to cry out against all things religious, and declared that he believed not in God; yet she reared up a number of children by his side, and they all became Christians. Some friend asked if she would tell how she managed this. She said, "I never set my word against their father's, but when he says anything against God's service, I hunt up a passage and say, 'Your father says so and so, but here is what your heavenly Father says,' and then I read it to them." That was all the secret she had, but what a blessed secret!

Parents, learn to have the Scriptures on your tongue's end for the benefit of your children. Good old John Wesley was a trifle superstitious, after the fashion of his time, when he used to open the Bible at random and make use of whatever text he happened first to light upon. Far better than that is it for us to have the mind so full of the Scriptures, their teachings so familiar to our thought, that whenever we need one of them it will come by natural association of ideas. And so Mr. Moody has taught all of us that if we can get some happy quotation of Scripture, it will be worth more than all our wisdom in explaining a difficulty to an inquirer.

4. I pass on to say a word as to a later point in Mary's history. She seems to have unwarrantably interfered in the ministry of her son. At the wedding at Cana she suggested for him a course of action, and he said: "Woman, what have I to do with thee," or rather "What have we to do with each other?" There was nothing harsh in this, but there was an intimation that they had entered into new relations, that he who had

been to her as a child to its mother could not be controlled by her in his public action, and she must draw back. A year or two later, when Jesus was teaching all the morning in a crowded house, and there were so many questions to be answered that they had not time for the mid-day meal, we read that "his friends" went forth to seize him, for they said, "he is beside himself." Now, put the Gospel histories together, and it appears that those friends were his mother and his brothers; and when they sent him a message over the heads of the crowd in the house, that his mother and brothers were without and wanted to see him, the answer, too, is very remarkable. He said: "Who is my mother, and who are my brothers?" And he looked around in a circle upon those that sat about him and said: "Behold my mother and my brothers; for whosoever shall do the will of God, he is my brother, and sister, and mother." His kindred were seeking to interfere with his work, and said he was beside himself. No wonder men call Christian earnestness fanaticism. Jesus himself, the founder of it all—they said he was crazy. His own mother and his brothers said this because he was in earnest. What a comfort there is for all of us in the application he made of their request: "Whosoever shall do the will of my Father in Heaven, he is my brother, and sister, and mother." How does a man love his brother? Think of the warm affection with which a man cherishes his brother. Then think of the tenderness with which a manly nature loves a sister. Then add to these, yea, compass them all around with the love that a real man has for his mother—a love that will ever grow as he grows older—and now consider. Jesus has said—it may include you and me, with all our unworthiness—" Whosoever shall do the will of God is as dear to me as brother, and sister, and mother." The Scriptures contain many wonderful things, but what more wonderful than those words?

5. There is one other theme, of which I know not how to speak—Mary at the cross. Description is here dumb. Imagination stands in mute wonder. There are many points of view from which to look at the cross, and one not the least instructive, no doubt, would be to try to place yourself in imagination beside that sorrowing mother, through whose heart now—according to old Simeon's prediction long before—a sword was passing, a sword of cruel suffering and death. You would remember how suffering is the inevitable consequence of sin in this world, how suffering was the necessary condition of human salvation, even that poor mother's suffering as she looked upon her atoning son. Then remember how out of his death came life again, and out of that sorrow came springing joy. I cannot speak of that; who can? But you might sit down sometime and think it all over. Try to stand beside the mother at the cross, try to imagine how she felt, and try, also, to imagine how he felt towards her; for amid all the strange sorrow of that dark hour, he that was dying thought of his widowed mother, and felt, as every true man feels, that he must make some provision for her future. Yea, amid that great event of the universe, with that darkness settling down upon all his soul as the sin-bearer, he made provision for his widowed mother. Yet, what a

simple provision it was! He had a loving friend, and to him he said: "Take her; do you be her son and she will be your mother," and that was all.

6. And now, finally, think a moment of Mary in heaven. If ever there comes a pang to the glorified ones, methinks Mary must look down with unutterable grief upon the thousands and millions that almost worship her instead of worshiping her son, the Saviour.

> "O centuries
> That roll, in vision, your futurities
>   My future grave athwart,—
> Whose murmurs seem to reach me while I keep
>   Watch o'er this sleep,—
> Say of me as the Heavenly said—'Thou art
> The blessedest of women!'—blessedest,
> Not holiest, not noblest—no high name,
> Whose height misplaced may pierce me like a shame,
> When I sit meek in heaven!"
> —Mrs. Browning, *The True Mary.*

It is not unnatural, it is because they have forgotten that he, the divine one, is himself human. The human heart longs after human sympathy, and the consciences of guilty men make them wish for a human mediator between themselves and the God they shrink from. Luther tells us that in youth, with his Romish education, he was afraid of Christ. He never heard a word said about Christ, save as the babe in the mother's arms, or the sacrifice on the cross, or the Judge in the last day. His idea was that he must call upon the saints, and especially upon the Virgin Mary, to pity him and intercede for him with Christ. When people have such views of

Christ, no wonder they seek some human mediator. The only cure for it all is to know that Christ the divine was truly human, that Mary was no more truly human than was Jesus, the Son of Mary. Truly divine and also truly human, he is able to sympathize with us in our infirmities, to lay a hand of love and pity upon our poor sinful heads, and yet, with the other hand, to lay hold upon the very pillars of God's throne, and to be our Advocate with the Father, our one Mediator,—all the Mediator we need or should desire. O Jesus, son of Mary, and yet Son of God, before the mystery of thine Incarnation we bow, and trusting in the mystery of thine intercession, we pray thee make us, make us, wholly thine!

X.

THE APOSTLE PAUL AS A PREACHER.*

Unto me, who am less than the least of all saints, is this grace given, that I should preach among the Gentiles the unsearchable riches of Christ.—Eph. 3 : 8.

NUMEROUS as were the functions of the Apostle Paul, he was, most of all things, a preacher of the gospel. The fact is prominent in his history, and was deeply felt by himself. Everything, with him, was made subordinate to this vocation. His whole life was wrapped up in it. Though often sad and weary, and not unfrequently (it would seem) desponding, he never turned aside from this great work. When difficulties and dangers gathered around, when foes were threatening and timid friends entreating, he could say, "But none of these things move me; neither count I my life dear unto myself, so that I might finish my course with joy, and the ministry which I have received of the Lord Jesus, to testify the gospel of the grace of God."

And Paul was the greatest of all preachers. Of course, we omit from the comparison him who spake "as never man spake." There was in *his* preaching such a continual self-assertion, such a sublime and holy egotism, that in this, as in every other re-

* Sermon as chaplain to the University of Virginia, May, 1857. Printed in pamphlet form at the request of many students and of the professors.

spect, his character is unique and peculiar, and we never think of comparing him with any mere man. There have been many gifted men, gifted by nature and grace, who have devoted themselves to the work of the ministry; God be thanked for them all, and God grant that there may be many more hereafter! but in the estimation of every one who diligently studies his character and history, Paul must stand, among all preachers, unrivalled and alone. Thoroughly to analyze his great powers is a task for which I have no talent, and my hearers, under present circumstances, would perhaps have little inclination. I mean only to present some points in connection with Paul as a preacher, the consideration of which I trust may be blessed to our benefit.

1. The first of these points is mentioned mainly because of its relation to what will follow. It is the remarkable adaptation of his preaching to the particular audience. He has himself stated the principle upon which he acted in seeking this adaptation: "I am made all things to all men." This saying has come to be grossly perverted, being constantly applied as a reproach to the fickle and time-serving. The apostle has just before said what perfectly explains it: "To the Jews I became as a Jew, that I might gain the Jews; . . . to them that are without law, as without law . . . that I might gain them that are without law. To the weak became I as weak, that I might gain the weak: I am made all things to all men, that I might by all means save some." He elsewhere declares the same principle as regulating his general conduct: "Even as I please all men in all things, that they might be saved."

We have striking illustrations of this, in some of his recorded discourses.

At Antioch, in Pisidia, he preached first in the synagogue, to Jews and proselytes. Here he conformed, as did Stephen in his address before the Sanhedrin, to the Jewish custom of commencing with a sketch of the national history. This would conciliate his audience, by bringing to mind facts of which they were all proud, and in which he and they had a common interest; and from one point or another of that history the speaker could easily and gracefully turn, as did Paul on this occasion, to the subject on which he wished to dwell. The promised seed of David he declared was come in the person of Jesus. He pointed out the fact that the condemnation, death and resurrection of Jesus were in fulfilment of prophecies which they all believed. He proclaimed to them through Jesus the forgiveness of sins, and that complete justification, to the believer, which could not be obtained through the law of Moses. He warned them not to neglect this proclamation, in language quoted from a prophet. All is from the Jewish point of view, and after the Jewish method; to the Jews he became as a Jew, that he might gain the Jews; and thus regarded, nothing could be more felicitous than the conduct of this address.

At Lystra, when he had wrought a miracle of healing, and the astonished and ignorant pagans were about to offer sacrifice to him and Barnabas, as being "the gods come down in the likeness of men," he spoke, to restrain them, a few words which contained the simplest truths of natural religion: "Sirs, why do ye these things? We also are men of like passions with you, and preach unto you that ye should turn from these vanities unto the living God, which made heaven, and earth, and the sea, and all things that are therein: who in times past suffered all nations to walk in their own ways: nevertheless, he left not himself without witness, in that he did good, and gave us rain from heaven, and fruitful seasons, filling our hearts with food and gladness." These truths were obviously appropriate to the occasion, and we learn that they sufficed to accomplish the apostle's object. But it is stated, concerning the same visit to Lystra, that "there they preached the Gospel," and that when he had been stoned, "the *disciples* stood round about him." We see then that his general preaching at that place was by no means confined to natural religion.

At Athens, every one has been struck by the skill with which he sought to avoid offending the prejudices or violating the laws of his hearers. He began by complimenting them as in all respects an uncommonly religious people. He availed himself of an altar "to the unknown god," to speak of the true God without incurring the penalty denounced against the introduction of new deities. In a few brief sentences, he assailed, pointedly but courteously, several leading errors which prevailed among the Athenians, particularly their idolatry and their proud conceit of distinct national origin. He quoted, not inspired Hebrew prophets, but a sentiment found in the writings of two Greek poets, one of them from his native Cilicia. And he carefully delayed to the close his declaration of the fact, so important, yet so likely to be rejected, that Christ had been raised from the dead. Was ever any discourse more skilfully adapted?

So, when standing before Felix, he did not directly denounce the tyrant's vices, for of course he would not have been heard for a moment, but he dwelt upon the opposite virtues. To a wicked man he spoke of righteousness; to an incontinent man, of self-control; to an unjust earthly judge, of the judgment to come.

A similar skill in adaptation, and care to conciliate, is observable in the Apostle's letters. You can form a tolerably complete idea of the history and present condition of a Church, or of the character and circumstances of an individual, from his letters to such an individual or Church. And you see everywhere how observant he is of all courtesies and charities, how careful first to commend what he can in those who must on other accounts be censured, how anxious to win and save even amid his severest rebukes.

The limit to this desire to please, the Apostle has clearly defined; as when he reminds the Thessalonians that he had not practiced any trickery in preaching, nor used flattering words, nor sought glory of men; "but as we were allowed of God to be put in trust with the gospel, even so we speak; not as pleasing men, but God, which trieth our hearts." However great his disposition to conciliate, he would not sacrifice principle—would never offend God, to please men.

Now, with all this variety of adaptation to particular hearers, connect

2. His adhering constantly to the great central truths

of the gospel. That cross, in which alone he "gloried," which alone he "determined to know," is always before his mind. Widely as he ranges over the fields of truth and duty, he never loses sight of that grand central object; never ceases to feel himself in its presence. Every doctrine, and every precept, is presented in such a way that we feel it to have relation to the atoning work of our Saviour. For instance, servants are urged to be honest and obedient, "that they may adorn the doctrine of God our Saviour in all things." Husbands are exhorted to " love their wives, even as Christ also loved the Church;" and wives to "submit themselves unto their own husbands, as unto the Lord; for the husband is the head of the wife, even as Christ is the head of the Church." When pressing upon the Corinthians the duty of giving for the relief of their poor brethren, he adds, "Thanks be unto God for his unspeakable gift."

The example of Paul in this respect is not always followed. In seeking for adaptation, how often do men fail to adhere to these same great truths? Very anxious to make the sermon appropriate to the occasion, accommodated to the prejudices, or suited to the taste of the audience, they neglect to have it present the essence of the gospel—to have it full of those truths which relate to sin and salvation. How much preaching, by able and earnest men, is thus comparatively lost, as to all the most important ends of preaching the gospel! Those men, and classes of men, who have been eminently useful as ministers, in actually converting sinners and building up believers, have been remarkable for constantly reiterating, in however various connections, and with whatever freshness of illustration, the same fundamental, saving truths. A glance at the history of the most successful preachers would show this to be true. It is true now of all the really useful among "revival preachers;" and of many a plain man, whose extraordinary success it is difficult to account for, until we observe the constant recurrence in his discourses of the truths which belong to salvation. Surely the most gifted and cultivated ought to imitate this excellent peculiarity; surely right-minded hearers ought to prefer and encourage it. Let the preacher, like Paul, adapt, conciliate, please; but let him, also like Paul, bring everything into relation to our Lord and Saviour, for otherwise he is not preaching the gospel at all.

3. Observe, again, the Apostle's simplicity and directness in presenting the truth. Every one is familiar with his defence, in the beginning of the first letter to the Corinthians, of his course in this particular. We know how he was complained of for the plainness of his mode of preaching, and how he resisted all the pressure, and would not practice the artificial rhetoric which was then fashionable.

Indeed, we are unwilling to think of him as acting otherwise. Whether we consider Paul's personal character, or the fact of his inspiration, it is felt to be inappropriate and unworthy that he should be searching after mere prettinesses, should be seeking to heighten the simple loveliness of heavenly truth, by the meretricious adornments of a would-be eloquence. And there is significance in this strong, instinctive feeling. If it would have been wrong for Paul, how is it right for others, who, though humble and uninspired, are yet proclaiming the same divinely-given truths, and should be keeping in view the same sublime object, to save men's souls?

At the same time, all know that the Apostle's speaking and writing possess much of real beauty. It need not be misunderstood if we say that Paul is an eminent example of the *right use of imagination*. Among his remarkable combination of mental qualities, it is clear that he possessed imagination of a high order. It is not shown by elaborate and multiplied figures for mere ornament. Occasionally we meet with an unobtrusive image of exquisite beauty; as when, in the address at Athens, he represents men as groping in their blindness after an object that is near: "That they should seek the Lord, if haply they might *feel after him, and find him*, though he be not far from every one of us." But his power of imagination is seen mainly in the shaping of his thoughts in general; in the clear and delicate outline given to each particular thought, whether argument or precept, as it came moulded from his mind. It is in the same way that we find the finest imagination employed by all the men who have been most truly eloquent, by Demosthenes and Daniel Webster, by Chrysostom and Robert Hall. They could not have been eloquent without possessing this faculty in an eminent degree; but they have used it, not to send off mere fireworks of fancy, but to heat into a glow the solid body of their thought. The beautiful is thus by no means abjured, but subordinated. The gratification of our æsthetic sensibilities may render great service, as auxiliary to the instruction, conviction, persuasion, which are the great objects of preaching the gospel; but it must always be held auxiliary. The poet and the novelist aim to please, and incidentally to instruct; the preacher to do men good, and to please only as contributing to this higher end.

I have a practical object in saying all this, which may justify what would else be perhaps out of place. Not a little of the preaching done by good men is weighed down by rhetoric, falsely so-called. The evil is widespread and well known. Its existence and continuance are not wholly due directly to those who preach, but result in some measure from the wrong taste of the people. The preacher is very naturally led astray by this. He sees that the people for a time flock to hear, and loudly praise, those who speak in this fashion. He cannot do them good by his preaching unless they will hear him. It seems necessary to yield to what appears to be the popular taste, though known to be false. Especially where one possesses more imagination than sober judgment, such a process of reasoning is very likely to convince him. Some little allowance, therefore, may commonly be made for those who show this ambitiousness of style, this effort after eloquence.

The evil must be corrected, partly by preachers themselves; but those among them who perceive and deplore it, are able to accomplish comparatively little except in their own case. It is so easy to break the force of the most unanswerable argument, coming from them, by a sarcasm, as that they only oppose that style of preaching of which they do not happen to be masters. The cure must come mainly from intelligent men who are not preachers. They can powerfully influence public sentiment, and they ought to speak their mind. There can be no question as to what all such men think on the subject, but they are often restrained from strongly expressing their opinion by a false delicacy, a mistaken respect for the ministerial office. In our age and country the relation of preacher and hearers must be freely discussed, like everything else. And the half-cultivated are everywhere doing this. The merits, not so much of different modes of preaching as of different preachers, form a prominent topic of conversation in many circles. That bad taste which forms the most erroneous opinions on the subject is also boldest in expressing them. Thus the evil is greatly augmented by loud voices of praise or blame. Cultivated men must exert themselves to correct it, though the task should sometimes painfully conflict with their reverence for the sacred office. They must freely commend or condemn, not only general methods, but individual examples. I call upon those who have, and those who soon will have, influence over public opinion, as they value God's great appointed means of converting the world, to do what they can towards correcting the popular taste; to take every opportunity and means of showing the people what good taste requires, what alone is appropriate to the most solemn of all earthly positions, that of the man who stands up to preach the gospel.

4. Observe, in the next place, the Apostle's tenderness as a preacher. Hear him speaking of false profes-

sors: "For many walk, of whom I have told you often, and now tell you *even weeping,* that they are the enemies of the cross of Christ." Hear his farewell words to the elders of the Church at Ephesus: "And remember, that by the space of three years, I ceased not to warn every one night and day *with tears."* What a scene was that—this great and inspired man, speaking to the people both "publicly and from house to house," warning them with tears; telling them of God's amazing love, and his tremendous wrath; of their guilt, their helpless condemnation, and the one way of salvation. Christians, too, he warned of the false teachers that should enter from without, like grievous wolves into the fold, and that should rise up among themselves; and he would weep as he entreated them to hold fast the truth as it is in Jesus, to adorn their profession, to live for the salvation of men and the glory of God. Thus, night and day for three years, he ceased not to warn every one with tears.

And why should not Paul weep? and every preacher and every Christian weep? See the condition of our fellow-men, our friends, our kindred, as depicted, not by our wild fancy or morbid fears, but by the calm teachings of the Word of God. They are "condemned already," "the wrath of God abideth on them," their "steps take hold on hell." Can we half realize what is meant by these fearful sayings, and not weep? But worse. We tell them of the Saviour, who died that we might live, and who ever lives to save; we tell them of free pardon, of full salvation, to every penitent believer in him; of his redeeming love, his gracious invitations and precious promises. We tell of eternal bliss and eternal woe, of their own imminent and increasing danger. We urge all that is terrible in God's wrath, all that is moving in his mercy. And they listen as calmly, they turn away as unconcerned, as though it were all a trifle or a dream. O, where is our pity, where our love, that we do not weep tears of blood? that we do not say with the Psalmist, "Rivers of waters run down mine eyes, because they keep not thy law?"

It is well that the gospel induces tenderness, since the preacher has to speak such awful truths. It is no light thing to look into the eyes of one you know, and respect, and love, and charge him with being a vile sinner—charge selfishness, and pride, and pervading ungodliness, upon what he accounts his best actions; to warn him of the wrath to come; to bid him tremble lest he receive deserved damnation, and reflect now what will be his unavailing remorse if "in hell he should lift up his eyes, being in torment." It is well that the gospel, which, along with its promise of salvation to the believer, requires us to say, "He that believeth not shall be damned," should also inspire that feeling of tenderness with which the painful duty ought to be performed.

But let us look again at the Apostle's tears. Why should Paul weep as he warned? He feared that his warning might be in vain; and often it was in vain. With all his abilities and inspiration, men often heard without heeding; and all his exhortations in many cases failed to restrain even professed believers from shameful sin, from utter apostasy. Need we be surprised that the same thing happens now?

5. The remaining point of which I would speak is, the disadvantages under which Paul labored. This greatest of all preachers appears to have had some serious physical disqualification. Let us consider the evidence of this fact, and the lesson it teaches.

In the second letter to the Corinthians, he quotes the disparaging language of his enemies: "For his letters (say they) are weighty and powerful; but his bodily presence is weak, and his speech contemptible." Making allowance for the exaggerations of a hostile spirit, it is yet plain, even from this, that his presence was not commanding, not impressive, but rather the opposite.

In the course of his letter to the Galatians, he seeks to revive their personal affection for himself (which the Judaizing teachers had endeavored to destroy), by reminding them of the time when he commenced his labors among them. Notice his language: "Ye know how, through infirmity of the flesh, I preached the gospel unto you at the first." The word *through* must be here taken to mean *on account of*—the original naturally conveys this sense, and will hardly bear another—so that we understand him to say: "Ye know how, *on account of bodily infirmity*, I preached the gospel to you at the first." When he first arrived in Galatia, he did not propose to tarry there; but some bodily infirmity making it necessary to remain, he began to preach the gospel to them. He adds: "And my temptation (trial) which was in my flesh ye despised not, nor rejected; but received me as an angel of God, even as Christ Jesus." The physical affection before mentioned, he here calls his trial. He had evidently feared that on account of this physical trial they would contemptuously reject him and his message; and he sets in strong contrast with that expectation the fact that they had received him with the greatest possible respect and reverence.

In Second Corinthians, again, he speaks of certain remarkable visions with which he had been favored, above fourteen years before, which would be soon after his conversion, adding: "And lest I should be exalted above measure through the abundance of the revelations, there was given me a thorn in the flesh, the messenger of Satan to buffet me, lest I should be exalted above measure." Nothing could be better calculated to humble a preacher, in danger of being elated on account of his extraordinary privileges, than to suffer from some grievous bodily affection—some marked distortion, it may be, of form or feature—which destroyed all impressiveness of appearance, which made him continually fear lest men should "despise" and "reject" him. If it were a mental defect, or a fault of character, he might hope in some measure to correct it. But this physical disqualification, which he is utterly unable to remedy, must be a constant source of distress and humiliation. The apostle deeply felt it, and prayed earnestly for the removal of the affection. "For this cause I besought the Lord thrice that it might depart from me. And he said unto me, My grace is sufficient for thee; for my strength is made perfect in weakness." The distressing disadvantage was not removed. He was taught that under all disadvantages Divine grace would be sufficient to uphold and prosper him, for the strength of the Lord attains its perfect manifestation when exercised through feeble instruments. And he had learned by this time to endure patiently his infirmity, as useful for his own humbling; yea, he had learned to exult in it, as conclusively showing that his great successes were due to no human influence, but to Divine power. "Most gladly, therefore, will I rather glory in mine infirmities, that the power of Christ may rest upon me. Therefore I take pleasure in infirmities, in reproaches, in necessities, in persecutions, in distresses, for Christ's sake; for when I am weak, then am I strong."

All men appreciate the great advantage, to a preacher as to any other public speaker, of a commanding and engaging appearance. We feel the effect of it, as soon as such a man arises to address us. And if the speaker's presence be not merely unattractive, but painfully and ridiculously peculiar, it inevitably diminishes the impressiveness of what he may say. Yet, be it well observed, and forever remembered, that the most useful preacher that ever lived, was in this respect signally lacking. God's strength is indeed made perfect in weakness. Let the man who truly desires to preach the gospel, and who mourns that he does not possess those physical gifts which seem almost indispensable to eloquence, take to himself with humble joy that blessed assurance, "My grace is sufficient for thee."

My hearers, one word more. The same glorious gospel which Paul preached has been handed down to us. However feebly presented, it is "the power of God unto salvation, to every one that believeth." Paul felt himself but a vessel of clay, bearing the precious treasure of the gospel. That same precious treasure is offered to you. O, reject it not—I beseech you—I warn you. O, believe on that Saviour, whose ministers labor awhile, and one after another pass away, but who is himself "the same, yesterday, and to-day, and forever."

XI.

THE HOLY SCRIPTURES.

And that from a child thou hast known the holy Scriptures, which are able to make thee wise unto salvation through faith which is in Christ Jesus.—2 Tim. 3: 15.*

WHATEVER we may say, it is to be admitted that there are wide and potent differences among the races of mankind. The Galatians who received Paul so joyfully, with such impulsive affection, and a few years afterward had turned away from him, were the same Gauls whom Cæsar described not long before, the same as the Gallic races of mankind to-day, impulsive and changeable: and no small part of what we prize most in our civilization is to be discerned in our German forefathers, as Tacitus describes them in a beautiful little treatise he wrote about the manners, customs and character of the Germans. Many other elements of our civilization, the things that contribute most to make our life desirable, come to us from the great classic nations of antiquity. Grecian philosophy, Grecian art, Grecian poetry and eloquence, have made their mark on all that we delight in; Roman law and the Roman genius for government have much to do with what is

---

*The author has quite a different sermon from the same text, entitled, "Three Questions as to the Bible," published in tract form by the American Baptist Publication Society, Philadelphia.

best in our law and government. And yet, when you have made allowance for all these, ample and cordial allowance for race characteristics, and for the effect of all that is Grecian and all that is Roman, who can deny that a large part of what we prize most and enjoy most in our life of to-day has not been explained from any of those sources—that it comes from the Bible, that it comes from Christianity? There are many men who think they are now so refined that they have gotten above Christianity, and yet it is Christianity that gave them the said refinement. Now, if all this is true, it ought never to be out of place nor beyond our sympathies to speak of the Bible—the Bible that has done so much for all that we like best in our homes, our social life, our public institutions—the Bible that has been the comfort and joy of many of those we have loved best in other days—the Bible that is the brightest hope of many of us for time and for eternity—the Bible that gives the only well-founded hope for mortal, and yet immortal man, in regard to the great future.

"Thou hast known the holy Scriptures." That did not mean the same thing for Timothy, exactly, as for us. It meant our Old Testament; for of course when Timothy was a child the New Testament was not yet in existence. How do I know that it meant our Old Testament? How do I know that our Old Testament is a book of Divine origin? Is there any way to prove that, which is not dependent upon scholarship, which can be easily stated? apart, I mean, from its internal evidence of its own inspiration through its wisdom, power, and blessing. I know it in this way. The term "Scripture" or "Scriptures" was in our Lord's time a technical term, just as it is among us. When a man among the Jews spoke of the "Scripture," when Jesus said, "The Scripture cannot be broken," everybody understood that it meant a certain well-known and well-defined collection of sacred writings known to all his hearers. Jesus and His Apostles have testified that the "Scriptures" are divine. Now do I know what writings they were? Yes; I know from outside sources, very varied and ample. I know from the great Jewish historian and scholar, Josephus, who expressed himself very distinctly as to the sacred books of the Jews, and declares that no man would venture to add to the number or to take away from them. I know from the Jewish writings of a later period, embodying their traditions of the New Testament time and of earlier times, the Talmud, in which the collection of sacred writings described is precisely our Hebrew Old Testament, neither more nor less. I know from Christian writers of the second century and of the third century, who made it a specialty in Palestine itself to ascertain what were the sacred books of the Jews in the time of Christ, and who definitely stated the result to be our Old Testament. Now I am not pinning my faith to the Jews and saying that these books were divine because the Jews thought so. I am trying to ascertain what books they were which Jesus and the Apostles declared to be divine, and I learn beyond a doubt that the Jews who heard them understood, without fail and without exception, that it meant precisely what we call the Old Testament. That is a clear statement of the matter, which cannot be gainsaid and which leaves no occasion for doubt. A man may say, "Well, I find a good many things in the Old Testament that I don't see any use in, that I don't see the good of, some things that I object to." But hold! The founder of Christianity and his inspired Apostles have spoken about them, and whether you understand everything in the Old Testament or not, they have declared that the Scripture cannot be broken; that all Scripture is given by inspiration of God, and is profitable; that the holy Scriptures (the Old Testament) are "able to make wise unto salvation through faith which is in Christ Jesus."

There is a great deal of wisdom in this world. It is wonderful that mankind, considering how foolish they are, should be so wise; and oh! it is wonderful that mankind, considering how wise they are, should be so foolish. There is a great deal of wisdom in the world; wisdom that commands the admiration of all who are fitted to appreciate it. Men are so wise about their business affairs! Just look at the great business schemes, the grand business combinations! How easily men discern the new openings for business which new inventions and discoveries offer to them! How clearly we ordinary people see, after a while, what some extraordinary man saw years before, and seized upon it and made himself one of the great business men of the time by his wisdom! I was reading, only yesterday, the life of Sir Moses Montefiore, embracing something of the life of the first great English Rothschild, and was reminded how wise those men were in understanding their times at the beginning of the century, during the

Napoleonic wars, in seeing deeper into the probabilities than even great statesmen saw. There is a great deal of wisdom in the world; and this makes it all the sadder to think how few, comparatively, seem to be wise unto salvation. Nay, these wonderful human endowments and energies of ours seem often to be directed toward wisdom unto sin. Men take their splendid powers and prostitute them in the service of wickedness. The longing to know evil is so intense in human nature! What is that early story in the dim light of the first history of mankind? We do not know much about it. We can ask a thousand questions about it that no one can answer. But this much we see clearly: A fair woman in a beautiful garden, gazing upon a tree and its fruit, and the thought suggested that it is a tree to be desired to make one wise; eat of that, and they will be independent of God, they will be themselves as God, knowing good and evil for themselves—good *and evil*—and not having to ask Him for guidance. She takes and eats, and gives to her husband, and he eats—in flat, bold defiance of the great Father's prohibition. Then their eyes were opened—opened unto sin, opened unto shame. And ever since —why, it is just wonderful to watch your own children and see how early they show a keen relish for knowing about wrong things; how they will get off with some villainous servant or off with some bad schoolmate, and get themselves told a lot of things that it would be so much better for them never to hear of. They do so want to know the bad things! The growing boys are so curious about places that are characteristically places of evil. Wise unto sin! There are a great many things it is better never to know. There are things about which ignorance is bliss; yea, and ignorance is wisdom. There are things of which those who know least are the wisest people, and those who know most are the most foolish people. It is a matter to be thankful for, and in a good sense proud of, if a man can say, that as to the popular forms of outbreaking vice he never knew anything about them; that he never entered a place of debauchery; that he does not know the names of the instruments of gaming; that he does not know the taste of intoxicating liquors. Happy the man who can humbly declare to a friend such blessed ignorance, such wise ignorance as that.

While men are so busy in being wise unto sin, how desirable, surely, that we should be wise unto salvation! My friends, let us wake up a little. We sleep, we dream along through life. We say, "O yes, yes, I believe that there is another life, a future." You believe it is eternal? "Yes, I believe it is an eternal life." And you believe in God? "Yes, I believe in God." And you believe in Jesus Christ? "Well, yes; I suppose that is all so." And yet, living in this brief, fleeting, uncertain life, in this strange world, and admitting all these things to be true, and not wise unto salvation, and not praying to be wise unto salvation!

"The holy Scriptures, which are able to make thee wise unto salvation through faith which is in Christ Jesus." That is the way in which they do it—*through faith which is in Christ Jesus:* for the holy Scriptures of the Old Testament are never half understood except as they are seen in the light of Christ Jesus. They all pointed forward to Christ Jesus; they all found their fulfillment, the key of their interpretation, in Christ Jesus. The Old Testament history is not merely a history of some wandering patriarchs and of a strange, wayward people of wonderful powers and wonderful propensities to evil. It is not merely a history of Israel. The Old Testament is a history of redemption, of God's mightiness and mercies, and of a chosen nation, all along toward the promised, long-looked-for time when God's Son should come to be the Saviour of mankind. We cannot understand the Old Testament, except we read it in its bearing upon Christ, as fulfilled in him. I remember once a neighboring professor sent us invitations to his house for a summer evening, saying that he had a century plant which seemed about to bloom, and asking us to come and watch with them till it blossomed. It was a delightful occasion, you may fancy. With music and conversation we passed on through the pleasant summer evening hours, on till past midnight. Then we gathered around and gazed upon the plain, wonderful thing that had lived longer than any of us had lived, and now, for the first time, was about to blossom for the admiration of beholders. And oh! I think sometimes that Jesus Christ was the blossoming Century Plant, the beauteous Millennium Flower. All the long story of Israel meant him; and if you do find many things in the Old Testament that you do not see the meaning of, remember that they all pointed forward toward him.

Then, besides, the Scriptures not only have to be understood through him, but they make us wise unto salvation only through faith in him; because if we do not believe what the Scriptures say concerning him, how can they have their full power over us? They have a certain power. Just as the moon, when it is eclipsed, yet has some light shining upon it, reflected from the atmosphere of the earth, so the people, who do not themselves believe in the Scriptures, and do not believe in Christ Jesus with living faith, get much benefit reflected from the Christian people around them, and the Christian homes in which they grew up, and the Christian atmosphere they breathe; but they never get the full benefit which the Bible is able to give, except through personal faith in Christ Jesus. Ah! that dark lie in the garden would never have brought its baneful results for our race of mortals, if our first mother had not believed it. A lie rejected is powerless; a lie believed is ruin. And so truth rejected cannot have its full effect upon us. How can we get the benefit of Scripture if we do not believe in Him who is the centre and the heart and the essence and the life of Scripture, even Christ Jesus?

There is another line of thought here: "And that from a child thou hast known the holy Scriptures, which are able to make thee wise unto salvation through faith which is in Christ Jesus." Happy Timothy! His mother and his grandmother had shown an unfeigned faith, to which the Apostle himself testified. From a child they had trained him to know the holy Scriptures; and in his early youth he had met the blessed Apostle and learned from him the faith which is in Christ Jesus, and thus had become wise unto salvation. Happy Timothy! Happy, every growing child that has devout people around to point it toward the knowledge of God's Word. My friends, we who are growing old, what do we live for in this world, but for the young who are growing up around us? What would be the use of life to us, if it were not in the hope of making the life of those whom God hath given us, and those who spring up under our view, brighter and better and purer and worthier? We ought not to think it a small matter to train the growing children—in our homes, in the Sunday-school, as we meet them in society, wherever we can reach them by our influence—to know the holy Scriptures. You are not doing enough if you merely tell your children sometimes, "You ought to read the Bible," and perhaps scold a little because the child does not read the Bible; that is not half enough. Ah! we ought to set the child an example of reading the Bible, as some of us neglect to do. We ought to make the children see, by our own daily assiduity, our own living interest, that we believe in reading the Bible and get good out of it. We ought to *talk* about what is in the Bible; we ought to point out to the child this or the other portion that is suited to his age and character and wants. We ought to talk to the child about what he is reading, to show him the application of this or that text to his daily life. Out of the abundance of a heart that is full of the knowledge of God's Word, our mouth ought to speak often in the conversation of the family, so as to make the child feel that the Bible has gone into our soul, and that it shows itself in the glance of our eye and in the tone of our voice and in the tenor of our life. Are there many of us that do that? Dear children! there come times when our hearts grow soft and tender toward them, and we feel that we could die for them if that would do them any good; and yet here is something by which we could promote their highest, noblest, eternal welfare, and—we do not have the time! Happy Timothy, who, ere he became grown, learned the faith which is in Christ Jesus. Happy every one who from a child has known the holy Scriptures, has learned early—and God be thanked! the earlier the better—to give the young heart to Christ Jesus and dedicate the young life to His blessed service, and now is going on, trying to persuade others to love and serve Him too.

But ah! there are many who from a child have known the holy Scriptures, and now are passing on into mature life, wise about a great many earthly things; and some of them are gray-headed and wrinkled, and some of them tottering towards the end—not yet, oh, not yet wise unto salvation through faith which is in Christ Jesus! There are many peculiar circumstances about growing old: the parents gone, long ago; maybe the brothers and sisters all gone, and one stands alone, like some pine smitten of the lightning in the field—alone of what was once the family circle; and the friends of youth most of them gone, alas! and some of them estranged, and others so far away; new things growing up, like the bushes growing around an old pine tree, that are not akin to it; new features, new interests, new pursuits; and he who grows old finds it hard to interest himself in these things and feel the spring and buoyancy and the sweetness of life as he felt it in other days. Alas for a man who from a child has known the holy

Scriptures, and now is growing old, and has not become wise unto salvation! Alas for a man who can bear, like Atlas, the burdens of the world's affairs in the maturity of his strength and his wisdom, and who is neglecting to be wise unto salvation! Ah! if I speak to any one such person in middle life, or growing old, might I persuade him to say this day, out of an honest and humble heart, "O Jesus, of whom my mother taught me in my childhood, take me now to be Thine!"

And alas! that there are so many, even in our own country, which delights to call itself Christian, who from childhood have not known the holy Scriptures; that in this, which is in some respects the brightest land of earth, and in some respects the foremost nation of earth, there are some children who do not know the looks of the outside of a Bible! They are growing up in homes where no Bible was ever seen; and there are plenty of such homes. Ought it not to be a pleasure to us to try to spread the Bible among our fellow-men? One will say, many copies are destroyed and many copies are slighted. Certainly: not every venture in business pays. There has to be a head in the books of every establishment for loss as well as for profits. There are many blossoms on the tree that bring no fruit, and many seeds fall into the ground that spring not up; but that does not prevent us from planting nor hinder us from gathering. Grant that some copies will perish, and many copies will be slighted: yet scatter the Bible, and many will read it, and not a few, by the blessing of God's grace, will thereby become wise unto salvation. It is hard sometimes to tell what is the greatest privilege of earthly life, but it does seem that just the greatest privilege of earthly life is to give to some fellow-creature the blessed Word of God, and then to try, by loving speech and living example, to bring home to the heart and conscience of those whom we can reach, the truths it contains. If we do love the Bible ourselves (and many of us do), then ought not such to delight in scattering the Bible among others? If some of us know too well that we are but poor sticks of Christians at best, and that we do not love the Bible as we ought, and do not live by it as we ought, yet shall we not at least feel, " Now here is something that I can do; here is something that I *will* do. I do not treat the Bible rightly myself, but I will gladly give the Bible to every one, high and low, rich and poor, in all the land, in all the world, whom I can help." O that it may be true of your children and mine, of your acquaintance and mine, that we have done them some good in bringing them to a knowledge of the holy Scriptures, and that they have all been brought, by God's grace, to the blessedness of being wise unto salvation.

XII.

ON READING THE BIBLE BY BOOKS.*

THE main support of all individual Christian life, the main-spring of all high Christian work, must be the truth of God. Truth is the life-blood of piety. Truth is always more potent and more precious when we draw it ourselves out of the Bible. I rode out yesterday afternoon with a kind friend among the glories of the famous avenue of Cleveland, and then away into the beautiful country region which they hope is to be Cleveland Park some day, until we passed presently a little fountain where the water, coming fresh and sweet and bright, was bursting from the hillside. The water we drink in the houses here from the lake is delightful, but there it was a fountain. There is nothing like drinking water out of a fountain. And I remembered what my Lord Bacon has said: " Truth from any other source is like water from a cistern; but truth drawn out of the Bible is like drinking water from a fountain, immediately where it springeth." Ah, this Christian work we have to-day in the world will be wise and strong and mighty just in proportion, other things being equal, as

* Address before the International Convention of Young Men's Christian Associations at Cleveland, Ohio, May 25, 1881. This may be had (with some additional analyses of books) in tract form from the International Committee, Twenty-third Street and Fourth Avenue, New York City.

it is directed and controlled and inspired by what we draw ourselves out of the Word of God! I have come to speak to people who want to study the Bible, who do study the Bible, who love the Bible, and would fain love it more and know it better. I am not to speak to Biblical scholars, though such are present, no doubt; I am not to speak to persons of great leisure, who can spend hours every day over their Bible; but to busy workers, most of them busy with the ordinary pursuits of human life, in their homes or places of business, and all of them busy, I have no doubt, in the varied work of Christian people in the world, and they wish to know how busy people, often interrupted in their daily reading of the Bible, and often limited for time, can make the most of this daily reading. Therefore, they will be willing, perhaps, to listen.

I am to undertake, by request, to set forth one of the many ways of reading the Bible, which I think may have special advantages, which is often too much neglected, and which may contribute to give us intellectual interest in the Bible, and to make its study spiritually profitable. I want your kind aid in doing this, my friends. I am going to speak of an intensely practical matter in as thoroughly practical a manner as I know how, and when I am done, I shall be exceedingly glad if one and another of you will ask me questions about the subject, or about anything that has been said.

The Bible is one book; but the Bible is many books. It is an interesting subject of reflection to look back upon the process by which men ceased calling it books and began to think of it as a book. You know that the Greek name for Bible, *Ta Hagia Biblia,* means the sacred books; and when they borrowed the Greek term into the Latin *Biblia Sacra,* it was still plural—the Sacred Books. How has that *Biblia* come to be a singular word in our language? When the various writings of inspired men had all been completed and began to be thought of as one collection, complete in itself, and when men began to know that singular and beautiful harmony which pervades so wonderfully all this great collection of books, written by so many men, through so many long centuries, perceiving that it was not only a complete collection of books, but that they were all in perfect harmony with each other, then the idea grew upon the Christian mind that this was really one book. A very noble thought that is, to be cherished and made plain to each successive generation—the internal harmony of all these various writings of inspired men.

But then we must not forget that, after all, it is many books. They were written separately; they were most of them published separately; they were originally read separately from each other; they had a separate character, a substantially separate meaning and value, a practical influence over those who read them, and they ought to be read as separate books.

Then each one of them must be read as a whole if we would understand them well. You cannot understand any book if you read it only by fragments—I mean the first time you read it. A cultivated gentleman of this city remarked at dinner to-day that he was reading for the third time that beautiful book of piety, "The Memorials of a Quiet Life,"—reading it for the third time, fifteen minutes of every day, he said. That is very well when he is reading it for the third time; but if he had read it fifteen minutes of every day the first time, he could not have entered so fully into the meaning of the book. The celebrated John Locke has a saying on this subject in the preface to his commentary on the Epistles of Paul. He said he had found from his experience that in order to understand one of the Epistles of Paul, it will not do to take it in fragments. Why, suppose (the philosopher goes on) that a man has received a letter from an absent friend, whom he loves very much—a letter full of valuable instruction to him, and that he reads a page to-day and then lays it down; the next day he takes another page and begins at the beginning of the second page, and does not notice much what was at the end of the first page; the third day he begins at the top of the third page and reads that. How much will he know about the letter when he is done. He tells you, perhaps, "I have been reading a letter from So-and-so—a letter full of valuable instruction," and you ask him what it is about; he does not quite know what it is about, and no wonder, with such a process of reading. You must take the Epistles, says Locke, as you would take any other letter. You must take them each as a whole, and sit down and read each from beginning to end, and see what it is about. And then, if it is very valuable, you will take it afterwards in parts, not necessarily in pages, but in parts according to the subject of which it treats, and you will see what it says about this subject, and what it says about that subject, etc. That seems to be very plain common sense, and yet what a pity that the idea has not struck more widely into the minds of the Christian world!

Will you pardon a little personal reminiscence? I think that those who grow old ought to take occasion to bear their humble personal testimony to the way in which good is sometimes done for and through young men. It is a long time ago now—I am almost afraid to tell you how long ago—that I was a college student at the University of Virginia. One day, coming home from a lecture, Dr. McGuffey, Professor of Moral Philosophy, speaking to a student who was contemplating the ministry, said, "I want you to get Horne's Introduction, and hunt up a paragraph quoted there from John Locke about the importance of reading the Bible, a book at a time, taking each book as a whole. Now, be sure to get it, and read it." The young man got it, and read it, and the thought went into his heart of reading the Bible in that way, and took hold upon him; and in order to show the impression that was made, he must mention as result that a few years later, by a series of Sunday night sermons on the life and writings of the Apostle Paul, before Conybeare and Howson were heard of in the world, treating each epistle as a whole, in the place where it occurred in the history, he crowded the aisles and crowded the doors of the church and built a new church; and a few years later still, another result was that the young man was drawn very reluctantly from the pastoral work he loved, and will always love better than anything else in this world, to be a teacher of others in this same work; and the man cannot tell to-day, as he looks back, how much of the direction his life has taken is due to the recommendation the professor gave to his student, as they walked home from the lecture.

Oh, ye people that have to do with the world's young men, you never know what some little word you speak is going to do in shaping the whole character and controlling the whole life of the man who walks by your side!

But I wish not to argue this matter, but to offer some practical illustrations of it. Let us just take up together, now, some books of the Bible, and by your very kind permission, I will address myself to the average reader, the person of average intelligence.

Take the First Book of Samuel. You want to read that book through at a sitting. How long will it take you? Forty-five or fifty minutes. Read it as you would read a Sunday-school book that one of your children brought home from Sunday-school, right straight through before you rise. Say to yourself, "What is this book about?" You find it is about Samuel, and presently it passes on to tell about Saul. Samuel continues to be his contemporary. After awhile young David comes into the history, and it goes on so till Samuel passes away and you reach the death of Saul with the end of the book. So that book has treated about Samuel, Saul and David, and you have got some idea of the general history of each of these persons, up to the death of Saul, and the time when you know that David succeeded him. Then you go to reading it again, the next day we will suppose, for you are a busy person. You take the book the next day, begin at the beginning and say, "Well now, the first part of this book is about Samuel. Let me look over it here, and see into what portions of Samuel's life it divides itself." You see pretty soon that you have first an account of Samuel's birth and childhood; secondly, you have an account of Samuel's active life as ruler of Israel; and then, thirdly, you have an account of Samuel's old age, when he had anointed Saul as King of Israel, and lived on as Saul's prophet, and finally came in contact with the youth of David. Those are the three periods of Samuel's history presented—his youth, his active life as ruler, and his old age as a prophet. You take up the account of his youth, and you purpose to read as much as you can of that for this first reading. Now the best way would be to read the book three times, if you are patient enough. I know this is a terribly impatient age, and I am afraid you will not do that. I am afraid you will wish to make only two readings of the book, and we will suppose that you adopt that course, although the other is better. While you are reading this life of Samuel, then, in its several portions, you will be studying Samuel's character as a prophet, a ruler and a good man. You will be paying some attention to Samuel's mission and office in the unfolding of the history of the people of Israel; for he occupies a very unique and interesting position. You will at the same time be attending, paragraph by paragraph, without bothering yourself much about chapters, to the practical lessons which are presented to you. "What is there here for me to imitate? What is there here for me to learn? What is there in this trait of

Samuel's character, what in this experience of Samuel's life, that I ought especially to lay to heart?" You are now getting the lessons out of one portion of the life, but with a reference to the other portion, taking it all as a whole. When you have completed the life of Samuel in that way, you pass to the life of Saul. You find you have Saul's early years and Saul's later history as a division into two parts. Perhaps you mark down on a bit of paper with a pencil, or you mark down on the fly-leaf of your Bible itself, the divisions in this way. Then you take one after another and study them. And so with the history of David as it comes in; the struggles of David's early years; then passing as you would have to do into the other book, Second Samuel, the history of David's prosperity in middle life, and finally, the history of his sore adversities in his later years. You will thus see how the struggles of his early years prepared him for his day of prosperity, and how the sins of his day of prosperity brought on his adversity and bitter sorrow, and you begin to take David's life as a whole, and see the connection of the different parts of it—see how the different traits of character, good and evil, come out one after another, and apply each, one after the other, to yourself. Now, I suppose that this would be a much wiser way of reading the First Book of Samuel, than just to read one or two chapters to-day, and the next day begin to read at the next chapter, and not stop to see what there is in the former, which is the way (present company, of course, excepted!) a great many people read their Bible.

But let us turn to another kind of book. Take one

of the Epistles of Paul. You will find that the books of the Bible must be treated, for our purpose, in a great variety of ways, according to their peculiar character. Take, now, the First Epistle to the Corinthians. We will suppose that you sit down and read it straight through, and just let the chapters go. What are the chapters, and who was the chapter-maker? Not the inspired writer, as everybody knows. Chapters and verses are convenient enough, provided we use them as servants and do not allow them to be masters. You read it straight through and see what it is all about, and you will find as you read that Epistle that it treats of a number of entirely distinct subjects. They have nothing to do with each other so far as you can see. You take your pencil and mark them down as you go along. You find there are four chapters—for the chapter-maker made but one grave mistake in that epistle, which is saying a good deal to his credit, more than can be said in other places—there are four chapters which treat of the divisions among the Corinthians, and the fact that they made these divisions with reference to the several preachers. This leads Paul to speak of his own way of preaching. He would not accommodate himself to their notions of preaching, a lesson which preachers sometimes have to remember in this cranky world. Then you find two chapters in which he speaks of special evils that existed among them —evils of licentiousness, and evils of getting their personal difficulties settled by heathen judges, instead of getting them settled by their own brethren for the honor of Christianity. He said, in the first place, that they ought not to have personal difficulties to settle, and, in the next place, if they had them, they ought to get them settled by their own brethren and not go to the heathen for it. Then you find the seventh chapter treats of questions pertaining to marriage, about which they had written inquiring of the apostle. Then you go on and you will see that chapter 8, 9 and 10 talk about the question of eating meat which had been offered to idols. That was a grave practical question among them, far graver than many questions that we dispute about now-a-days, though to us it is dead and gone, just as many of our questions of dispute will be dead and gone in the coming centuries, and men will wonder what in the world made those good people of the nineteenth century spend so much time over matters that will seem to them of no consequence whatever. Those three chapters treat of the eating of meat offered to idols, and in connection with that the apostle indicates the right course by the course that he pursued. By the way, let me mention what his argument is there. It is familiar to most of you. He says: "Now grant that this meat offered to idols is not different from any other meat. The idols are nothing, and the meat is just the same as it was before it was laid on the altar. Yet if your weak brother cannot get over the old idolatrous associations, cannot eat it without a revival of the old reverence for the idol, and without its carrying him back to sin, oh! had you not better let it alone, even if it is innocent for you, for the sake of your brother?" And I think sometimes, Oh! that we could content ourselves with that principle in regard to some practical questions of to-day—that argument which our fathers employed about the use of intoxicating drinks, for instance; grant that it may be innocent for you, yet if it leads your brother into sin, cannot you let it alone for your brother's sake? "Then besides," the apostle says, "you had better not be too sure that this thing is innocent for you, for, before you know it, it may get you into trouble too." That is what I should call "A calm view of Temperance." But this by the way.

Then, to proceed with the Epistle, you find that chapters 11 to 14 treat of abuses that had arisen at Corinth in connection with their public worship. A variety of abuses are mentioned. Most of them refer to the disorderly conduct of their public worship, when ever so many of them would want to speak at once, and they would not sit down as gracefully as I saw gentlemen do this afternoon in the social meeting. They would go on talking together, and were not willing to give up to each other. Some of them were proud that they had special gifts, and others jealous because they did not have the like, and the apostle tells them that all this must be managed in decency and in order, and that Christian love is a far brighter, sweeter, nobler thing than all the special gifts. Just here please let the chapters alone, for what you call the 13th chapter of I. Corinthians comes right in as a part of his teaching about this matter of the displaying of gifts, the ambition, the jealousy, etc., and you have no business reading the first portion of that chapter without noticing how it links on with what precedes at the end of the twelfth chapter, and without noticing how the end of it is connected with the chapter that follows. It blazes like a diamond on the bosom of Scripture, but then it fastens Scripture together.

The fifteenth chapter of I. Corinthians treats of the Resurrection, and the sixteenth contains some practical information, etc.

Now you have half a dozen entirely distinct subjects here. You have observed that, and you have marked it down. Then you take the subjects up one at a time, and study them.

You will find some other epistles in which you cannot make that sort of absolute division—this topic, and then another topic, and then a third topic—but the writer goes from one thing to another, and then perhaps comes back to the first subject. Still, in a good many of those cases, you can find that there is some one thought that is the key-note to the whole. Take the Epistle to the Philippians, for example. It is quite short; you can read it all through in less than half an hour. You ask yourself, What is this all about? What is the main idea here? for you perceive that you have not here several topics, as in First Corinthians. The main idea, however, is Christian joy. "Rejoice in the Lord." Wonderful idea, when you remember that the man who wrote the letter to the Philippians was a prisoner chained, his life subject to the caprice of the most terrific tyrant the world has ever seen. And he was writing to a church poor and persecuted, which had sore trials awaiting it in the future. Yet, in the midst of all this, Paul writes to his persecuted brethren, and the key-note of what he says is, "Rejoice in the Lord." It is true that, in the middle of the Epistle, he apologizes for saying it so often. He says, "To write the same things to you, to me indeed is not grievous." He thought it might be grievous to them.

Before he gets through with it he says it two or three times more, and at the end he breaks forth, "Rejoice in the Lord always, and again I say, Rejoice!" Our beloved brother Paul, inspired by the Holy Spirit of God, was yet a man of like passions with ourselves, and as our Saviour himself showed humanness none the less genuine because so blended with the Divine nature, in the unity of his one person, and that humanness of his sweetly draws us toward the Divine; so it is with the humanness of the sacred writings too, and we may feel the touch of human thinking, and the glow of human feeling, and not lose at all our reverence for the divinity that is in it all.

What is the key-note of the Epistle to the Ephesians? It is the unity of Christians. The dispute of many years whether the Gentiles should become Jews is not ended, but the apostle urges that the Christians are one, Jew or Gentile. That was the widest idea that ever existed among Christians in this world. None of our divisions of sect, of country or of race is half so hard to overcome as was that question of the junction of Jewish Christian and Gentile Christian, and the apostle's great thought in that Epistle is that all are one in Christ Jesus. The Epistle was intended apparently to be sent around as a sort of circular letter to many churches, but that is the key-note. I do not say that everything in Ephesians is about unity directly and immediately, and if you get hold of that idea, the danger is that you will carry it too far, and will find it in many places where it is not. At least, if you do not, brethren of the laity, you will be wiser than brethren of the ministry often are.

But you will find another kind of books. We are supposing you are examining for yourself. Of course, it will be very convenient if you get some of the works which give analyses of the books of the Bible, and tell the topics they treat of. That is helpful, especially helpful in enabling one at the outset to see how to take hold of the matter. But, oh, it is so much better to have a little rude analysis you have made yourself; because that treats of the thing the way it looks to your mind, and you are able with that, though it may not be half so good as one you may find in the work of another, to get more of the sacred thought which this book suggests to your own mind. In many of these sacred books you cannot find one key-note, nor a division into separate topics, but you will find some subject that pervades the whole and gives unity to it in some other way.

Let us take the great Epistle to the Romans. Some people think the Epistle to the Romans is tremendously hard to understand. I remember a time when I found it right hard to *believe*. I used to say that certain portions of it were the most difficult writing I knew of in any language—that is the way young fellows talk, you know, and sometimes old fellows have not gotten over it. I used to say that certain portions of it were surpassingly obscure. And why? It seems to me now— and I mention it because the thought may be worth considering—that there never would have been any great difficulty in seeing what the apostle meant to say, if I had only been willing to let him alone and let him say what he wanted to say. But I had my own notions as to what ought to be said on that subject, and what ought not to be said, and you see the plainer he was in saying what he wanted and what I did not want, the harder I found it to make him mean something else.

You find at once, as you read this Epistle rapidly through, that it breaks into two parts. Eleven chapters contain doctrinal arguments and instruction and then five chapters treat of practical matters only slightly connected with the doctrinal matters. The first eleven doctrinal chapters treat of justification by faith, and the first three of them give the whole substance of this doctrine. They show that the Gospel reveals the righteousness of God, which is by faith, and then they show why men need justification by faith—because they cannot find justification in any other way—their works will condemn them, and if they find it at all, it must be by faith. This takes up the first and second chapters and a part of the third, and then the remainder of the third chapter tells about this provision which God has made for justification by faith, and how beautifully this provision works to take all the pride out of repentant souls and humble them into receiving the great salvation that God gives. The fourth and fifth chapters only give further illustration of justification by faith. They say that Abraham himself was really justified by faith (one whole chapter is given to this), and that this matter of our being justified through the effect of Christ's work of salvation is only paralleled by the effect of Adam's sin upon his posterity. This takes a great part of the fifth chapter. These are mere illustrations, you see, from the case of Abraham and from the effect of Adam's sin—illustrations of the idea of our being justified through faith in the Saviour. Then you come to chapters 6, 7 and 8. You find that they treat of justification by faith from another point of view, viz.: In its bearings on the work of making men holy, *i. e.*, of sanctification. Then the next three chapters are on the privileges of the Jews and Gentiles. So you see that the Epistle divides into different departments of the one topic, and after you have read it through several times, and tried to find out the line of thought in it, and been willing to let the apostle mean what he wants to mean, whether you like it or not, I think you will find that the subjects considered are not so very difficult. Of course, there are questions we can ask about them at once that nobody can answer, but we must content ourselves with what is taught us.

Take another kind of book: The Epistle to the Hebrews. There you find there is a line of argument, and one set of practical applications that runs through the whole letter, so that there are not half a dozen sentences in the Epistle which you can properly understand without reference to the entire thought of it as a whole. You must have that before your mind all the time. Now what is the practical object of this Epistle? Well, after trying persecution upon the Hebrew Christians, they tried argument, and persuasion; they used cunningly devised reasoning against Christianity. You can see it yourself, if you look at the Epistle and think about it. They said, We used to think that your Christianity was only one form of Judaism; but since you seem to have got the idea of cutting loose from Judaism and setting up your Christianity as a religion by itself, why, don't you see that it is no religion, that it is entirely inferior to the religion of our fathers? You had better give it up, and come back and be Jews and nothing but Jews. The religion of our fathers was given through the holy angels at Mount Sinai. Are you going to turn away from it? The religion of our fathers was given through the great and revered Moses. Are you going to abandon Moses? The religion of our fathers *is* a religion, with its magnificent temple, its smoking altars, its sacrifices, its incense, its robed priesthood, its splendid ritual. The religion of our fathers is a religion indeed! And what is your Christianity, if it is to set up for itself? Hadn't you better abandon Christianity? And the sacred writer replies, Nay! I will take their own arguments, and turn them all against them. He says, "The religion of our fathers was given through the angels at Mount Sinai, but Christianity was given through the Son of God, and as the Son of God is revealed in the Old Testament to be incomparably superior to the angels, so is Christianity superior to Judaism. The religion of our fathers was given through the great and revered Moses, but Moses was only, as it is said in Deuteronomy, a faithful servant in all the house, and the founder of Christianity is above him as the son of the household is above the servant. The religion of our fathers has its outward forms of worship, but they are only the pictures of the realities in the glorious world beyond those clouds through which our great High Priest passed, like the Jewish high priest through the vail of the temple, where lies the true Holy of Holies in the other world. And thither he has gone, bearing not the blood of bulls and goats, but his own precious blood, offered not every year, but once for all, and all sufficient, and there he stands, not for a little time while they wait without till he appears again, but there he ever liveth interceding for them that come to God through him, and so is able to save to the uttermost." Don't you see that he takes every one of their own arguments and turns them right against them to show the superiority of Christianity? And the practical bearing of it, all the time, is, Therefore don't abandon Christianity and go back to be a mere Jew; don't give up your faith in Christianity; see the evils of unbelief and apostasy. As I said, there is hardly a sentence in the whole Epistle, the full purport of which can be understood unless you bear in mind its relation to this line of argument.

Let me give another illustration in that direction. I think in practical experience one of the hardest books in the Bible to treat as a whole, is the book of Job. Yet I do not think it very difficult to get the general outline of the book if you address yourself to that task, provided you will not allow the beautiful poetic phraseology to prevent you from seeing the line of thought. You see that in the first place you have the prosperity of Job described, and then the sore trials that were allowed to come upon him. How sore they were, and how he stood all the trials! Then you have his friends coming to him and treating him better than people among us sometimes treat their friends who are in affliction. For they go and talk them half to death, and Job's friends sat—

how many days and nights was it?—before they even spoke a word; and then they go to talking about him. The theme of their talk is one of the greatest subjects of sorrowful human thought in all the ages of the world. What is the meaning of sore afflictions when God lets them come upon men? It is a question that has not been answered yet—one of the questions the full answer to which, if it ever enters into finite minds, must be reserved for the better light of the better world. But how much light is given upon it in that book? You see that these friends of Job are mistaken on this subject, and they say many things about it that are not strictly true. They are said from a perverse point of view and with a mistaken idea of the matter. I have heard people quote sayings of those men as sayings of Scripture, when it ought to be understood that the Scripture says that those friends of Job said certain things on that occasion, and how far they are exactly right will have to be judged by looking at the book as a whole, and cannot be judged otherwise. Now take one man at a time and ask, what does he say? And then how does Job reply to him? You will find that at first they take hold of the subject delicately. They say: "The Almighty is just; he prospers all good men; he never sends sore trials upon a man unless that man has deserved it." They do not say yet, "You have deserved all these sore afflictions." They hint it. And then Job begins to reply; he gets warm with the argument; he sees what they are hinting at; he says: "I have not committed any enormous sins, greater than men around me, to bring on me these great afflictions." Then they come squarely to the point and say, "Oh, Job, you had better confess it. The Almighty has found you out. We never knew that you were a very bad man; we thought you were a very good man. Everybody thought so; but the Almighty has laid his finger upon you, and that shows that you have committed great sins, and you had better confess them now, and maybe you will be forgiven." Job warms still more; he lifts his hand to high heaven, and says: "God knows that I have not committed any such great sins as you speak of at all. Oh, that I knew where I might find him, that I might get away from you who will not do me justice, and do not understand me. Before him I could argue my case." And so the discussion goes on, in an extremely interesting way, the great thought being, whether great sufferings do prove that a person has been guilty of extraordinary sins. Then a young man comes in, and—it is a lesson which old men would do well to lay to heart—the young man talks more wisely than all the old men had done, though he does not explain the matter yet; still he says: "Ah, the Almighty is greater than we, and we must not expect to understand all about him; we must try to submit ourselves to his ways, even though we do not understand them." And then Jehovah himself appears. I remember how, when I was a lad, I was first reading the book of Job, with some help in getting the idea, and when I reached this point my heart took a leap. I said: "Now Jehovah himself appears, and he will clear the whole matter up." But he does not; he simply says: "Who are you? What are you talking about? What do you know? What power have you? What wisdom have you to survey the universe and compass eternity? Why should you expect to understand everything? Remember how great am I and remember how little are you, and bow yourselves in humility, even where you cannot understand." And oh! friends and brethren, amid all our wide, wild questionings in life— and rightful questions too, if they are not mad—the loftiest knowledge in human life is to learn how to be willing, when we cannot understand Jehovah's ways, to bow to Jehovah's will, and put our sole trust in him.

There is only one more book that I shall mention for illustration. Do you read the book of Revelation in your family much? Do you preach about it much in your pulpit? I do not know whether to hope that you do or do not, because a great deal of the preaching about this book, and writing about it that I have come in contact with, would better have been let alone, according to my judgment; but the greatest evil that happens about it is, that a great many good people are led to neglect the book of Revelation. I asked a very able minister once, "Do you pay much attention to the book of Revelation?" He said, "No. I have no opinion of these calculations of prophecy, that have been made a hundred times over, and a hundred times over have turned out failures. I don't believe those men know anything about it, and I am sure I don't. And so I think I had better read somewhere else." Meantime, get your little child to say, if your child has heard the Bible read much, whereabouts you shall read the next time, and see if the child does not say, "Please turn over there to that last part and read that again."

There is much in the book of Revelation that takes hold upon children. Allow me to mention a personal reminiscence of something that touched me very much. Years ago, when my family included servants, I used to try very hard to get the servants and the children interested in the family worship. I tried the parables; I tried the life of our Lord; I tried many other parts of the Bible; sometimes they were interested, and sometimes not, and at length it occurred to me, "Now I will see if they will not be interested in the Revelation, that contains so much beautiful imagery." So I began, and I found that the servants and the children were very much interested for several days. I tried to explain a little, and I could do that very well for the first few chapters about the churches, etc., and could explain the scene of worship in heaven in the fourth and fifth chapters. Then we got on into the opening of the seals and the sounding of the trumpets, and I stopped explaining, for a reason that you can perhaps conjecture. But I did not stop reading. They told me to go on with it. They all seemed to be interested. At length, after many days, we were far over in the middle of Revelation, and I was reading some of that splendid, solemn, impressive imagery that is there presented—like the unrolling of a mighty panorama, scene after scene of wonder and power, and struggle and conflict, and hope and promise—and one day as I was reading I looked up through my tears and all the circle, from the aged grandmother down to the little child, were in tears too. You may say we did not know exactly what it was about. Yes, we did. It was about God—about God looking down on this world of ours, about the sorrows and struggles of this human life and the fact that God sees it all, is watching and controlling it all.

I have mentioned this for a purpose. I beseech you, read the book of Revelation. If you have no definite views as to the predictive portions of the book (and I have not, I confess), let them alone, but read for the sake of practical instruction ; that the book may bring Jesus, the exalted Redeemer, close to you ; that it may make clear to you the idea that heaven is the headquarters of the Christian, from which the angels come as messengers to bring the word of command, and carry back word as to what is going on in this battlefield of life. The book of Revelation tells us that these sorrows, temptations and trials are to end at last in complete victory, and in everlasting peace and joy. And to get sentiments like these, oh ye cultivated men and women, in this cultivated age of ours—to get tender, devoted, loving sentiments like these deeply impressed upon loving hearts, is worth all culture that falls short of them.

Now, I have just two or three remarks to make in conclusion. If we read the Bible by books, first taking each book as a whole, then seeing how it is divided up, then taking the several divisions and treating them, and so coming down to details, we shall learn in that way, and learn for ourselves how to interpret the several parts of Scripture with reference to their connection. Everybody will agree that you ought to look at the connection of a passage of Scripture. I remember one day my father said he did not like to find fault with preachers, but he wished some of them would pay more attention to the connection of the text, as the preacher that morning did not do. I suppose they have grown wiser since that day, and always do pay attention to the connection now. But in talking about it my father said, "Now, I can prove to you out of the Bible—it was an illustration to a little child—that there is no God." He got his Bible, opened it to a certain place, put his finger down and said, "Come here and read;" and the boy read, "There is no God," and it began with a capital T, too, as if it were a complete sentence. Then my father lifted his finger and said, "How is that? 'The fool hath said in his heart, There is no God.'" "Now," he said, "don't you see, you must always attend to the connection." That was a very simple lesson, certainly. What is the connection of a passage of Scripture? Only the other part of the sentence? Well, there are preachers sometimes who do not attend even to the other part of the sentence, and it may be true of some other persons besides preachers. But is that all the connection, only a sentence before or after a particular passage you are considering? Sometimes that is all, but in other cases it is a page or two that is the connection, and, as I have said, in the Epistle to the Hebrews, and in the book of Job, it is the whole book that is the connection; you cannot be sure that you are getting the precise point of view and the real meaning of any one of the sentences, unless you take it as a part of the whole, and with reference to the whole line of thought and practical design. You see how important it is that we should learn to study every particular expression of Scripture in its connection. It is a very beautiful thing to pick out the passages of Scripture that treat of some particular subject, as you can do with the help of a concordance, and put them together in a mosaic. It is like taking many pebbles and combining them, as the Romans were fond of doing, into a mosaic. That is a very delightful thing, only be sure about your material. Take care that you see where these things come from, and that you have got them right. No man would be so unwise as to take out of the Epistle of Paul, "A man is justified by faith without the works of the law," and then take a fragment out of James, "We know that a man is justified by works and not by faith only," and lay those two together and say, "How beautiful is the harmony of Scripture!" We know we must see what Paul was talking about and to whom he was talking, and to what sort of persons James was talking, and what he was talking at, in order to judge what each meant by this particular form of expression; we dare not put those two passages side by side and neglect the connection. Now in many other cases the difficulty and danger are not so obvious, but they may be just as real. So often, when a man with his concordance is picking out passages that all contain a certain word or refer to a certain subject, and laying them all together in a beautiful picture to please the eye, it is as if he made a mosaic in this fashion: Here is a pebble and there is a diamond; here is a crumb of sugar and there is a flower bulb; and those make a mosaic, do they? A mosaic is a beautiful thing, but your materials must be harmonious. You must know where these things come from. You must understand their connection, or else you will break living things all to pieces, in order to build up the dead fragments into a dead thing.

Then another remark. Each of these sacred books has its special aim and practical value, and we ought to try to get the practical impression that each of them is designed to make. For instance, each of the Gospels presents certain aspects of the life, character and work of our Lord. Those aspects are often overstated in the books about them, but you can catch the matter practically. Next year when we shall all be studying the Gospel of Mark, in Sunday-School lessons, the attention of half the Christian world will be turned to those particular aspects of the life, character and teachings of Jesus which are presented in that Gospel. You read one Gospel to see how that presents Jesus, and each of the other Gospels to see how it presents him, and if you have done that and then try to blend them all together in your loving faith, and reverence and humble desire to live like him, God being your helper, and to bring others with you to follow him too, you have made the most beautiful harmony of the Gospels that ever is made in this world. So as to other portions of the Scripture. We ought to get the devout and practical inspiration which each particular book is designed to give, and these, one after another, will unite themselves together in the symmetry of a complete Christian character, and the fulness and power of a true Christian life.

It is not an accident, brethren, that in this age, in which infidelity has anew become blatant and arrogant, the Bible is more studied than ever it was before. It is not an accident that there is a new demand, throughout the Christian world, springing up for Biblical, expository preaching. There has not been such a desire outside of Scotland, the great and noble home of expository preaching, for many generations. It is not an accident that these Bible-readings, which have done so much in our time, and will do so much, have become popular just now. People don't know about believing the preacher nowadays, and a great many people don't know about acknowledging the authority of a church as they once did; but the people who come to hear the gospel, if you bring them something right out of the Bible, not a broken, dead fragment, but a part of the living whole, full of the true, divine life, and show them its meaning as God has taught it, and lay that meaning, explained, upon their hearts and their lives, the people everywhere respond to that; they like it; they feel that that is good. It is not an accident that in a time when infidelity is so bold and noisy, there has come this revived love of Bible-study and Bible-preaching, Bible-readings, Bible-classes and Bible-work in general.

They say that the cultivated mind of the age has had enough of the Bible. Does it look as though people had stopped reading the Bible? You see men in the street-cars reading the New Testament. When I passed through Cincinnati on Monday, I ran to a book-store to get a copy of the Revised New Testament, and I saw a man buy, before my eyes, the last copy they had, out of a thousand sold over the counter that morning. God be thanked for this revived demand for it. But, oh, men and brethren, we do not read the Bible as we ought to read. It is easier to eulogize the Bible than to love it. It is as easy to praise as it is for some poor, silly opposer to make sport of the Bible. Dr. Johnson said that a man of real wit would be ashamed to make jests about the Bible, because it is too easy to do. It is just as easy to eulogize the Bible and then to neglect it.

I have spoken with the hope that I might by God's blessing awaken in some of you at least a greater desire to read the Bible attentively, and I pray God that we may all turn away with an earnest promise in our own souls, before him who knows the heart, that in the remainder of our lives we will try to love his word more, to read it more wisely, and to live more according to its blessed teachings.

If anybody wishes to ask questions about these matters, and you are willing to listen a few minutes, I shall be glad to answer them if I can.

Q. You spoke of analyses. What analyses would you recommend?

A. The analyses which are contained in Horne's Introduction are very good for this purpose. It is an old book which can be picked up anywhere. The analyses in Angus's Bible Hand-book are short and very good for this purpose.

Q. If a person has read the Bible through two or three times, and has a general idea of it, would you advise his stopping that plan, and spending the time on separate books?

A. The best of all ways, of course, would be to read the Bible in three different ways at once, if a man had time for it—to read very rapidly through the Bible once or twice a year, also read some books carefully, and daily some small portions as a part of private devotions. But I should say that most persons would find it better, instead of continuing to read it through in the way you mention, to take a book and study in the way I have indicated.

Q. What book would you advise a young convert to begin with?

A. Well, that would depend upon his previous Bible knowledge and general intelligence. But I think that there is nothing so important for the young Christian as to read the story of Jesus himself as told in the Gospels. The whole thought and feeling of our time seems to gather itself about the idea of Jesus. That is the citadel of the Scriptures for attack and defence, and that is the heart of the Scriptures for love. I should say to the young convert, "Read the Gospel of Mark; then read Matthew, Luke and John."

Q. Would you advise haste in going from one book to another before you have got the best judgment on one?

A. It would depend upon your knowledge of Scripture whether you should go rapidly. It would depend upon your own staying qualities, too.

Q. If you wanted to impress a skeptical man, who was seeking sincerely for light, with the inward truth of the Scripture, what book would you advise him to begin with?

A. Oh, I should give him the Gospels, and tell him, "Try to get near to Jesus Christ; try as you read it to seem to be looking at him and listening to him."

Q. Would you advise the reading of books of the New Testament and books of the Old together for the light they throw on one another?

A. That is very desirable sometimes. Leviticus and Hebrews may be read together very profitably; or Matthew and Isaiah. There are different expedients that each person will discover and adopt according to his own judgment and advantages.

Q. Do you recommend the use of the marginal references?

A. They are very desirable indeed, provided you pay attention to the connection which you find referred to. You must not take them as scraps, and put them where they are cited as if they belonged there. You must remember where they do belong.

Q. What brief word of counsel would you give in regard to the use of commentaries?

A. Well, it would be this: Be sure you get the very best commentaries there are; for there are commentaries and commentaries.

Q. Will you please recommend one?

A. Well, that is a very hard thing to do here. Use your commentaries all that you can, provided you do not read them instead of reading the sacred text. Read the Bible itself in its own connection, and commentaries to help. I remember a singing-master from whom I took lessons when a lad. When the ladies would not beat time, he used to stop and say, "Why don't you beat time? Ladies, if you can't sing and beat time both, stop singing and beat time." If you can't read the Bible and commentaries both, let commentaries alone.

Q. Would you advise the marking of Bibles?

A. Yes; mark them in every way.

Q. Would you not advise much prayer and communion with God in the study of the Bible, in order to a better understanding of it?

A. Oh, assuredly I should advise prayer and communion with God. I ought not to have taken that for granted. I blame myself that I did not say that. We ought to pray to God every time, for that is the heart of the matter.

Q. A young man asked me to ask you, how should we learn to love the study of the Bible?

A. Well, that is a good question; but, like a good many others of the wisest questions, the answer cuts deep. To love the reading of the Bible more, we must love him more of whom it tells us. And then, by reading the Bible more, we shall learn to love him more. And then, by trying to live the way the Bible tells us to live, we shall read it with more satisfaction and understanding. For if any man is willing to do the will of God, he will know concerning the doctrine.

Q. Would you advise regular hours for Bible study?

A. Oh, yes, yes, yes. Regular hours for reading the Bible, and irregular ones to boot. It depends upon your mode of life what hour is to be chosen.

Q. Would you recommend the morning hour rather than the evening?

A. That depends upon whether you are an early riser. I do not think you can lay down any law in regard to that matter. Everybody must find out for himself what his circumstances and his habits will allow him to do most profitably.

XIII.

MINISTERIAL EDUCATION.*

Give diligence to present thyself approved unto God, a workman that needeth not to be ashamed, handling aright the word of truth.— 2 Timothy, 2: 14.

I WISH first to indicate some of the leading thoughts in this passage of Scripture, in the second chapter of second Timothy, beginning at the 14th verse. The apostle is speaking to Timothy, not only with reference to his own duty, but to the qualifications of the men who are to be selected as ministers of the gospel, and whom he must instruct. Addressing Timothy himself, he says: "Give diligence to present thyself approved unto God, a workman that needeth not to be ashamed." The image is obvious to all. A minister of the gospel is compared to a mechanic, a skilled workman, a man who has stood the test and is approved, and then his skill in his work is shown by the added phrase, "a workman that needeth not to be ashamed, handling aright the word of truth." The term means literally "cutting straight," as you read in the margin. Perhaps the phrase came from the idea of a carpenter cutting a straight line with his saw; possibly from Paul's early trade. It required a very skillful workman to cut straight with scissors

---

* Sermon before the Missouri Baptist Educational Society, at Liberty, Mo. (the seat of Wm. Jewell College), in 1881.

the rough hair cloth of which they made the Cilician tents. Whatever be its origin, the term denotes, in a general way, skillful work—a workman that needeth not to be ashamed, cutting straight, handling aright the word of truth. A skilled workman is the minister. Then the apostle proceeds to indicate for Timothy himself, and for the faithful men to whom these things are to be committed that they may teach others also, the importance of knowing how to avoid seductive and ruinous errors. He says of these, " charge them that they strive not about words," mere logomachies, " to no profit. Shun the profane babblings." Presently he mentions examples, Hymenæus and Philetus, who had thought that the resurrection was a mere spiritual resurrection and past already, and had overthrown the faith of some, and Timothy and the other ministers must know how to shun these hurtful errors. If they do so, they shall be like the gold or silver vessels, honored in the Master's house. Another point about them is that they must not be given to mere babbling. " Foolish and ignorant questionings refuse, knowing that they gender strifes." The word is literally " fightings " or " battles," and the Lord's servant must not strive, must not be a fighter. In another sense, of course, we all know that the Scriptures teach that we must fight, but you see what is meant here. It is so easy for a man to be a fighting minister! Some men are fighting ministers for the very reason that they have not what the apostle here enjoined. The Lord's servant must not be a fighter, but must "be gentle, apt to teach, forbearing in meekness, correcting them that oppose themselves." Many a man is a fighting preacher because he does not know how to do anything else. It requires some wisdom and some skill to teach aptly, to correct with gentleness and meekness the errors of those who oppose themselves, and try to win them to the truth; but just to fight requires no skill at all.

You see, then, this passage presents very varied qualifications for the minister of the gospel—spiritual and mental qualifications combined. Of the mental qualifications, you see that it indicates some that belong to men by nature and others that come by cultivation; and as to the qualifications that come from cultivation—acquired skill—these come partly in the actual exercise of the duties of the minister, but they may come all the better if there be special early training for it. Take the image of the mechanic. "The only way to learn to preach is to preach," the fathers used to say. Certainly. The only way to learn to saw is to saw, or to learn how to make horse-shoes is to make them. At the same time, it is the experience of mankind that while some men take up these pursuits and acquire some skill merely from their practice, yet it is usually better for a man who proposes to be a mechanic, to work in his early attempts under the guidance and with the correction and encouragement of those who are far ahead of him in experience; and if men have found that so in all the mechanical arts, why should we be surprised to find it so in the great work of life of which the apostle speaks? "A workman that needeth not to be ashamed."

Our passage, then, brings before us the great subject of the qualifications and the training of ministers of the gospel. Where do we stand to-day, my brethren, as to ministerial education? What is the duty of to-day in regard to it? As to our past, there is in it much to be thankful for, and of course much to lament. I believe, for my part, that the theory of the Baptist churches as to the ministry of the gospel is a right theory, substantially. That theory has always been that the ministry of the gospel ought not to be restricted to men who have been over a certain fixed course of mental training in order to it, but that every one should be encouraged to preach who feels moved to preach, and whom the churches are willing to hear. At the same time, it has always been the theory that every minister of the gospel should seek to be a competent and enlightened man in general, and in particular that he must be a man who has sound views of the teaching of the Scriptures, and knows how to explain them to others. Our brethren have never held that it was a good thing for a minister to be ignorant, but they have held that it was not a disqualification for a minister to be destitute of this or that particular kind of mental training, provided only that he had some power to preach, and people were willing to hear him. That theory I think is right. It is what the Scriptures enjoin. It is what was true of the early teachers of the gospel—not only the inspired men, but others. It has been an absolute necessity for this new country of ours. I have profound respect for the ministry of the Presbyterian and Episcopal brethren, for instance, but I wonder sometimes what in the world would have become of the masses of the people in America if all the religious persuasions had done as they have done with reference to the ministry. They have had for themselves a cultivated ministry, in general, and they have had all the benefit of this select and exclusive arrangement as to the ministry, and some of them all the pride of it—which is natural. But if it hadn't been for the great Methodist and great Baptist bodies, and some others like them, who have encouraged men to preach that were destitute of this artificial course of training, what in the world would have become of the masses of the people? It has been bad enough as it was; it would have been flat ruin if all denominations in our new country, where most of the lawyers and most of the doctors have been men without any special training, had insisted that it should be otherwise with the ministry. I am not ashamed, therefore, of the fact that I belong to a body of Christians which has a great number of comparatively uneducated ministers. I think that in our past this has been unavoidable. I think it has been a necessary part of trying to see the gospel as it is and do our duty to the people among whom we were cast. But things are changing. Oh, how fast they change! A man who comes from my part of the world to this, finds that all his knowledge of geography has vanished. He does not know anything about the country at all. States that were thought new when some of us can remember, are old States now, and all around me I hear people talk of "going West," which seems strange to me. Things are changing, changing fast as to education, and we must change with them, and if our Baptist churches have not wisdom to see that the conditions which justified our past as to our ministry are changing and rapidly ceasing to justify them, then they will pay the penalty of their lack of wisdom. It may be that we have gone too far even in the past, and that some are going too far now in encouraging the entrance of men into the ministry who are unfitted for it; some unfitted by their grievous ignorance, and others still more ruinously unfitted—I pray you agree with me in the statement—by their lack of sense. For I can find you ignorant men who ruin the Queen's English and yet have sense and character and have done great good; and I can find you men that can speak passable English enough, and even prate about the learned languages, but from sheer weakness and silliness have always been a disgrace to the ministry. It may be that some of us are going too fast now, in some parts of the country, towards the opposite extreme—inclining too much to take up the other idea, that all ministers ought to have a certain artificially-fixed kind and grade of preparation for their work. It may be, my brethren, that in connection with institutions of learning we are somewhat prone to go from the one extreme to the other; and if that be so, we ought to look the danger in the face and guard against it.

What I wish to speak of, then, is our present duty as to ministerial education. And I have three points of remark about it.

First,—Ministerial education must go hand in hand with general education. It ought to keep in advance; but it cannot be, as a general thing, far in advance of the education of the people. They must go together. Why, with our free system of choice, you cannot get the churches to prefer a well-educated man, unless they have some education themselves. A man who has been reared among intelligent people and has been well educated, and who then goes to preach among the very ignorant, is startled to find how prejudiced they are against his ideas and against him. You will pardon a very homely illustration of it, egotistical in addition. I remember to have had the honor, twelve or fifteen years ago, to be elected pastor of a very large country church in Upper South Carolina—the largest country congregation I ever saw—where there were many noble people, too; but they had just been gathered in by hundreds, by good men, and never taught from the pulpit that there were any Christian duties to perform. At the end of a year of earnest attempt to preach there, with many encouraging results, I had the cheering intelligence that a good sister in the neighborhood had said, with reference to the justly beloved old man who had preceded me, that she "had rather hear dear old Uncle Toll give out one verse of a hime than to hear that 'ar Greenville preacher go through a whole sarmon." You will pardon me, for I wanted to illustrate the fact that ignorance, like a shell-fish, secretes a coating of prejudice that hardens all around it. If you could make all your ministers educated, as long as the mass of people are comparatively uneducated, they would often not want them. So the two must go together. Moreover, it is a thing very easy to happen, and which sometimes does happen with all our precautions against it, that a certain class of men are educated away from the people. It is not true of the highest class of men. The highest class of men, whatever they may learn, will not forget the language of the people, and will not fail to be able to bring all their highest efforts in reach of common minds. But it is true of some men of very respectable ability that, struggling themselves after what they call "education," they get away from all sympathy with the common mind. They don't know how to talk to the people. This happens with some, not from lack of intelligence of some kinds; it is from lack of imagination, from lack of intellectual sympathy with other minds, from lack of the power to comprehend the way that people in general look at things. I have known men—very noble men in all their aims and aspirations, and men very wise in some respects—who could not get hold of the people at all, because they didn't know how people in general think about things, and couldn't present things as the people have to see them. And then I suppose it must be admitted that sometimes a man who is educated away from the people thereby shows his essential lack of sense.

Here is another difficulty. Our ministers can seldom receive their boyhood education with a view to the ministry. They are usually called into that work when they have about reached young manhood; and if now they are to be educated, all the education of their boyhood must have been such as they have obtained without reference to the ministry. As long as people in general have but little of education—nothing beyond elementary instruction—so long will most of the young men who come into the ministry and wish to prepare for it have, for their earlier boyhood training, only what is to be had among the people at large. I speak of one of the most familiar—painfully familiar—phenomena to all who are called to instruct young ministers. What a common thing to see a fine young man under this disadvantage! You can see it in his eye that he is a man. You can see it in his tones that he wants to make the best of himself. You can see how he works; but there are the disadvantages of his comparative lack of training in his boyhood, and how to overcome them is the question. Many men never can fully overcome them, and they are humiliated sometimes because they cannot spell. Only some people can spell the English language, I believe. It is a torture and an outrage upon human nature that ought not to be perpetrated many generations longer, that people should be required to spell the English language as it now stands. I say, then, that if our ministers are to have earlier education —boyhood education—of a valuable kind, they must obtain it without reference to the ministry, and so there must be facilities for this among the people at large. I wished to explain how it is that ministerial education ranks itself necessarily with the general education of the people, and the experience of our churches has shown the fact. Almost every institution of learning that our Baptist people in America have founded has been founded with special reference to the ministry of the gospel; but then they have found that they must associate this with the education of others also. One of the wants of to-day is high-schools that shall be preparing our half-grown youths for whatever they are to do in the world, and then as many of them as are afterwards called into the ministry of the gospel will have the benefit of these schools; high-schools—whether they are to be supported by the public at large or founded by Christian people, is a question of locality and circumstances—high-schools that will forbear to call themselves colleges; that will not attempt to take upon themselves the functions of colleges; that will consent to do the humble, but so needful work of giving really thorough instruction in the elements of knowledge, and if they must add some other things for those pupils who will study there alone and will never go to college, they should still give to these mainly the thorough training in the elements of knowledge; high-schools that will teach history—for I find more fault with my pupils from lack of knowledge of history than almost anything else; for how can a man know anything unless he knows history?—high-schools which shall give thorough training in English composition, so that people can speak and write decently their own language; which for those who wish to study the classic languages, shall teach the elements of those languages. President Wayland used to say—I am using familiar incidents for my purpose—that there must be a mystery about Greek grammar. "For," he said, "a boy learns Greek grammar at the common school. Then he goes to the academy, and learns Greek grammar; then at college Greek grammar again, and then to the theological seminary, and still he must learn Greek grammar. There must be something very mysterious about Greek grammar." If there were only high-schools in which the teachers were willing to teach Greek grammar to those who are attempting to learn it, I know a certain class of men who come a little later on in our ordinary processes of education, who would have much occasion to thank the teachers of the high-school.

This, then, is my first point of remark, that ministerial education must go hand in hand with general education; therefore people who are specially interested in the education of the ministry must be equally interested in the education of the people; and our colleges need few things so much to-day as the help of high schools that shall prepare young men to enter college with a due knowledge of the elements of education.

My second point is this—*Ministerial education must not be—cannot be—the same for all.* Let us not go from one extreme to the other. There are differences that are felt, and what are you going to do about them? You have no power to coerce your young men. Some of them don't feel that they need this; how can you make them feel it. There are wide differences in circumstances. Some men are called into the gospel ministry comparatively late in life, and we must not get away from that good idea of our fathers that this is the right thing. Some of the noblest ministers of the past have entered on the work of preaching when they were of middle age, but not a few of us are getting towards the idea that every minister must go through a certain artificial course of training, fixed exactly, and have even thought that the idea of a man's entering the ministry at middle age must be discarded. Many enter the ministry somewhat late in life, and are so embarrassed by their domestic relations that, for an extended course, they are without the necessary means. Then there are differences in men's natural mental structure which make it unwise that you should carry them all through the same process of education. There are men who would really be hampered by an attempt to make scholars of them. I have known —far away from here, of course—ministers of the gospel who really were worse for having learned Latin, because they wasted their time in attempts to do that which they never did do successfully, or they were conceited with the notion that they knew something which they really did not know, and there is an old saying, which you must pardon again, that "there's no fool like a fool that knows Latin."

So, then, I insist upon it that we Baptist people, in trying to elevate our ministry, must not go from the extreme to which our churches once inclined towards the other extreme. If we do, we shall be false to all our history; we shall be false to what we conceive to be the teaching of the gospel; we shall be recreant to the demands of the approaching future. My brethren, we must not have some artificial notion of education, and allow it to be converted into a mechanical process, which is always the tendency. People talk as if educating a man was just taking him through a certain fixed machine, all men through the same machine, and coming out at the same point with the same training. That is false to all the prodigious variety in the faculties and tendencies of mankind. We must constantly guard against the tendency to make education, in all its departments and in all our institutions, a mechanical process, instead of a process of growth and the training of a living thing. Every body who knows anything about teaching knows that the main thing in all our early instruction is not knowledge, but discipline, and yet how constantly people are overlooking this! You ask the ordinary average person what children go to school for, and he will tell you that they go there to get a knowledge of certain things. That is not the main thing. The main thing is the discipline of mind, as every body who will think about it must perceive. When a young man goes out, after his course of training in a carpenter's shop do you inquire how many tools he has, or whether he has a lot of lumber ready to make up? You inquire whether he has learned his trade and knows how to handle tools and work the material that he will get as he needs it. The analogy is not perfect, I know, because in the training of the mind that which we use in the training becomes tools and materials for the work of the future, and we have in this to combine the acquisition of materials with the discipline of our faculties and the acquirement of skill. But while we combine them we must beware of confounding them, as men are prone to do.

Come now to my third point—*Our institutions for ministerial education, or, more generally, our institutions of higher education, must be greatly improved without delay.* There are no men who feel that so much as the men who have been struggling on amid a thousand difficulties, and have often done very noble work, and brought about, by God's blessing, quite good results, amid all their disadvantages. If you knew, as I could tell it, of the sore struggles through which many of our professors have passed, called to attempt three times as much in teaching as one man can possibly do to his own satisfaction, and yet how, under all these burdens, they have put forth their utmost power and have done good work—I think you would find it a theme for pathetic reflection. Our institutions need *more instructors*, in order that the work may be divided out, in order that each man may have the opportunity to devote himself to certain things and know them thoroughly, and work at them with the intense delight that comes to a man when he feels that he is making progress in the subject he loves. The tendency of our time is to specializing knowledge, as every one knows. I have a friend, a geologist, who gained his professorship in one of our leading American institutions by the fact that he was not only a geologist, but had confined himself to the department of geology which pertains to fossils and, among fossils, to fossil botany. And so by working at fossil botany he has gained a name in Germany and a noble place at home. This illustrates the tendency of all knowledge now. Men have to work more and more within narrow limits, if they are to make progress in these times or even to keep up with the progress that others are making; and so, in order that our professors may become "specialists" in our colleges—the only thing that can be satisfactory—we must have more professors. This is a crying need of the present time. And they must have more time in order to be better prepared. If you expect your professor in a college to meet classes three or four hours a day like a school-master, how can he lecture? How can he come with his mind all full of one theme, and all the reserved nerve force of his body and energy of his soul gathered up and concentrated upon one burning hour, in which he will carry home his subject to the hearts of those who hear him, and kindle in them that glowing enthusiasm which is the joy of a young man, and will be the inspiration of his life? Your hard-worked professor may kill himself in the effort to do that, but he cannot do justice to himself nor to his pupils nor to his Master nor to you.

And we must have professors who are *better paid*, so that they shall have the means of commanding comforts, without intense solicitude about it; so that they shall be able to live fitly in the better society of their community without finding it a burden; so that they may give their undivided energies to their duties.

Well, you see the absolute necessity that follows. Our institutions must be *better endowed*. They must be far more largely endowed. We must get hold of many of these people of ours who mean right, but who are not informed in this respect, and we must widen out their minds like the broad Mississippi Valley, to see the greatness of education, that they may give largely. Some of our brethren think that they have large notions already of what institutions of learning ought to be, but they have only begun to see, and it is our duty to hold up a high standard, and spread out a broad view of what these institutions must be made. The endowment of institutions of learning is a thing needed for the sake of the poor. There are many who fancy that somehow these colleges and universities are gotten up for the benefit of the rich; but it is not so. They are for the benefit of the poor, and I speak for the poor. As for the rich, they do not need any word from me. Here, for instance, is a man who wants education, and first-class education. He must go to a great city to find that, if there are no endowed institutions. He could find that nowhere but in a large city. If the professors are to be supported by the tuition, that tuition must be very high, and if the student is to have three or four teachers of eminent talents, he will have to pay three or four hundred dollars in tuition. The son of a rich man can do that, but what is to become of the son of a poor man? The institutions of learning come in to open their halls free of rent. The chief support of those professors will be from the endowment, and the man who is comparatively poor can thus obtain the benefit of contact with master minds, and instruction from men of high talents, which would otherwise be for him absolutely impossible. It is for the poor, I say, that our institutions are endowed. When you go to a rich man say, " Do your duty as one whom God has blessed with riches, and endow an institution for the sake of the poor all around you," and you may add, "Maybe your own son, that goes there from the home of his wealth and with all the benefits around him of ample means, will learn to study from some of those poor young fellows, his associates, who make him work by showing him what it is for a man to work." Last February I was a great deal in contact for some weeks with eminent men of business, and there came to me this thought about our institutions of learning, which you may have for what it is worth. When we go to a man of means and ask him to give largely for the endowment of an institution of learning, we are not begging. I protest I am no beggar. When I go to a rich man and say, "Come help us, won't you, in this enterprise," I present to him a joint-stock concern, a very popular idea now-a-days, an investment which will yield him large dividends, and which will last a long time. I say, "Here are our men who have given their whole lives to the work of instruction. They have toiled early and late through long years to qualify themselves for teaching certain things, and they are willing to put their lives into this—not simply a little of what they are, but all of what they are they will put into it, and the very fortunes of their families. Now, if you will put some money into it, then you and they will be in a joint-stock company, and you will be doing together what you cannot do without them, and what they cannot do without you, but together you will be doing a work that will bless humanity. They are no more dependent on you than you are on them, but you will be brothers united in a common work and receiving results in common." I think that is the right view of the matter, and that there are great-hearted men of wealth who would rejoice in the idea that they were investing in that which would yield large dividends to them and the world and which would last through long ages. For there are no investments in the civilized world so permanent as investments in institutions of education and religion. The old universities of Italy and of France and of England have lived eight or nine centuries—have lived through all changes, through all revolutions of governments, through all upheavals of society, and there they are to-day. No revolutionist has ever dared to attack them. No new government has ever done aught but wish them well, and perchance help them on. A man who wants to put money which God has enabled him to gather where it will last when he is gone, doing the work that he has chosen for it in the long centuries to come, must choose a mode of investment in some institution of education or religion; and if it be combined, an institution of education and of religion, of course all the better.

Now, my brethren—ministers and laymen, men and women—we must take hold of such thoughts as these, which would come to any of us upon reflection, and go among our people and stir their souls with the thought of the opportunity there is for them, the many to give a little, but especially the few to give much, for it is only from the large gifts of the few that institutions of education have received ample endowment; to stir their souls to see what God gives them opportunity to do, and what God's high providence sends down, like the sunbeams out of heaven, for a direction to them. Not all rich people are selfish or mean; not many rich people are narrow-minded or ignorant; but they are busy—busy with their own affairs, burdened with their own great burdens—and somebody must go and tell them of these openings for investing money, better than they can invest it anywhere else in all this world, for the highest good of man and for the highest glory of Christ.

XIV.

THE AMERICAN BAPTIST MINISTRY OF A.D. 1774.*

THERE are few things so advantageous, in the detailed study of history, as to establish ourselves at some definite point of the past, and look carefully around, until all that lies within the horizon of that time is thoroughly known. The period just named for this purpose is of peculiar interest to American citizens, as lying at the threshold of American independence, and also to Baptists, for then our brethren were just drawing near the end of their struggles and sufferings, and preparing the way for more joyous and prosperous work in a new and blessed day of freedom. The limits of a lecture will of course not allow any general study of that grand epoch. Even confining ourselves to the one theme of the Baptist ministry at that time, we shall be able only to glance rapidly along the outlines of this single department in the wide field of view.

It requires a great effort of imagination to go back one hundred years. In 1774 there was nothing of our present magnificent country but the thirteen colonies along the Atlantic coast, from New Hampshire to Georgia. In many of these, as we look back, we see that only the eastern part of the territory is settled, even in

* Public lecture in opening the session of the Southern Baptist Theological Seminary, then at Greenville, S. C., September 1, 1874.

Pennsylvania and Virginia hardly one-half, and in New York and Georgia, only the southeastern corner. The first feeble settlements in Kentucky and Tennessee are but a few years old. There has been in the colonies great political discontent for some fourteen years, particularly manifested in Massachusetts and Virginia, which has grown into a widespread opposition to the home government. The "Boston tea party" occurred last winter, December, 1773. The first Continental Congress is to meet in Philadelphia three days hence, September 4, 1774. The colonists intend to maintain their rights by force if necessary; but very few are as yet looking forward to independence. The Virginians have been engaged all summer in a great Indian war, which will end a few weeks hence with the "bloodiest and most decisive" of all the Indian battles at the mouth of Kanawha.

Let us now survey the leading Baptist ministers of the several groups of colonies. Many able and useful men have long ere this passed away. In the previous century Hansard Knollys and Roger Williams were Baptist preachers in New England within less than twenty years after the landing of the Pilgrims, and John Clark founded the church at Newport in 1644, only twenty-four years after the landing. Still others were coming over from England and Wales, and by the end of the seventeenth century there were seventeen American Baptist churches in existence, situated chiefly in Rhode Island and Massachusetts, but several of them in Pennsylvania and New Jersey, and one in Charleston, S. C. Passing to the eighteenth century, we find that Elisha Callender, a graduate of Harvard College and a pastor beloved by all denominations in Boston, died in 1738, which is thirty-six years ago. A few years afterwards died Valentine Wightman, a man of marked ability and extensive attainments, who founded many churches in Connecticut. And still earlier in the century was Abel Morgan, who came over from Wales to Philadelphia in 1711, and was greatly respected for his ministerial knowledge, zeal and usefulness, until his death in 1722. These three—Morgan, Callender and Wightman—are all that we have time to glance at of the departed worthies, though various other good ministers of the time are known to history.

Coming to those who are still alive in 1774, we must look first at leading ministers who are by this time growing old, or already widely known—those who belong mainly or largely to the past.

A number of these are found in New England. Timothy Wightman succeeded his father, Valentine Wightman, in Groton, Conn., and though a man of less power than his father, has been very devout and useful, and has brought his church into a very healthy condition, with repeated revivals. He is now fifty-five years old, and is greatly beloved and full of pastoral work. Gardiner Thurston, of Rhode Island, is a little younger, and has spent all his life at Newport. He was not educated at college, but has always had a great thirst for knowledge, and been very diligent both in general and in theological studies. At first assistant to an aged pastor for eleven years, and giving part of his time to business for a support, he afterward succeeded him and has for fifteen years been full pastor and entirely supported by the church.

He is a charming man in private intercourse, and in preaching is not only interesting and instructive, but pathetic and solemn, and plainly depends much on the special support and blessing of the Holy Spirit. In Massachusetts is the famous Isaac Backus, now fifty years old, and in the fulness of his powers. Reared a Congregationalist in Connecticut, and converted during the "Great Awakening," produced by the preaching of Whitefield and others, he presently went off with the Separatists or New Light Congregationalists, who contended for a converted membership and strict discipline, and for an internal call to the ministry. After preaching some years in this connection he became a Baptist, and at length pastor of a new Baptist church in Middleborough, Mass., in which position he has now remained for eighteen years. Two years ago he was chosen agent for the Baptist churches in Massachusetts, to labor for securing religious liberty, and has done the work with great zeal and ability, corresponding with the English Baptists on the subject, and also corresponding with the patriotic Samuel Adams, as the Virginia Baptists are doing with Jefferson and Madison. He will shortly be in like manner appointed agent to attend the Continental Congress, which is about to meet in Philadelphia. Mr. Backus has already published several sermons and a number of pamphlets on questions of Scripture doctrine or of religious liberty. And he has been busily collecting materials for a history of the Baptists in New England, the first volume of which will be ready in two or three years. Very diligent and painstaking in the collection of materials and laborious in general, his writings are full of reliable information and vigorous argument, though somewhat deficient in literary finish. He is a man of powerful physique, strengthened by early work on a farm and by much travelling on horseback. His commanding appearance, deep-toned voice, grave argumentative style, earnest and masterful nature and fervent piety make him, though not exactly an attractive, yet a highly impressive preacher. And, altogether, he is at this time probably the most influential Baptist minister in New England. Fifteen years later he will spend six months in Virginia and North Carolina, strengthening the churches. While passing over various others, we must not fail to notice Noah Alden, of Massachusetts, now forty-nine years old, who was originally a Congregationalist, but has been for nineteen years a Baptist minister, greatly respected for his wisdom in regard to politics as well as religion, and very useful in his pastoral work.

These are the older men among the leading Baptist ministers of New England at the time of which we speak, Wightman, Thurston, Backus, Alden. Several others are younger, though already well known and influential. Foremost among them are Manning and Stillman.

James Manning was born in New Jersey thirty-six years ago, attended the famous Baptist School at Hopewell, N. J., conducted by Rev. Isaac Eaton especially "for the education of youth for the ministry," and graduated with the highest honors at Princeton College. He speedily grew very popular as a preacher, and before long became pastor at Warren, Rhode Island. Here he was the most active person in founding, just ten years ago, Rhode Island College, which in a few years was removed to Providence, and is destined at a later period to be known as Brown University. Of this first Baptist College in America Mr. Manning was made President and Professor of Languages, and he and the college have already gained a warm place in the affections of the people of Providence and of the Baptists of all the colonies.

Samuel Stillman, a native of Philadelphia, was brought by his parents to Charleston, S. C., when eleven years old, and converted under the ministry of Rev. Oliver Hart, of whom we shall hereafter speak. He received a classical education from Mr. Rind, "a teacher of some celebrity" in Charleston, and then spent a year in studying theology with the assistance of his pastor, Mr. Hart. He began to preach in Charleston sixteen years ago, and settled first on James Island; but his lungs becoming diseased, he went to New Jersey as a better climate. After preaching there two years he visited Boston, where he was at first assistant in the Second Church, and soon afterwards, nine years ago, was made pastor of the First Baptist Church. Here he rapidly sprang into great popularity and influence. His preaching is attended for the sake of its eloquence by men having little sympathy with his thoroughly evangelical doctrines, including prominent lawyers and politicians. Highly cultivated and careful in preparation, he yet often indulges in "sudden bursts" of unpremeditated, impassioned eloquence, and constantly makes free use of anecdote and other illustration. His religious visits are valued and solicited by persons of all denominations. He is also taking an active part in the support and management of Rhode Island College, and in all the work of the Baptists of New England, and has already published quite a number of excellent sermons. He is now thirty-seven years old. Universally admired and beloved, full of ministerial work in public and in private, in his own church and elsewhere, deeply devout and richly blessed, we shall find in all this survey no Baptist pastorate so truly brilliant as that of Samuel Stillman in Boston. Indeed, it is doubtful whether the age in question presents a more popular preacher of any denomination in America.

Hezekiah Smith, by birth a New Yorker, was educated, like Manning, at Hopewell School and Princeton College. After graduating, he traveled South for his health, and was ordained in Charleston, S. C. After preaching a while in the Pedee country, with great acceptance, he returned northward, went to New England, and finally built up a new and strong Baptist Church at Haverhill, Mass., of which for the last eight or nine years he has been the beloved pastor. He has also made numerous preaching tours as far north as Maine, and his dignified, solemn, truly eloquent preaching everywhere makes a great impression. He maintains an affectionate correspondence with Oliver Hart and other brethren in South Carolina. He is now thirty-seven years old, about the same age as Manning and Stillman.

There is little time to speak of Samuel Shepard, who was a young Congregationalist physician in New Hampshire, but was converted to Baptist views by reading a tract found at the house of one of his patients; and soon beginning to preach, founded three new churches in New Hampshire, and three years ago became their pastor. Nor of John Davis, the younger of that name, a native of Delaware, prepared at Hopewell School, and graduated at the College of Philadelphia, and after some years made pastor of the Second Baptist Church in Boston—a man remarkable for learning, abilities and usefulness, cut down by death two years ago, when but thirty-five years old.

Leaving New England, we come to the Middle Colonies. Of the older men who are still living three or four must be mentioned.

Ebenezer Kinnersley, an Englishman by birth, and brought to this country in childhood by his father (himself also a Baptist minister), is now sixty-seven years old, and has spent his life in and about Philadelphia. Never engaging much in preaching, he has been otherwise a very distinguished man, both as a zealous coworker with Franklin in discovering the properties of what they call the Electric Fire, and as the highly popular professor of English and Oratory in the University of Pennsylvania. He has delivered scientific lectures in the chief cities, which attracted great attention. In 1772, two years ago, he resigned his chair in the college, and retired to the country in feeble health. Abel Morgan, Jr., nephew to the older minister of that name, whom we mentioned, was born in a Welsh settlement in Delaware. After his ordination he came with a company of Baptists to South Carolina, and "was a constituent member of a church called Welsh Neck, in 1738."

Returning, he became pastor in Middletown, New Jersey, and has now been there for thirty-five years. He never married, giving as a reason the wish that "none of his attention and attendance might be taken off" from his mother, who lived with him more than thirty years, and died only three years ago. His learning is really extensive, and he is especially skillful in disputation. Years ago he had a public debate on Infant Baptism with Rev. Samuel Finley, afterwards President of Princeton College. It was Mr. Finley that proposed the discussion, and as he afterwards printed a pamphlet, Mr. Morgan replied, and each of them replied again. These were probably the first works issued in the New World in vindication of the baptism of believers only, and they are said to show decided ability and good learning. Though now sixty-one years old, Mr. Morgan is still a very laborious and useful minister. John Gano, born in New Jersey forty-seven years ago of a Huguenot family, after determining to preach, spent two or three years in studies preparatory to that work, meantime frequently preaching, even before he was licensed. In response to earnest requests from the South for ministerial help he was induced, twenty years ago, to come southward, and traveled extensively. In Charleston he preached in Mr. Hart's pulpit in the presence of a brilliant audience, including twelve ministers, one of them being George Whitefield, and for a moment (as he has recorded) felt the fear of man, but soon remembered that he "had none to fear and obey but the Lord." Two years later he made another tour to the South, and settled for two years in North Carolina, but being driven out by the Cherokee Indians, returned North, and for a while preached alternately in Philadelphia and New York. Twelve years ago a church was at last organized in New York, and Mr. Gano became its pastor, in which position his labors have been greatly blessed. A small man, yet of manly presence and commanding voice, of good mind, respectable attainments and deep feeling, he is a highly popular and effective preacher.

It is worth while to notice how late the Baptists were in establishing themselves in New York City. They organized a church in Boston in 1664; in Charleston, S. C., 1683; in Philadelphia, 1698; in New York no permanent church was formed till 1762.*

Somewhat older than Gano is Morgan Edwards, a native of Wales, a preacher from his sixteenth year, and educated in the Baptist Seminary at Bristol, England. After preaching a number of years in England and Ireland, he was sent to America thirteen years ago by the famous Dr. Gill, in response to a request from the Baptist Church at Philadelphia that he would send them a pastor. The story is that in writing to Dr. Gill the church "required so many accomplishments" in a pastor, that the old gentleman told them he did not know that he "could find a man in England who would answer their description," but that Mr. Morgan Edwards "came the nearest of any that could be obtained." After remaining eleven years in Philadelphia, he removed, two years since, to Newark, N. J. Mr. Ed-

---

* There was preaching in New York as early as 1669, and a little church appears to have been formed there by Valentine Wightman about 1714, but it was afterwards dissolved.

wards is a man of genius and scholarship. His Greek Testament is "his favorite companion," and he has also a good knowledge of the Hebrew Bible, being accustomed to say that the Greek and Hebrew are "the two eyes of a minister," while his extensive travels and wide general reading have contributed to make him a very interesting man, both in public and private. He has thus far published three sermons and a History of the Baptists in Pennsylvania, besides collecting much material for other works; and he is very careful and critical in respect to English style.

Besides these four older men in the Middle Colonies —Kinnersley, Morgan, Gano and Edwards—we must notice two who are somewhat younger, but prominent and promising—both of them named Jones.

Samuel Jones is a native of Wales, but was brought to this country in infancy. His father, himself a pastor in Pennsylvania, and a man of wealth, was determined to give his son a thorough education, and accordingly Samuel was graduated A.M. of the College of Philadelphia in 1762. For the last eleven years he has been pastor of a church near Philadelphia, and also occupied in teaching, being very successful and highly honored in both vocations. By his excellent judgment and remarkable self-control he is particularly useful in meetings of the Philadelphia Association, and other ecclesiastical assemblies. This is noteworthy, for successful preachers much oftener possess fervor and fire than sound judgment and equanimity. David Jones was born and reared in Delaware, and educated at Mr. Eaton's Hopewell School in New Jersey, where he says he "learned Latin and Greek." Having determined to become a minister, he went, thirteen years ago, to Middletown to study divinity with his kinsman, Abel Morgan. For the last eight years he has been pastor in Monmouth County, N. J., but two or three years ago made three different journeys to the distant country about and beyond the Ohio River, preaching to the Indians, though without much effect. At the time of which we speak he is full of zeal for the political rights of the Colonies, as are the Baptist preachers everywhere, with rare exceptions. Some years ago he made a visit to New York City, and had an amusing experience which may help to show how scarce were our brethren in that place:

When I first came to New York [so he is said to have told the story] I landed in the morning, and thought I would try if I could find any Baptists. I wandered up and down, looking at the place and the people, and wondering who of all the people I met might be Baptists. At length I saw an old man, with a red cap on his head, sitting on the porch of a respectable-looking house. Ah, thought I, now this is one of the old residents, who knows all about the city; this is the man to inquire of. I approached him, and said: "Good afternoon, sir. Can you tell me where any Baptists live in this city?" "Hey?" said the deaf old Gothamite, with his hand to his ear. Raising my voice, I shouted: "Can you tell me, sir, where I can find any Baptists in this place?" "Baptists, Baptists," said the old man musing, as if ransacking all the corners of his memory; "Baptists! I really don't know as I ever heard of anybody of that occupation in these parts!"

We now leave the Middle Colonies, and come to speak of some leading ministers in the Southern Colonies, from Maryland to Georgia.

In Charleston, S. C., we find, as already several times mentioned, Oliver Hart, who is now fifty-one years of age. He was born and reared in Pennsylvania, and when a young man often listened with great profit to Whitefield. Ordained at the age of twenty-six, he heard "the loud call for ministers in the Southern Colonies," and coming South, found the church at Charleston vacant, and becoming their pastor twenty-four years ago, has, in that position, been highly respected and widely useful. He takes an active part as a citizen in the movements for the maintenance of colonial rights and liberties, but does not "mix politics with the gospel, nor desert the duties of his station to pursue them." We are to think of him as a man of tall and graceful figure, with a pleasing countenance and voice, and while not exactly eloquent, yet an exceedingly instructive and impressive preacher. Though not bred in college, he has been a diligent student of the classics and of physical science, and has been the instructor in general learning and in theology of several other ministers, among them Samuel Stillman. Of these, Stillman and some others were furnished with the means of support by the "Religious Society" which Mr. Hart organized in Charleston nineteen years ago (1755) for this purpose.

Shubael Stearns and Daniel Marshall were intimately associated in North Carolina, and are naturally spoken of together, though the former died three years ago. Shubael Stearns was born in Boston in 1706, and under the influence of the Great Awakening, attached himself, in 1745, to the Congregationalist Separates, or New Lights, and began to preach. In 1751 he became a

Baptist, in Connecticut, and after two or three years more, longing to carry the gospel to more destitute regions, he came, with a small colony of brethren, to Berkeley County, Va. Here he was joined by Daniel Marshall, who was of the same age with him, and had also been a Congregationalist and a Separate in Connecticut. Believing that the second coming of Christ was certainly at hand, Marshall and others sold or abandoned their property, and hastening with destitute families to the head-waters of the Susquehanna, began to labor for the conversion of the Mohawk Indians. After eighteen months he was driven away by an Indian war, and went to Berkeley Co., Va., where, finding a Baptist Church, he examined and adopted their views about 1754. He had married, while in Connecticut, the sister of Shubael Stearns, and the two became associated in Virginia, and soon sought together a still more destitute region in North Carolina, not far from Greensboro. Here they and their little colony taught the necessity of the new birth and the consciousness of conversion, with all the excited manner and holy whine, and the nervous trembling and wild screams among their hearers, which characterized the Congregationalist Separates in Connecticut. Though at first much ridiculed, they soon had great success, building up two churches of five hundred and six hundred members. Retaining their New England name of Separates, they called themselves "Separate Baptists," and these spread rapidly into Virginia and into Georgia, though destined, when their enthusiastic excesses should have been cooled down, to be absorbed, before the end of the eighteenth century, into the body of regular Baptists. Stearns died in North Carolina; but Marshall, ever looking out for new fields, came, after a few years, to Lexington District, in South Carolina, where he built up a church, and finally, three years before the time of which we speak, removed to Georgia, not far from Augusta, where he has already formed a considerable church. Among the unusual customs of the Separates, both Congregationalist and Baptist, was the practice of public prayer and exhortation by women; and in these exercises Marshall's wife is said to have been wonderfully impressive.

In one of his preaching tours, from North Carolina back into Southern Virginia, sixteen years ago, Daniel Marshall baptized Colonel Samuel Harriss, of Pittsylvania. This gentleman had a good social position, holding numerous civil and ecclesiastical offices, and possessing some wealth. He at once threw himself earnestly, with serious pecuniary sacrifices, into the work of preaching, and in the course of these sixteen years has made preaching journeys through a great part of Virginia as well as portions of North Carolina. His overwhelming earnestness and wonderful pathos produced so great an effect that highly judicious men declared that even Whitefield did not surpass him in addressing the heart. He has also taken an active part in Baptist efforts to secure religious freedom, none the less that he himself has been shamefully persecuted for preaching in Culpeper and Orange. He is a favorite presiding officer in the associations and other business meetings of the Separate Baptists, and in this very year,

1774, these enthusiasts having concluded that the office of apostle ought to be perpetual, Samuel Harriss and two others have been elected and solemnly set apart as apostles, an office which will be silently abandoned by all concerned the following year. Such a transient notion is but a spot on the sun of his noble Christian character and life. He is now fifty years old.

There are other well-known men in Virginia at the time in question of whom it would be pleasant to speak, such as David Thomas, forty-two years old, a Pennsylvanian, educated at Hopewell School, and removing when still young to Virginia, where he has been very useful; but we must pass them by, as we have passed by many good men in other colonies. In Maryland we find John Davis, the older of that name, fifty-three years old, another Pennsylvanian, who removed eighteen years ago to Maryland, and has built up a strong country church. There is as yet no Baptist Church in Baltimore.

It must have been noticed that with the single exception of Samuel Harriss, all the older ministers we have mentioned as particularly distinguished in the Southern colonies came originally from the North. When the early Baptist settlers came over from England and Wales, the English went chiefly, for reasons not hard to discern, to New England, and the Welsh chiefly to Pennsylvania, New Jersey and Delaware. Next to these the colony to which Baptists earliest came in considerable number was South Carolina, and here the number was small compared with New England and the Middle Colonies. Thus the Baptists were at first far more numerous at the North than at the South, and naturally produced a larger number of ministers. Besides, there were already more general opportunities for education in the Northern Colonies, so that ministers from that region were more likely to become distinguished. And furthermore, the work of Whitefield and others awoke the slumbering Congregationalists of New England, and brought out the enthusiastic Separates, many of whom became Baptists, and traveled southward, in a missionary spirit, to supply the destitution. These considerations will help to account for the fact mentioned. And already, in 1774, if we look at the younger men just coming forward and giving especial promise of usefulness, we shall see a very large number in the Southern Colonies. Some of these young men we must briefly notice.

William Fristoe, hardly thirty years old, is already famous in Virginia, with many seals to his ministry, and in this year is chosen moderator of the great Ketocton Association. "Swearing Jack Waller," thirty-three years old, once a dissipated young man of good family, and a persecutor of the Baptists, was converted and baptized seven years ago, and some time after was long imprisoned for preaching. He blazes with unquenchable zeal, and turns many to righteousness in his native State, and has doubtless little idea that he will be buried in Abbeville District, South Carolina. James Ireland, aged twenty-six, a Scotch school-master in Northern Virginia, and very wicked, was in a singular manner convicted and converted, and five years ago was baptized by Samuel Harriss, and beginning to preach with great zeal and effect, was soon after seized and imprisoned at Culpeper Court-House, where his enemies tried to blow up his room in the jail with gunpowder, and to suffocate him with fumes of sulphur, all for preaching the gospel; and he retaliated simply by preaching through the jail window to the people who would gather around. He is now at liberty and zealously at work. William Marshall, of Fauquier, now thirty-nine years old, was converted six years ago. Being of an influential family, and having been a conspicuous man of fashion, it made a great noise when he became a Baptist preacher, and the crowds who came to hear him have always been deeply impressed, and great numbers of them converted. He has a young nephew, John Marshall, who will in coming years be Chief Justice of a new nation. Lewis Lunsford, near Fredericksburg, is only twenty-two years old, but began to preach five years ago, being called "the wonderful boy," and his preaching attended by great crowds. With all this, and while he must have been conscious of possessing extraordinary talents, he has not been spoiled, but is full of humility and devotion. But the time would fail to tell of Picket, Conner, Williams, Taylor, the brothers Craig, Courtenay, Koontz, Garnett, Webber, and many more of these promising young men, who have, in 1774, recently entered upon the ministry in Virginia.

We know of similar men in South Carolina and Georgia. Edmund Botsford, a young English soldier, came to Charleston some years ago, was converted under the ministry of Oliver Hart, and for the last three years has been preaching with great acceptance in the south-western part of the State, until in May, 1774, he moved across into Georgia, whence we know that he will, after some years, return to spend his useful life in South Carolina. Richard Furman, *clarum et venerabile nomen*, is now nineteen years old. His father, a surveyor at the High Hills of Santee, has carefully taught him mathematics and the Bible. Uncommonly mature in intellect and piety, he began to preach at the age of sixteen. Some youths of the same age tried all the arts of insulting ridicule, but without seeming to move him at all; his father earnestly strove to dissuade him, being anxious that he should become a lawyer, and fearful that he was carried away by temporary excitement; but he respectfully urged an irresistible feeling of duty. Soon invitations came to visit destitute places in the country around, and he has been preaching far and near. Tall and handsome, serious and dignified even in youth, his grave and impressive eloquence commands the attention of young and old, and men can see that he will be a prince and a great man in Israel. Abraham Marshall, son of the Daniel Marshall we spoke of, is living with his father in Georgia, aged twenty-six, and has been preaching several years. His educational advantages were confined to forty days at an "old field school;" but his native gifts of mind, his athletic frame and noble voice, his knowledge of the Bible and of the human heart, make him a highly effective and promising young preacher.

In Philadelphia we find William Rogers, a native of Newport and graduate of Rhode Island College, who began to preach three years ago, and for two years has been pastor of the Philadelphia Church—a young man of fine gifts and culture, and refined manners, very useful as a preacher, and destined to distinction as a professor. Burgess Allison, of New Jersey, has been preaching, in fact, though not formally, since the age of sixteen, and now, at twenty-one, is studying classics and theology with Dr. Samuel Jones, near Philadelphia. He is fond of music and painting, and has great mechanical ingenuity, and with his singular good sense is likely to turn out a useful preacher and teacher, and a distinguished man of science. Thomas Ustick, a native of New York, is also twenty-one years old, was baptized at thirteen, and graduated at Rhode Island College, has been teaching school in New York and studying for the ministry, and in this year has begun to preach. Modest, gentle, devoted and diligent, he promises to be very useful.

In New England, likewise, we hear of several very promising young men. Silas Burrows, of Connecticut, has been preaching nine years. Without much education, he is a man of good sense and the deepest feeling, and is wonderfully gifted in prayer and exhortation. Charles Thompson, a native of New Jersey, belonged to the first graduating class of Rhode Island College, five years ago, and for the past four years has been pastor at Warren, R. I. Vigorous in intellect, and very diligent in study, with a fine figure and magnificent voice, full of tender pathos and of lofty passion, and devoted to his work, he is a young man of mark. His classmate at college, William Williams, of Welsh descent, was baptized three years ago by Thompson, at Warren, and licensed to preach, and in connection with the ministry will become famous in Massachusetts as a teacher.

It has seemed a long list, of older and middle-aged and young Baptist ministers, who were living in 1774. Yet it has been made short by reluctantly omitting names well worthy to be known and honored.

And there are youths who have not yet entered the ministry, but will one day be heard of. John Leland, twenty-one years old, was baptized in June, in Massachusetts. Thomas Baldwin, of the same age, is living in Connecticut, a diligent student, but not yet a Christian. Silas Mercer, in Georgia, is twenty-nine years old; originally an Episcopalian, he has become a Baptist in sentiment, but will not be baptized until next year. Henry Holcombe is a boy of twelve years, and his father has recently removed with him from Virginia to South Carolina. Jonathan Maxcy is six years old, in Massachusetts, a very precocious child, who will not die early. Robert B. Semple is five years old, in King and Queen. Andrew Broaddus is four years old, in Caroline County, Va., and his father, a zealous member of the Establishment, designs that his son shall be a clergyman.

Glance a moment, too, across the water. Whitefield died four years ago. Wesley, though over seventy, has many years of work in him still. Of the English Baptists, Dr. Gill, the great Talmudical scholar, author of a giant commentary on the whole Bible, an elaborate Systematic Theology and many other works, and yet all his life a hard-working pastor, died three years since in London. Robert Robinson, at the age of twenty-nine, is already a well-known author, an omnivorous reader, and a highly popular preacher under the shadow of the University of Cambridge. Stennett and Beddome, authors of so many excellent hymns, are in their prime. Andrew Fuller is twenty years old, having been baptized at sixteen, and after several years of providential leading towards the ministry, has just begun to preach regularly. Robert Hall, son of an able and honored minister of the same name, is ten years old, and loves, when out of school, to read over and over again such books as Edwards on the Will and Butler's Analogy.

Let us now single out for brief observation some points in the opinions and practices of American Baptist ministers in 1774.

1. These men felt themselves inwardly *called* to the ministry. Some of them indulged wildly enthusiastic notions as to the nature and evidences of this call, but at bottom it was a thoroughly correct conception which prevailed among them. And on this account it is not well to speak of the ministry as a *profession*. One ought not to choose the ministry at all as he might choose to be a lawyer, physician, teacher or editor, but it ought to be entered upon from a sense of *duty* to God and man. We are not claiming any special sanctity for the pursuit itself as compared with the professions, but only urging the importance of carefully avoiding the notion that to enter upon the ministry is merely "making choice of a profession."

2. They endured great hardships in the prosecution of their work. Frequent and immensely long journeys on horseback, through thinly-settled districts, devoid of

comforts, were taken by almost all the pastors in their evangelizing labors, and burning zeal often impelled them to severer toils than they were able to bear. Besides, there was not seldom persecution, involving indignities, discomforts and sometimes positive sufferings. Many of us are familiar with the story of such persecutions in Virginia; but they began far earlier in Massachusetts, and were violent there at the time of which we speak, the Cavalier and the Puritan establishments being equally harsh and cruel. The Baptists are one of the few religious denominations that have never persecuted. We cannot say they have been personally too good, seeing that some of them have shown great bitterness towards other religionists and even towards their own brethren who differed from them; but their immemorial principle of opposition to all union of church and state has always made it impossible that they should persecute. In so doing they would at once cease to be Baptists.

These hardships, from persecution and from ministerial labor, often told upon health. Many suppose that the frequent deaths from paralysis, for instance, are a peculiarity of our times. But among the men we have been speaking of it is mentioned that Backus, Alden, Gano, Harriss, Stillman and Manning all died of paralytic affections. True, these had all passed through the long agony of the Revolution.

3. Many of our brethren of that day erred about *ministerial support*. What they called the "hireling ministry" of the establishments was an abomination to them, and they frequently went to the opposite extreme,

some of them even proclaiming that they wished no contributions for their support; and not being wise enough to see and explain, like the apostle Paul, the difference between the course which for temporary reasons they pursued, and the general right of ministers to be supported. Their undiscriminating teachings were but too acceptable to human selfishness, and left deep-rooted errors which we are still toiling to eradicate.

4. Our ministers, in 1774, were in general heartily in favor of *ministerial education*, and many of them were themselves highly educated men. This last had been true from the beginning. Hansard Knollys and Roger Williams had both been clergymen of the Church of England, and educated at the English universities, and John Clarke was a diligent student of the original Scriptures. In the eighteenth century Elisha Callender was a graduate of Harvard, Samuel Jones and the younger John Davis of the College of Philadelphia, President Manning and Hezekiah Smith, of Princeton, and Charles Thompson, William Williams, Thomas Ustick and William Rogers, of Rhode Island College. A number of others, though not college graduates, were diligent students and really well educated; for example, Valentine Wightman, Thurston, Kinnersley, Gano, Abel Morgan (senior and junior), Morgan Edwards, David Jones, David Thomas, Oliver Hart, Stillman and Furman, several of whom were eminent for their general and theological attainments and teachers of others. The only men we have spoken of who became leading ministers without being what we might fairly call educated, were Isaac Backus and Silas Barrows, Shubael Stearns,

Daniel Marshall and his son Abraham, Samuel Harriss and some of the younger men in Virginia, and Edmund Botsford; and some of these were highly intelligent and well-informed. Great interest was also shown in institutions for higher education. An English Baptist merchant, Thomas Hollis, gave a large donation to Harvard College to found a professorship, about 1720. Besides the famous Hopewell School in New Jersey, established by Isaac Eaton with express reference to the preparation of young men for the ministry, and which we have had occasion to mention so often, several high schools, conducted by Baptists, are known to us as in existence at the time. Rhode Island College (Brown University), established in 1764, awakened the liveliest interest among the Baptists everywhere. The Pennsylvanians, in fact, claimed to have originated the movement. The college was located in Rhode Island because there only was there absolute religious liberty. It received contributions of money, soon after its establishment, from Virginia and South Carolina, as well as from New England and the Middle Colonies. We find the associations also early expressing interest in ministerial education. At the Philadelphia Association, in 1722, "it was proposed by the churches to make inquiry among themselves if they have any young persons hopeful for the ministry and inclinable for learning, and if they have to give notice of it to Mr. Abel Morgan, that he might recommend such to the academy, on Mr. Hollis his account." Mr. Hollis, besides endowing the professorship in Harvard, had apparently authorized Abel Morgan to send young men preparing for the ministry to the academy in Philadelphia, and look to him for the money. The association wishes to co-operate in this, and the rather quaint phrase of their minutes is worth remembering,—" Any young persons hopeful for the ministry and inclinable for learning." In 1756 the Charleston Association, South Carolina, recommended that the churches raise " a fund to furnish suitable candidates for the ministry with a competent share of learning." And we have seen that in the previous year, 1755, a society had been formed for that purpose by the church in Charleston, which aided Stillman, Botsford and others in pursuing studies for the ministry, Oliver Hart being their instructor in theology.

But while in so many ways showing that they valued, and striving to promote, the education of the ministry, our brethren were never disposed to confine the office to those who had passed through any specified course of study. They believed that God calls men to become preachers who have not had, cannot obtain, opportunities of regular preparatory education ; and that the only test which the churches ought to apply is the practical one suggested by the apostle's expression, "apt to teach." At the same time, they generally maintained that every minister ought to gain all the knowledge he can. But a hundred years ago there was among the Baptists in some quarters a disposition to underrate general education in ministers, arising principally from two causes. First, the Congregational and Episcopal establishments had both shown a strong tendency to treat a course of education as not only an indispensable, but the only requisite preparation for preaching, many of their ministers making no pretension to an inward call, and some of them not even to personal piety. The Congregationalist Separates and the Baptists, opposing themselves strongly to this, naturally tended toward the opposite extreme, making piety and the inward call everything, and caring little for the general and theological education which was associated in their minds with so many unspiritual, and not a few immoral, clergymen. Secondly, the country was new; the people themselves were in general quite uneducated, sympathizing most strongly with preachers who were but little superior to themselves in general culture; and many of those among them who were efficient in other intellectual callings were self-taught men. These last considerations, to some extent, still hold good in large portions of our country. The masses are still comparatively ignorant, and men who are even partially educated must take great care or they will fail to have the complete sympathy of this important class of their hearers. Alas! for the education of ministers of Jesus if it ceases to be true that the common people hear them gladly. And in a country where so many of the ablest and most successful statesmen, lawyers, physicians, teachers, journalists have had no regular education, there is a great want of propriety in requiring that no one shall be a preacher who has not gone through a certain fixed course of study. But it *is* proper to insist that every minister, as well as every other who aspires to instruct his fellow-men, must in youth and in age be a learner, a diligent student.

One thing our brethren have always expected and required,—that the minister, whatever else he knows or does not know, shall study the Bible. To explain and impress the teachings of the Bible is his great business. It is very desirable for the lawyer to know classics and history, but necessary that he know law. It is highly useful for the physician to know psychology, but indispensable to know medicine. The teacher of mathematics is much profited by classical training; but he can do nothing unless he is acquainted with mathematics. And so the minister of the gospel will find all knowledge useful, and general training of mind eminently desirable; but the Bible he must know. And how much it means to know the Bible!

Let us add that a large proportion of these ministers were highly educated in another sense: they had the spirit, habits and manners of *gentlemen*. If it is not important for a preacher and pastor to be a gentleman, for whom is it important? It is, in this respect, a great privilege to have been reared in refined homes. But as Henry Clay and others of our American statesmen, so have many of our ministers shown that a man may come up from very inferior advantages, and by force of native delicacy and generosity of feeling, and by diligent use of the best social opportunities, may become a noble gentleman.

5. Finally, notice the character of their preaching. It was eminently *Biblical*. Whether learned in other things or not, they all, as we have said, tried to know the Bible. Those ignorant of Hebrew and Greek were yet most diligent, loving and life-long students of the English Bible. And some who had read few other books were yet "mighty in the Scriptures," often teach-

ing opposers the truth of the old adage: "Beware of the man of one book." They were familiar with the text of Scripture, able to turn to any passage they wanted without a concordance, committing to memory long passages, and some of them whole books of the Bible. It is an abuse of our multiplied helps if we fail to gain like loving familiarity with the sacred text. There is point in the words of an Elizabethan poet:

> I would I were an excellent divine,
> That had the Bible at my fingers' ends;
> That men might hear out of this mouth of mine
> How God doth make his enemies his friends.

And the preachers of whom we speak used their ready knowledge of Scripture in this way, both publicly and privately, whether men would hear or whether they would forbear. "May it please your worship," said an irate lawyer in Virginia, "these men are great disturbers of the peace; they cannot meet a man on the road but what they ram a text of Scripture down his throat." Their preaching was also eminently *doctrinal*. The great Scripture doctrines of depravity, atonement and regeneration were almost unknown to many of their hearers, and disputed by many others. And so the preacher felt called continually to preach these and the related doctrines, proving and enforcing them by liberal quotations from the text of Scripture. Whenever men cease to preach these great doctrines of the Bible, drawing them directly from the fountain head, believing something definite, knowing what they believe and why they believe it, and how to prove it from the Inspired

Word, then the pulpit soon loses its power. Their preaching was, at the same time, eminently *experimental*. It was very common for the preacher to tell the exercises of his mind at the time of his conversion. When modestly and wisely done, as it has been done by Bunyan, Augustine, Paul, this can never fail to be full of interest and impressiveness. The Washingtonian temperance speakers carried too far their narratives of a drunkard's experience, and so may our old preachers have sometimes gone too far with their experience-telling; but the thing is natural and lawful, and is mighty, if fitly managed.

As to their *manner* of preaching, but little need be said. They had all the methods of preparation and delivery which we have, and differed about them as we do. Some of them, particularly of those who traveled widely and preached much in the open air—and chiefly, it would appear, among the Separates—acquired certain offensive mannerisms of delivery, the most striking of which was a peculiarity of tone, commonly called the "holy whine," which may still be heard in some very ignorant preachers in certain parts of the country. This unpleasing and, to some persons, very ridiculous practice had a natural origin. When men spoke to crowds in the open air, on a high key, with great excitement for a long time, the over-strained voice would relieve itself by rising and falling, as a person tired of standing will frequently change position. This soon became a habit with such men, and then would be imitated by others, being regarded as the appropriate expression of excited feeling. The same causes produce the same sing-song tone in the loud cries of street-vendors in our cities. But the whine of the preacher, associated for many ignorant hearers with seasons of impassioned appeal from the pulpit, and of deep feeling on their own part, has become a musical accompaniment which gratifies and impresses them, and, like a tune we remember from childhood, revives "the memory of joys that are past, pleasant and mournful." Why should we wonder at all this? Extremes meet. What is the *intoning*, which modern ritualists in this country so much admire, but just another species of holy whine, originating long centuries ago in very similar natural causes to those just stated, and impressive to some people now by reason of its association with what is old and venerable in devotion? If any one doubts that it is the same thing, let him hear the intoning in the Armenian Convent Church at Jerusalem.

It suffices to add that the preachers of that day depended much on the aid of the Holy Spirit to give them liberty in speaking, and the hearts of their hearers. Some of them carried this to an enthusiastic extreme. But every truth is perverted by somebody. And it is a great fundamental truth, to which we must cling, that God will help us in preaching and himself "giveth the increase."

The American Baptist ministers of one hundred years ago labored not in vain. The denomination was growing rapidly in the years before the Revolution, and it has continued to grow. In 1774 the total membership of Baptist churches throughout the colonies is estimated to have been not more than (30,000) thirty thousand, and many think this estimate too high. Thus the membership was less than one per cent. of the population. In 1884 we had in the United States of regular Baptists, exclusive of cognate outlying bodies, at least (2,500,000) two million five hundred thousand members, which is nearly five per cent. of the population. More than one-half of our present population is of German, Irish, French, Italian or Spanish descent, and thus originally altogether averse to any such opinions as ours; there has been no Baptist immigration except from England and Wales, and to a small extent from Scotland; yet in the face of all this we have an increase in our *membership* from one per cent. to five per cent. of the population, and the persons more attached to the Baptists than any other persuasion must be from one-fifth to one-fourth of the entire population. This shows that the work of our fathers' hands has been blessed.

And yet how many of these church members are comparatively useless. And throughout the country what growing masses of noisy infidelity—what a spread of irreligion and corrupted Christianity, of immorality and vice, of political corruption and social pollution! Not only the example of the past age, but the pressing needs of our own age, call us to diligent, self-denying, devoted labor. And are we ambitious? Do we ask whether a hundred years to come men will be searching our history, repeating our names, rejoicing in our work? It matters little, for "they that are wise shall shine as the brightness of the firmament, and they that turn many to righteousness as the stars for ever and ever." Nay, it matters not at all, if only we can hear at last that thrilling word, "Well done, good and faithful servant, enter thou into the joy of thy Lord."

XV.

COLLEGE EDUCATION FOR MEN OF BUSINESS.

THOSE sprightly, growing boys of yours, what are you going to do about their education? Let us think a little upon that question. Even if your mind is partly made up, there is no harm in listening to the notions of a man who has spent his life as an educator; of course you will decide for yourself all the same.

You have been looking about for now a good many years, and have pretty much concluded that it *is* desirable for those who are to be *professional* men to go to college. But your son will not enter a profession; he is going to spend his life in business. I ask,

HOW DO YOU KNOW?

You may have a very definite purpose on the subject, and so may he; but how can you be sure? Inquire concerning the men who have succeeded well in the several professions, and it will be very curious to see how small a proportion of them, at the age of sixteen or eighteen, had any notion of spending their lives in the professions they finally adopted. Parents and teachers ofter err egregiously in their judgment as to what a youth was born for. It is said, that when Mr. Moody first spoke in a prayer-meeting, his pastor advised him not to attempt that again, as he had evidently no talent for public speaking; and now, let the crowds that hear his preaching tell, and the thousands of converts. And the lad himself will often err likewise. At one period of my own boyhood I read Cooper's novels, of which my father was very fond, until I became enamored of Indian life, and fully resolved that so soon as I became "a man," I would go to the Missouri Territory (as they used to call it), among the Blackfoot Indians, get to be a great hunter and fighter, marry a squaw, the daughter of an old chief, and succeed him as chief of the tribe, and live and die in paint and feathers. Would any sensible father and mother have said, The boy has got his head on that; it shows the native bent of his genius, and so there is no use in sending him to boarding-school? How do you know, then, and how does your son know, though he may have no such silly fancies as the boy just mentioned, what is his destined calling for life? And especially is this true as to the ministry of the gospel. If a man must be divinely called to this work, that will often happen much later in life than the proper time for entering college.

I am very glad you hold that the professional men of the future ought, in general, to be thoroughly educated. Even in the past, the most eminent men have much more frequently had this advantage than most persons imagine. Of the leading Baptist ministers in America a hundred years ago, quite a number had been to college, and nearly all the rest were laborious students. Or take our statesmen. America has been the Paradise of what we call self-made men. In every calling such men came to the front, and in politics there was long a decided advantage in being a self-made man. The fraction of Americans who have been to college is extremely small; how large, in comparison, is the fraction of leading statesmen who were college bred, even in this "new country," with a prejudice in favor of the other class. Look at Congress, or the Legislature of this State, at any time during the last hundred years, or at the present day, and the comparison of these two fractions will be very suggestive. And then we must stop calling ours a new country. Things are rapidly changing. In medicine and law it will, in less than fifty years, be required by public opinion here, as it is now in Europe, that the acceptable practitioner shall have a good general education and a *thorough* training in his profession. The editorial profession, which is looming up into such importance, greatly needs thorough education, in order to breadth of view and sympathy with all truth, in order to correct handling of the ten thousand subjects which journalists have to treat, and in order that they may cease butchering the English language and shocking literary taste in the frightful fashion to which, with few exceptions, they are now accustomed. And *teachers*, what profession is more important than this? What greater need is there among us—except the need of Christian morality—than of really well-qualified teachers? Everybody believes in schools for children. But education has to work from above downwards. Where shall we get educated teachers, unless people more generally send their sons to our higher schools? As to our ministers, I think the Baptists have been quite right in encouraging some uneducated men to preach. It was a necessity, else the masses would never have been reached; for well-educated men were too few, and the illiterate could often command a fuller sympathy. A like necessity will still exist, but it will be constantly diminishing. An increasingly large proportion of our ministers must be thoroughly educated men, or Baptists will not keep pace with the times.

But, coming back to your son,

SUPPOSE HE DOES

spend his life as a man of business, an agriculturist, merchant, manufacturer or the like. I earnestly urge that in such a business life, higher education, or what we commonly call college education, will be of great advantage to him. So many doubt this, deny, even ridicule the idea, that I beg your special attention. Good and generous men, all over the land, are even giving their money to endow colleges to educate other people's sons, and then entirely failing to send their own sons to them. Now, I think, there is no little popular error about this something we call education, partly due to the wrong methods pursued and wrong ideas put forth by some professed educators. Pray consider, then,

WHAT DO WE MEAN BY EDUCATION?

This term is generally used among us in quite too narrow a sense. Thus, we hear a great deal about "educated men" and "self-educated men." But, in one sense, *every* man is self-educated who is ever really educated at all. It is only in the voluntary exertion of his mental powers that he gains development and discipline of these powers. John Randolph said: "Put a blockhead through college, and the more books you pile on his head the bigger *blockhead* he will be." A man has to educate himself, no matter how numerous and advantageous his helps. And then, in another sense, *no* man is self-educated. Even those who never have a teacher, if they really become educated men, have been educated by books (teachers who, being dead, yet speak), by the men with whom they converse, by the events which lead them to think, which draw out their powers into active exercise, by the ideas which are abroad in the atmosphere of their time. There is, then, no such broad difference between the educated and the self-educated as many suppose.

Now, when can we say that one is an educated man? My answer would make something like the following points: 1. An educated man is one whose mind is *widened out*, so that he can take broad views, instead of being narrow-minded; so that he can see the different sides of a question, or at least can know that all questions have different sides. 2. An educated man is one who has the power of patient *thinking;* who can fasten his mind on a subject, and hold it there while he pleases; who can keep looking at a subject till he sees into it and sees through it. If anybody imagines it easy to think, in this steady way, he has not tried it much. 3. Again, an educated man is one who has sound *judgment,* who knows how to *reason* to right conclusions, and so to *argue* as to convince others that he is right. 4. And finally—not to speak now of imagination and taste, important as they are—an educated man is one who can *express* his thoughts clearly and forcibly. Now, if this be a roughly correct description of an educated man, there are many among us who deserve that name, though they never went to college, and some of them went little to school. Look at our really successful business men. You will find that in most cases their minds are widened, so that they can take broad views. How grandly comprehensive are often the views of a great planter, merchant, manufacturer or railroad man! Also, that they can keep thinking of a subject till they see into it; that they can judge soundly, and reason and argue, reaching just conclusions themselves, and convincing others that they are right; and that they have command of clear and forcible expression. These, then, are really educated men.

But notice. They gain this education, in the school of life, very slowly in most cases, and usually cannot be called educated in this sense, until they have reached or passed middle age. Now is it possible to select certain branches of knowledge, and combine them into such an apparatus of mental training, that, by putting our young men through this, we can, to a great extent, *anticipate* the discipline which would be slowly gained in the school of life, can give to the young man of twenty-one or twenty-five much of that accuracy of thought, soundness of judgment and command of expression, which otherwise he would not have till he reaches fifty or more? Of course this cannot be *wholly* done, for some kinds of mental training can be gained only by experience and by slow degrees; but can it be done to a considerable extent? Wide and varied experiment has shown that it can be. And precisely this is the main object of all wise educational processes. The *knowledge* gained may or may not be directly useful in subsequent life: the main thing is to *educate*, to give the young man, in a few years, much of that development and strengthening and discipline of his principal faculties, that *use of himself*, which, otherwise, he would have only when almost an old man. And remember that if, in certain respects, we cannot anticipate the lessons of the school of life, in other respects we can prepare the young man to learn those lessons to better purpose than would otherwise, for *him*, have been possible.

See, then, how unwise people are when they keep asking: "What good will Latin and Astronomy and Metaphysics do a business man?" and keep saying that our youth must study only those branches of knowledge that will be "useful." What can be so useful to a young man as to improve his *sense*, to give him greater power of thinking closely and soundly, and of making other people think as he thinks, and do what he wants them to do? You wish your son to be a practical man; but you do not want him to spend his life as simply a day-laborer. Well, if he is to rise above this, is to acquire property and control the labor of others for his advantage, it must be done by *sense*. Not even industry and saving ways will suffice, unless he can see into things, judge wisely about complicated questions and talk sensibly to those with whom he deals. No doubt these powers depend partly on natural endowment; but, then, they can be greatly improved by education, and I insist that to improve them is the main object of all wise educational processes. In fact, the *method* of education is even more important than the material. A superior teacher could, to a great extent, educate a superior pupil with almost any branch of knowledge. But certain subjects, suitably combined, are found to have much greater educating power than others, and on this principle we select and recommend. If some of them are also of practical utility, that is, of course, very desirable. But, in very important respects, the mind may be better enlarged, invigorated, disciplined by subjects of study which have little to do with practical life; and I repeat that the effect on the mind itself is the principal matter.

RESULTS OF SUCCESS IN BUSINESS.

Besides, you do not simply wish your son to prosper in business, to accumulate property. Think of the *good he is to get* from his business success. He will wish to have a home, a bright and sweet home. Wealth alone cannot make this. I am not speaking now of the one thing that is needful, but consider how much *culture* contributes to the happiness and highest well-being of a growing family. Almost every man who has financial prosperity aspires to this. Some succeed, notwithstanding the lack of early advantages, but very few under such circumstances attain true and high culture. Many a worthy gentleman of middle age, fondly watching his growing children, and longing to inspire them with a relish for the delights of history, poetry, and popular science, to see them bathe their young minds in the sweet waters of literature, resolves winter after winter that he will read upon certain subjects—buys a number of books, begins, and next summer remembers that he has done almost nothing, and mourns, again and again, that he did not acquire reading habits, and a basis of literary knowledge, in his youth. And sooth to say, many of our girls are now receiving a fairly good education, and women are so quick in picking up and turning to account a knowledge of general literature, that our young men must get a better education than has been common, or they will in many cases find themselves unpleasantly inferior to their wives.

Still further, as to your son, think of the *good he is to do* in life. Success in business will give him influence in some respects, but how much more influential he will be, and how much more useful as a member of society, if he had in youth a good education. You have known here and there a man prosperous, intelligent and of high character, who in a country neighborhood or a village was worth as much as a school—he seemed to lift up the whole community. In our current politics one of the great wants is that of intelligent leading citizens. There is much humbug now-a-days about reading and writing. Some of our new-light philosophers seem to think that if we can only teach everybody to read and write, then the masses will always vote wisely and do right. But what do they read? The fact is, the masses need, and always have, leaders, to tell them what to do; and the only question is whether they shall be led by low demagogues, or persons not much wiser than themselves, or on the other hand by men worthy to lead, qualified to lead wisely. So, too, in our churches, the most crying need at present is for an educated *membership*. We have heard a great deal about educating our ministers, but educated private members, of both sexes, are just as necessary. These, where they do exist, give interest to Sunday-schools and prayer-meetings, diffuse correct ideas of Christian benevolence, and give sympathetic appreciation and moral support to an intelligent and active pastor. These can meet in conversation the subtle infidelity which is spreading its poison through all our society, which the pastor often declines to preach against lest he merely advertise instead of curing, and which is seldom mentioned to him in private because its advocates in general do not really wish to have their errors corrected. O how much we need a larger number of thoroughly educated and truly devoted men and women in all the churches!

DIFFICULTIES IN THE WAY OF HIGHER EDUCATION.

You say you are willing to send the boys to *school*, and want the teacher to do the best he can for them; but, when they are pretty nearly grown, you find they generally want to go into business, and you think they are about right—go to school while they are boys, and get to work as soon as they are men. But consider. We have agreed, have we not, that the mental conditions most important for business success are breadth of view, power of patient thinking, sound judgment. And I have insisted that the great object of wise schemes of education is to train the mind in these respects. Now, these powers cannot be trained till a person is nearly grown, for the excellent reason that not until then have they any considerable natural development. In a little child, the leading faculty is imagination, and the chief means of teaching it is story-telling. Everything must be put into that form, or, at least, must be sweetened with a story. If we do not tell the children stories, they will make some for themselves and tell them to each other. At the age of ten or twelve, the leading faculty is memory. That is the time to store the mind with knowledge of facts, explaining where it is not too difficult, but aiming chiefly to lodge the facts themselves permanently in the memory. But judgment, in any high and broad sense,—analysis, generalization, abstract thinking, reasoning,—these are, as a rule, not much developed until the age of eighteen or twenty. Of course, then, it is not until that age, as a rule, that we can begin to give those high mental powers any effective training. A great many efforts have been made of late years to have boys anticipate the studies proper only to comparative maturity. Children of a dozen years are found toiling over Evidences of Christianity, Rhetoric, English Syntax—subjects which they cannot possibly understand. All this is a grievous mistake, though it is a well-meant effort to supply a felt want. These things ought to be learned, and others of the same sort; but they can be learned, not at the beginning, but only towards the end of "the teens." Now see what happens. Our boys and girls go to school, and perhaps learn well, during the period when memory predominates, get a useful knowledge of facts (though this might be much better managed than it commonly is), but just when they reach the age at which we could begin to give them education in the highest, broadest sense—education that would really prepare them for the duties of life—they break away; the boys plunge head foremost into business, and the girls—well, they quit school! Here is an evil most lamentable and wide-spread. Who trains horses that way, or builds houses, or railways, or raises crops—laboring a long time with the mere preparations, and stopping short just at the time when the consummation of the undertaking comes within reach? What we call "higher education" is really the most *practical* part of the whole process; and yet our restless youths and our thoughtless parents neglect it, just because, forsooth, they are so anxious to be practical.

But, you ask, do we expect all the young men of the country to go to school until they are twenty-five years old? No, and we do not expect all the young men of the country to be highly successful in business, or highly influential and useful, as citizens or as Christians. Higher education is, of course, not possible for all. Besides, if college studies now keep many till the age of twenty-five, this is usually because our preparatory schools and our general methods of training children have been, for the most part, so poor and unsatisfactory. When better ideas are diffused throughout society, when a larger number of good teachers are trained, and more good schools are established, then most of our competent young men will be able to complete a fair course of higher education by the time they are twenty-one or twenty-two.

You remind me of another difficulty, that there is

need of some early training for business itself. Certainly, one who is to be a farmer ought to work on a farm in his early teens, watching every detail with a boy's sharp observation, and learning how to do all kinds of work himself; and he who is to be a merchant ought, while still a boy, to hop counters and tie bundles, to keep accounts, and observe the quality of goods and the tastes of customers. But this can be managed by putting such boys to work on Saturdays and in the greater part of vacation; and perhaps, also, it might be well, somewhere between thirteen and seventeen, to keep them at home a year, and make them buckle down to steady labor. I could tell you of men eminently successful in their callings, who were trained in just this way, with advantage to their health, and certainly no damage to their mental improvement.

And yet another difficulty occurs to you. It doesn't look reasonable that young fellows so different in turn of mind, and in their proposed callings, as the students of a college are, should all be put through exactly the same course of study. But remember, that the object is to develop and discipline faculties which all intelligent youths possess to some considerable extent, and which have to be exercised *in all callings alike*. Special training for particular pursuits may be distinct, going on partly at the same time with, and partly subsequent to, this general training, which will contribute to success in any kind of work. Besides, most of our colleges are beginning to provide for a change of the course, by making certain studies elective, or even by making the whole course elective, so that the studies of each youth may be more or less adapted to his peculiarities of mind, preparation, or destined pursuit.

OBJECTIONS TO COLLEGE LIFE.

But there is no use in talking, you say, about your son's going to college. It is too expensive—you can't afford it. Colleges are just intended for rich men's sons, or those that get their money easy in some way; you made your money by hard work, and can't afford to spend it so fast.

Why, the very object of college endowments is to *cheapen* education, for the sake of those who are not rich. If your son were to get instruction from a single one of these select professors, with his talents and high scholarship, it would cost him twice as much a year as his entire college fees. Rich men could employ several such instructors if they chose, but you and I could not. And if our sons can have the privilege of being taught by these professors, it is for the reason that a large part of their support is drawn from endowment; and usually it is a support most meagre and unworthy, when we consider their choice abilities and severe labors. In fact, college education is one of the cheapest things in the country; and we who are comparatively poor get a great bargain in it, a first-rate article for one-third the cost.

Ah! but you didn't so much mean the tuition; it is the other expenses. Yes, and you begin with counting all that is spent for clothing, and forget that the fellow would spend money for clothes if he stayed at home. If it be said that at home he would only need a

Sunday suit, and could wear plain and cheap clothes all the week, I answer, so he can at college. If a student's general appearance and personal habits are good, if his hair and his hands, his boots and his linen, are always scrupulously clean, and the rest of his clothing, however cheap and even coarse, is well brushed and free from stains and spots, then, with good manners, he will be accounted a thoroughly genteel young man, by all those whose opinion is worth regarding, young ladies included. Forty years ago, two young men entered the University of Virginia, paying their way with money saved from teaching, and during the first winter wearing plain jeans coats all the week, among those aristocratic and dressy youngsters from the Cotton States. Both found hearty welcome in the professors' families, and formed choice friendships among the students, besides gaining unsurpassed academic honors; and one of them is now a distinguished educator in Virginia. And to-day there are students in great number at our colleges who spend scarcely a cent more on their clothing than they would do in a country home, and yet make a good appearance, and are respected and well received in society.

As to the board, it is already very cheap at many colleges, and can be made cheaper still, if students choose to abstain from mere luxuries, and set their heads on economizing. A rapid and salutary change is going on in many parts of the country. It used to be the case that college fashions were mainly set by rich fellows, who went to college simply as a thing proper for a gentleman's son to do, and consequently others were ashamed to show their poverty by living plainly. I hope to see the day when, as in the German cities, a student can live on as few cents a day as he pleases, and it will be nobody's business; when not only those of moderate means, like your son, but the very poor, can work their way, by hard struggles and various helps and God's favor, through a college course. So it was centuries ago in Europe; so it is now in Scotland, in Germany, and to some extent in New England. The present head of one of our most important Baptist institutions stated in my presence that at one period of his student life he lived on bread and molasses for a considerable time. Kingman Nott, when at the academy, lived on bread and milk, and when prices rose, then on bread and water, and bought them with money made by sawing wood. Some English noblemen are remembered in history only by the fact that, when students at Oxford, they got their boots blacked by a charity student, named George Whitefield. Ho, for the poor young men! Look them out; call them forth where they have brains, and are cherishing vague, wild longings after an education which seems far on the other side of an impassable gulf; help them if you can, show them how to help themselves, and stir in them by encouragement that high resolution, which in the young and gifted laughs at impossibilities, and conquers the world.

But after all, your son is not utterly poor; and when you come to think of it, college education may be so managed as not to be very expensive. If, through his own good sense and your good influence, he is disposed to economy, he will assuredly find plenty of students at the present day to keep him company, and students who stand high both in the lecture-room and in society. If once you made up your mind that it was really and exceedingly desirable for him to go to college, you know very well that you could manage to provide the means. And how else, O thoughtful and loving father, can you use the same amount of money so much for his advantage? Pray, think that over. A college education, or a thousand dollars, in land or goods or cash—which would be most profitable to him as he enters upon active life?

There is another class of objections which some make. I know not whether you agree with them.

They say that at college the young man is very apt to form vicious habits and evil companionships. Now I have spent most of my active life in connection with, or in the immediate vicinity of colleges, and I beg to express the full conviction that a young man is safer, as to companionships and temptations to vice, in any good college than in the average home. Of course, there are a few exceptional homes; I speak of the average, of the general rule. Some young men will get into bad courses wherever they may be. All the good influences at college cannot prevent it—nor, if they stay at home, can father and mother and sister and pastor and sweetheart, all combined, keep them out of bad company and vicious practices. But in general, I repeat it earnestly, the morals of the average student are safer at a well-conducted college than at home. Some think this might be so if the college were at a retired village, but not when it is in a city; they tremble to think of the temptations of a city. But really there are no colleges now at retired villages. The railways that bring the students can bring all the apparatus of vice, and keep the students in easy and speedy communication with the cities themselves. Well may we tremble at the temptations to which our boys are now everywhere exposed; but when they are nearly grown, repression and seclusion are no longer possible; we must try to train them to sound principles and right habits from childhood, foster in them vivid recollections of a home where they are loved and prayed for, and let them fight their battle. Remember, too, that if they may meet evil companions at college, they will assuredly meet many among the noblest young men of the land, who will set them an example of true manhood and gentlemanly bearing, and draw them, if they be worthy and willing, into the bonds of high and inspiring friendship.

Others are afraid the young fellow will come home with "city airs." Perhaps he may, if he was born a simpleton, in which case I do not urge sending him to college. But if he has good sense, he will only get something of refinement, of graceful bearing and social ease, and power of agreeably entertaining others—will become more of a gentleman in his manners and tone; and will not that be an advantage to him?

A grave objection with many excellent people, and one having the appearance of good ground, is that if you give young men a college education, they will "get above business;" they will want to engage in one of the professions. Now, something of this sort has frequently happened; but there are several things to be considered about it. Sometimes the young man is right in turning away from what he and his friends had contemplated; for he has become intelligently conscious of being better suited to some other pursuit. In other cases, it is the effect of those wrong notions of which we have been speaking, and which I hope you will use your influence to correct; he thinks, as so many do, that college education is of no use to a business man, and perhaps foolishly imagines business pursuits to be less honorable and less worthy of his intelligence and cultivation than some profession. But the principal reason for such occurrences is that we have hitherto had a very inadequate supply of well-educated teachers and other professional men; the young man sees this, and his sense of the value of education makes him seek more directly to propagate it. When high cultivation becomes more common, and correct ideas more generally diffused, this evil will be, for the most part, corrected.

"But suppose my son *doesn't want* to go to college, what then?" If he needs it, if you see that he would be greatly profited by it, what is your duty? Argue with him, I should say, exhort him, plead with him, and if he is still unwilling, *make* him go. What, you cannot control a boy of sixteen or eighteen! Then you haven't trained him properly, and it is all the more important that you should get some professors to help you train him, before it is too late. Yes, *make* him go. And the time shall be when he will come to you, in your old age, or perhaps come and stand by your grave, and tell his gratitude that you did not leave him to the follies of his youth; that by all the power of parental love and parental authority you constrained him to that which has been such a blessing to him through life. Oh! the dear memories that come up in saying this of a father who did not need to constrain, but who broke up a pleasant home, and spent his last years in most uncongenial employment and amid pecuniary losses, solely that his son might receive the education for which he had not dared to hope. How that son thanks him more and more every year—how he thanks God for such a wise and noble father.

XVI.

EDUCATION IN ATHENS.*

THERE is nothing more natural or appropriate, at these annual meetings, than that our thoughts should mainly dwell upon topics connected with education. Not only must the very atmosphere we breathe, all the associations of the place and the occasion, recall the lively interest which years ago we felt in this subject, but our experience amid the activities of life must be continually impressing us more deeply with the importance of obtaining the most thorough mental culture and the most complete mental furniture. And if gratefully recognizing the benefits received from our own early training, we cannot but desire that others may enjoy yet more abundant privileges. We gather again, those who have wandered farthest and those who have remained nearest, around the domestic hearth; we look with pride upon these younger brothers who fill now the places that once were ours, and far from feeling any jealousy of their perhaps superior attainments, far from cherishing any aristocratic notion of rights of primogeniture in education, we can heartily wish that, as is wont to happen in this democratic and growing country, our cherishing mother may be able to provide

* Address before the Society of Alumni of the University of Virginia, 1856.

the best advantages for her younger sons. Whatever, then, is related to education in general, whatever promises to cast the least ray of light upon the higher education among ourselves, as it is and as it ought to be, can hardly fail, I have thought, to be for us a welcome theme.

Now the educational methods and machinery of cultivated modern nations have received large attention, since they furnish illustrative examples which are most nearly parallel and models which are most easily imitated. But it has appeared to me that something at least might be learned from considering the methods employed and the material possessed among the foremost nations of antiquity. A very little reflection sufficed to show that one particular people of the ancient world afford not only what is most interesting, but almost all that can be instructive; and for the sake of definiteness, it seemed best to confine the view to a single leading city and a comparatively limited period. I propose to speak, therefore, of the higher education in Athens during the period of its greatest prosperity, say the century from about 450 to about 350 B.C. It is a very brief, and I know a very imperfect account, which alone I can expect to give; but I have hoped it would possess some interest, and might perhaps suggest some profitable reflection.

A problem presents itself here for our solution. The Greeks, and especially the Athenians of this age, have left monuments of mental power which the world can never cease to admire. Though ignorance may sometimes sneer, and self-complacent modernism may sometimes assail, yet one need not be a mere praiser of the past to assert that the productions of the Athenian mind have hardly ever been surpassed, and not very often been equalled, by the noblest kindred works of modern times. Whence came this wonderful power? What was there, in the influences to which they were subjected, corresponding to these great results? Now if a distinction be made between what we call education in the technical sense and those more general influences which accomplish so much in developing the mind and directing as well as stimulating its activity, then it is to be observed that these last were perhaps more potent among the Athenians than any other nation of the world. If there be an exception, it is in our own people; and, indeed, the most superficial observer must always be struck by the numerous points of resemblance, in this respect, between the Athenians and ourselves. It is very difficult, in either case, fully to estimate the powerful effect of the influences in question. The peculiar genius of the race—its enthusiasm, its restless activity, its self-reliance—must form an important element. The working of their democratic institutions,—the fact that every citizen, besides frequently attending the popular assembly and having a voice in the direction of national affairs, so as to feel the dignity and responsibility of his position, was called to take part very largely in the administration of justice, sitting frequently in the immense juries of from five to fifteen hundred, and required, whenever a cause of his own was on trial, to appear not simply by counsel, but in his own person, and plead for himself,—all this would be an element of almost incalculable importance. And the circumstances of the age were not only favorable, but stimulating. Commerce and tribute, during the years which mainly gave character to this period, filled Athens with wealth, so that men possessed the leisure and the means necessary to intellectual pursuits. The yet fresh memories of that great struggle, in which their fathers had shown such bravery in battle and such heroical fortitude in suffering, in order to maintain their liberties against the terrible power of the Persian; the frequent successes and then maddening losses, and the final and almost hopeless ruin which made up the history of the Peloponnesian war; the anxiety and strife connected with the Theban and Macedonian supremacy,—these made it throughout an age of excitement. But after making the largest allowance for the unusual power of these general influences, one cannot resist the conviction, that there must have been something in their education, strictly so called, corresponding to the wonderful excellence of their intellectual achievements. We must look into the facts, so far as they have come down to us, in order to ascertain whether this conviction is just.

If one should begin by examining the scattered extant allusions to elementary education in Athens, he must be struck by the extraordinary attention which was bestowed upon the subject, and the very general acquaintance, among the citizens, with the elements of knowledge. Great philosophers constantly interested themselves in devising plans for the better conduct of elementary instruction. Schools for the young were always established by private enterprise, but there were special laws having reference to them, even from the time of Solon, and special supervisors for their control, appointed by the State. We read in Plutarch's Themistocles, that when the women and children of Athens fled to Trœzene at the time of the Persian invasion, a part of the hospitality with which they were entertained was, that the Trœzenians paid persons to teach the children. If the story can be relied on, it certainly affords a very remarkable proof of the interest felt, by the exiles and their hosts, in the constant instruction of the young. And, this being the case, one is not surprised to find that at the period of which we speak, a very large proportion of the citizens, in the proper sense of that term, appear to have been able to read and write. To notice no other evidence, the fact is proven by the introduction, as early as 510 B.C., of the remarkable institution known as the Ostracism. It would have been folly to resort to a secret ballot, in order temporarily to banish one or the other of two powerful political rivals and thus secure political tranquillity, if any large number of the citizens had been dependent upon others to prepare their ballots, and thus liable to be imposed upon by designing partisans.

With reference now to the higher education, there are two departments of inquiry, the supply of instructors, and the material of instruction.

Of instructors, we have reason to believe that there was a much larger number than the cursory reader of Greek history and literature might suppose. There were many included under the general name of philosophers. Among these, every one will think of Socrates and Plato, as belonging to this age. Though the former never constituted regular classes, yet we know that young men were accustomed to attach themselves to him, and to follow his daily wanderings in the agora and the gymnasium, conversing with him themselves, and listening to his conversations with others; so that besides the general influence he exerted, in awakening and stimulating the minds of almost the entire community, there was always a circle of those who might be considered, in a strict sense, his pupils in philosophy. Plato held conversations and lectures in the Academy, to which all could listen who chose. We read of him as on one occasion delivering a lecture in the Peiræeus on the Good; and one is more sorry than surprised to find that his audience gradually wasted away—the philosopher had chosen a subject too abstract for the popular taste. In addition to these public labors, he had a band of disciples who regularly assembled in his own garden at Colonus, there to partake of a frugal meal, and discourse together on subjects of philosophy. There are other famous philosophers of this age, who resided at Athens, and taught their peculiar opinions. Anaxagoras is stated to have been the instructor of Euripides and Pericles, and many others of the most eminent men of the time. Zeno of Elea is recorded to have spent some years in Athens, unfolding the doctrines of his philosophy to such men as Pericles and Callias, from the latter of whom he received for his instructions a large sum of money, and also to the youthful Socrates. The accomplished and excellent Democritus would seem to have sojourned there a while, and even casual intercourse for a limited period with a man of his extraordinary attainments and beautiful character, must have been a means of marked improvement to the rising young men of the day. And may we not take it for granted that there were many others, citizens and strangers, addicted to philosophical studies, and accustomed to give at least informal instruction to the young, whose names have not come down to us? They who have lived in history were the men of originality, the men of splendid powers, the men who introduced new doctrines in philosophy, or wrote valuable treatises on opinions already current; must there not have been a much more numerous class, just one degree inferior, who were well acquainted with all the teachings of the different schools, perhaps warmly attached to the doctrines of the Ionian school of Pythagoras or the Eleatics, and anxious to win over every young man of promise to their own opinions? These would often give far more information as to the true nature and extent of the various systems than the more original thinkers, who would commonly allude to the tenets of their predecessors, as Socrates does to those of Anaxagoras, only for purposes of refutation or ridicule. Thus we may see that the class called philosophers formed a numerous corps, so to speak, of able and active instructors.

Again, there were many persons who made teaching their occupation. A man who had gained some reputation, perhaps, as master of an elementary school, or had become specially fond of a particular subject, would undertake to give instruction to young men, separately or in classes. We find incidental allusions to some of these, as teachers of music (in the modern sense), of geometry, of oratory, &c. It is plain from the manner of allusion that they were numerous; but only one here and there is known to posterity, from his good fortune in having some pupil who became famous. As many an humble English clergyman has a name in history from his being the early tutor of a great statesman, as a plain New England schoolmaster will be remembered because of his connection with Webster, so there is now and then to be found, from among the old Athenian instructors, some name which had floated down the all-engulfing tide of time only because attached to the ever-buoyant, imperishable names of Pericles or Plato, of Aristotle or Demosthenes. It is a thought not strange to the bosom of any reflecting instructor, a thought tending to humility, and yet to honest pride in the true power of his calling, that centuries to come men may recognize as his chief claim to their gratitude, the influence he exerted upon another; yea, that highly and deservedly honored as he is now, posterity may remember him at all, only for having been the teacher of one who sits now, a modest lad, scarce noticed among his pupils.

Perhaps the most influential of these professional teachers, and certainly those who have the largest place in history, are the so-called Sophists. Among the numerous instances in which recent historical research has overturned received opinions, there are few more striking than the inquiry which Mr. Grote has made, in his unrivalled history, into the true character of these celebrated men; and it may not be amiss to state the conclusions he has reached and the outline of his argument. Doubtless, in attacking the popular notion, he has gone somewhat to the other extreme. We have more than one remarkable case of this among the distinguished historians of the present generation. Ever since the days of Niebuhr it has been the fashion to assail all established historical opinions; and wherever plausible grounds can be found for questioning, there at once to reject. Pleased at detecting the errors of ancient authorities, many a writer seems to forget that himself can err in the conclusions drawn from their statements; delighted to expose the prejudiced views of previous historians, he may yield, half unconsciously, to prejudices of his own. When weary of the misrepresentation and general injustice which so frequently attach to contemporaneous judgments, we often console ourselves by thinking of the future, and "the impartial voice of history." Yet it is but a poor approximation to impartiality that is ever actually found. No achromatic arrangement has been devised, whereby the historian, as he looks into the distant past, may be able to see things precisely in their true colors.

But to return. The term sophist, which is for us so opprobrious, and which from the days of Plato began to be confined to a particular set of men, originally denoted, in the general and honorable sense, a wise man, a man of talent. It was applied to poets and statesmen, and constantly used by Herodotus in speaking of the "seven sages." But where general ignorance prevails, there will always be a secret dislike to the few men of superior attainments and abilities, which gradually becomes more decided till it is avowed. Thus by degrees there came to be associated with the term sophist, a certain invidious feeling. Then other words, such as philosopher, were preferred for the good sense, and sophist became the stock term of reproach applied to any person, who possessed acknowledged power and was eminent as a teacher, but for whatever reason was personally unpopular. Thus Aristophanes, in the "Clouds," called Socrates a sophist; and in a subsequent age, "Timon, who bitterly satirized all the philosophers, designated them all, including Plato and Aristotle, by the general name of sophists." Now Socrates, and still more Plato, greatly disliking the eminent professional teachers of their time, have succeeded, by their justly powerful influence, in fastening upon them this odious name. The cause of their dislike was two-fold. The men in question taught for pay. Of course, those of them who became most celebrated would at times receive high pay; and in some cases they went from one city to another, where there was a prospect of obtaining large sums for their instructions. The result would be, that these ablest men commonly taught only the wealthy. All this was extremely repugnant to the notions of the two great philosophers. Socrates held that the relation between preceptor and pupil must be like that of intimate friends, or even of lovers; and that this could not possibly be the case, unless the instruction were gratuitous. With our modern ideas and experience, we should of course utterly dissent from this philosophic fancy. True, there is still a certain unwillingness to see men receive for the duties of this profession a compensation at all approaching to equality with that which the same ability and attainment and devotion might secure in some other calling; but we do not require them to teach altogether for love. We do not expect a profound and accomplished man, every day and all the day long, to leave his home to Xantippean care, and, poorly clad and with scanty fare, to wander among the people, giving instruction to all who might desire it. Not even to escape the horrors of a home like that of Socrates, nor to have the exquisite pleasure of proving other people less wise than themselves, could men be expected to lead such a life of privation and penury. In this respect, then, the prejudice against the teachers called Sophists, was certainly unjust.

The other ground of dislike was the peculiar character of their teachings, as contrasted with those of Plato and his great master. Socrates was a moral reformer, Plato a splendid social theorizer, proposing to re-model society altogether; while the persons they stigmatize undertook merely to prepare young men for performing their duties as citizens, for achieving success and reputation in Athens as it was. How much soever we may admire the doctrines of the philosophers, we cannot account the latter to have been in itself an unworthy task. There is no proof that the ethical precepts they inculcated were immoral; all the fragments which remain are of an opposite tendency. By the discipline they gave, and the knowledge they imparted, their pupils acquired a power which certainly could be used for maintaining the wrong as well as the right; but in cases where such perversion occurred, it was no more an argument against their teachers, than was the misconduct of Alcibiades a proof, as so strenuously urged, of some corrupting tendency in the teachings of Socrates. It may be that in training the young men for skill in discussion and effective oratory, they sometimes adopted the mistaken plan of teaching them to defend the weaker side and argue in favor of what was known to be untrue; but it cannot be shown that their instructions had any direct and purposed tendency to confound moral distinctions. The accusation that their pupils were trained to "make the worse appear the better reason," from which especially has come the modern use of the word sophist, was made also against Socrates, and as he himself remarks, was the charge constantly made against persons devoted to philosophy. And whatever reproach may attach to a readiness to defend either side of a cause, it must be borne by one of the most learned and honored professions of both ancient and modern times.

It may be concluded, then, that we have no evidence that there was anything corrupting in the influence of these much-abused men. And certainly the general effect of their instructions was very great. Thoroughly acquainted with all the learning of the age, devoting all their energies to the instruction, for the time being, of a few select individuals, Protagoras, Gorgias and their compeers were educators of no mean order. As to public speaking, some of them appear to have taught the analysis of a discourse into its parts, with various practical rules for the proper management of each; and this was a great advance upon all previous treatment, and a necessary preparation for the work of the great master of rhetoric. And they could add to their precept the example of an elaborate and ornate style of oratory which was not without its power, and for a time became very popular. Bad taste in this respect was perhaps the greatest fault of their teachings. Such a style was the very opposite of that beautiful simplicity and directness, that absence of all artificial ornament, for which Aristotle contended, which Demosthenes so strikingly exemplified, and which forms the chief charm of all the better Grecian literature.

Upon the whole, it must be evident that, at the period of which we speak, Athens abounded in men who occupied themselves as instructors in the higher education. Indeed, we know that from every part of Greece and the colonies, men of ability and ambition flocked to this great city, where their literary tastes would find sympathy and their labors reward, and the approbation of whose citizens would constitute the highest meed of fame. We learn, too, that men were accustomed to send their sons from distant cities to Athens to be educated; so that already the city began to be, what in the age of Cicero it had fully become, the University of the World.

The places at which instruction was commonly given were peculiar. When the hour of noon was fully past, and the business of the agora completed, almost all the men of leisure in the city might have been seen taking their way without the walls, to one or another of the three great Gymnasia. Some of these went to the bath, others to participate in, or witness, the gymnastic exercises, while many others tarried in the peristyle. This outer court of the Gymnasium consisted of a spacious lawn surrounded by buildings. On three of its sides were arcades with large halls, many of them open to the sky, and having stone benches, running along the walls, or arranged in a semi-circular form. In these numerous public halls, men would seat themselves for conversation, and here might be found many a philosopher or professor, with a band of pupils around him, and perhaps a crowd of listeners near, engaged in earnest dialogue or lecture. When weary of formal lecture-room instruction they would wander forth among the shade-trees of the lawn, conversing still upon the subject which had occupied them before. Socrates, if we may judge from his general course, probably frequented all the gymnasia in turn; though there appears to have been some one place where he was most commonly to be found, and which Aristophanes humorously called Socrates' thinking-shop. Two of the great gymnasia have become famous as the chosen resort of Plato and of Aristotle; and every little palæstra seems to have been employed for the same purpose, and often appropriated by some particular instructor. Besides, teachers of every class frequently gathered their pupils and friends at their own houses, or at the residence of some person of literary tastes, and there spent the hours in familiar conversation and at times in regular instruction.

But what formed the subject of these conversations and lectures? What educational material did the Greeks of this age possess? What progress had they already made in the several departments of knowledge? To this inquiry we turn. Instead of pausing to explain the peculiar phraseology which they employed, it will be more convenient to use the modern sub-divisions and terms.

With the most remarkable properties of Numbers, and the processes which admit of being performed upon them, the Greeks of this period had made considerable acquaintance. The fanciful theory of Pythagoras and his followers, that all things have their origin in numerical relations, that every physical existence and every mental attribute is due to some combination of numbers, would naturally lead them to investigate in that direction with the greatest diligence. Besides those several operations which lie at the foundation of arithmetic, they seem to have possessed methods of extracting the square and cube root, and to have been familiar with the theory of arithmetical and geometrical proportions and progressions. The elements of arithmetic were carefully taught in the schools for boys; and its higher questions appear to have awakened interest and received large attention among the most cultivated men.

Of Geometry they knew much more. Every one is aware that our modern treatises on synthetic geometry contain, to say the least, no very great improvements upon the work of an old Greek. It is true that Euclid wrote considerably later than the period we are contemplating (for it is now settled that he was a different person from Euclides of Megara, the pupil of Socrates), but we might be sure, from the very nature of the case, that a treatise so complete as his Elements cannot have been the creation of a single mind. And in fact there is abundant evidence that Geometry had been largely studied from the earliest times, especially from the time of Pythagoras, and that enough was known before the days of Plato to prepare for his reputed discovery of some of the properties of the conic sections. Somewhat earlier than the middle of the fifth century B.C. (460) we read of a systematic treatise on Geometry, prepared by Hippocrates of Chios, and similar works are ascribed to later authors. Plato insisted very much on the importance of this science, not only for practical, but for educational purposes, and (according to the familiar story) refused to admit any one into the inner circle of his philosophical pupils, who was not a Geometer. When in his old age he was invited to visit and instruct the younger Dionysius at Syracuse, he set the monarch his first lessons in Geometry. Thus it appears, that during this age geometrical studies were pursued with great zeal, and rapid advances were continually made even in the higher departments of the science, while there existed compends for elementary instruction.

Astronomy had likewise become a favorite subject. There is no good reason to doubt the truth of the story that Thales predicted an eclipse of the sun; of course it must have been by some empirical method. In the sixth century B.C., the age of Anaximander, there are said to have been instruments for determining the time of solstices and equinoxes; and as early as 432 B.C. the golden period was devised by Meton. They had divided the visible heavens into constellations, and marked out a Zodiac, which is still retained. Accurate observations upon the motions of the planets, though five of them were so familiarly known, do not seem to have been made till a somewhat later period. But already there were distinguished Geometers who taught something of astronomy, and whose instructions came to be in great request; and many minds were busy with astronomical inquiries. The clear atmosphere of Attica was very favorable for watching the heavenly bodies; and one or another of the surrounding mountains might well serve, as Lycabettus was used by Meton, for an observatory. In other branches of Physical Science very little was known that we should account satisfactory or valuable. A spirit of inquiry had been awakened, and miscellaneous observations were made in every direction, which doubtless aided in furnishing material for the numerous and valuable works of Aristotle upon physical subjects, as, for instance, upon Natural History. When we find the persons composing the so-called Ionian school, from Thales to Anaxagoras and onward, spoken of as natural philosophers, we must understand little more than that they occupied themselves with general physical speculations. Universal science had not yet been divided into various distinct departments; indeed, the making of such a division would require no small previous knowledge, even as one who is preparing a discourse has gone far towards mastering his subject when he has fairly marked out its natural divisions. Looking at the universe as a whole, and influenced by that desire for unity, which finds its true satisfaction in the idea of a great First Cause, the earlier Greek philosophers were constantly seeking some simple primordial principle, which would account for the origin of all existing things. When some of them taught that this principle is one of the more subtile forms of matter, as water or air or fire, it was not pure *a priori* speculation; but they seem to have always observed at least a small number of facts, and upon these built their theory.* So that we have here only an extreme result of that tendency to hasty generalization, and then unwarranted inference, which, in some departments of physical science, is not wholly restrained, even amid the correct principles and careful researches of our own day. And while these theories were, in many respects, absurd and utterly fruitless, and served to divert attention from that accurate and patient observation which alone can lead to any correct acquaintance with the material world, yet they were by no means without value as a sort of mental gymnastics.

We have thus entered upon the Greek Philosophy. Of course, no more can be attempted, in speaking of this great subject, than to call attention to its extent and value, as being indeed the chief material of Athenian education. It is a well-known matter of dispute how far the Greeks were indebted for their philosophy to the Orientals. Ritter contends, with great earnestness and force, that it originated almost entirely among themselves. Coleridge used to declare that he could not believe it was otherwise. Admitting, however, what seems at least probable, that a certain influence

* At the present day (A.D. 1886) even the most rapid sketch would make some mention of Democritus and his atomic theory, to which attention has of late been anew directed.

was exerted by Oriental ideas, both in the rise of Greek speculation, and subsequently through particular men, as Pythagoras and Plato, yet certainly their philosophy was their own, in the sense that it had a regular development, in accordance with the genius of the people and their general progress. Even in the pre-Socratic philosophy we find an orderly succession of doctrines, either by natural development or the antagonism of reaction, corresponding precisely with the alternations of philosophic opinion in all subsequent ages. There was ultra-sensationalism and ultra-idealism, with various attempts to combine the two. There was a school recognizing an imperfect sort of theism; another, with teachings more or less distinctly atheistic, and more than one whose tendencies were decidedly to pantheism. Whatever value, then, as an instrument of education, is assigned to modern speculation, belongs likewise, in no small measure, to even this earlier philosophy of the Greeks, presenting, as it did, the same subjects of investigation and essentially the same systems of belief, though with a much less extensive development, and in a much less perfect form. And it was not only valuable, but attractive. The men of that time were largely occupied, as philosophers have always been, with the interesting task of exposing the erroneousness and absurdity of opposite opinions, and this with no lack of the most pungent personality. The fact, too, that these speculations were so much at variance with prevailing opinions, would lead men not only to make acquaintance with them, but, when they possessed any plausibility at all, to investigate them with a sharp and searching attention. So great is the power of paradox in stimulating inquiry, that we have seen eminent instructors at times cast their ideas into a purposely paradoxical form, with the design of breaking up settled prejudices and arousing to examination. Now, when a young Greek, accustomed to those old legendary notions, which vaguely described all things as the offspring of certain imaginary persons, was made acquainted with the doctrines held by one or another of the early schools of philosophy,—when he heard, for instance, of some original substance and of impersonal forces, as accounting for all existences, he would almost certainly be led into curious inquiry and earnest reflection; and when these speculations came to be denounced and persecuted as impious, that would only give them an additional charm. Is there not in these considerations sufficient explanation of the fact that the doctrines referred to were through life eagerly studied by such a man as Pericles, and sufficient reason to believe that they largely contributed to the expansion and discipline of his great mind? That the philosophical teachings of Socrates and his illustrious pupil were immensely valuable for purposes of education will be recognized at once and by all. Let it only be observed that their most profound and difficult speculations possessed always some element suited to awaken the liveliest interest. They taught political and social philosophy to young men whose special ambition, in most cases, was for political advancement, and for whom these subjects formed a part, so to speak, of professional study. Their ethical and æsthetic inquiries were often made to spring from some actual occurrence or real object, which seemed to render them living questions. And every one who has read Plato will remember the vivacity of manner with which Socrates is represented as discussing the most abstruse subjects, and the familiar, quaint, even whimsical character of many of his illustrations. A delight in abstract inquiries, a love of dialectical investigation for its own sake as well as for its fruits, a consequent sharpening of all the mental powers, and a general elevation of spirit at least in some degree commensurate with the ennobling tendency of the doctrines themselves, must have been derived from any careful study of the Socratic and Platonic philosophy. Every well-informed man has doubtless already as exalted an idea of its educational influence upon that and all subsequent ages as any attempted estimate could possibly give.

There were other subjects to which much time was devoted among the Athenians, and from which they cannot have failed to derive large benefit. We have, however, no very definite information concerning the extent to which these were made matter of systematic instruction by the teachers of young men. They studied their own noble literature. In the elementary schools, a large portion of their time was occupied in committing to memory the writings of the great poets, epic, lyric and dramatic; so that we read of young men who were able to repeat the entire Iliad and the like. There is a well-known and touching story, that when the Athenian soldiers taken captive at Syracuse in the year 413 B.C. were sold into slavery, many of them gained the favor of their masters, and some their liberty, by repeating large portions of the dramas of Euripides, who was very popular in Sicily, and that several of these lived to thank the great poet on their return to Athens. Besides the obvious improvement of memory and refinement of taste, this exercise at school formed a means of acquiring that accuracy and elegance of pronunciation which the Athenians so rigidly required, and which, in the Greek language, must have been so difficult. It prepared them also for the introduction and appreciation of those felicitous quotations from the older poets which so abound in the orators and philosophers. But these early lessons were not all; in some cases, at least, lectures on literature were delivered by the higher instructors. Hippias is represented by Plato as lecturing to crowded audiences on Homer and various other poets, giving much archæological information which might illustrate those old writers, presenting critical estimates of the comparative value of different poems and of the character of the Homeric heroes. It seems reasonable to conclude that the practice was not unusual. The benefit derived from these lectures would be greatly augmented by the fact that every man who heard them had a familiar previous acquaintance with the literature which formed their subject. Add to all this the general effect of reading and of the drama, and it cannot be questioned that here was a most important means of education. Even so much as then existed of that glorious literature, whose thoughts of power and forms of beauty still afford valuable discipline and abiding delight to all civilized nations, must have been far more influential among a people who could perfectly sympathize with its inner spirit, a people familiar with the scenes it depicted and for whom it possessed the peculiar charm that always attaches to our national history and our native tongue.

Much attention was also given to the arts. Almost every Athenian youth learned something of the graphic arts and of music, and a philosophy of each was already recognized. Phidias, Parrhasius and others established canons in their several departments of art, and musical science, both in its physical and metaphysical relations, was largely studied. Aristotle has left us an elaborate argument on the importance of a practical acquaintance with these subjects, which in his day were beginning to be neglected. He says, for example, that taking the very lowest view, these accomplishments are a source of exceeding pleasure to ourselves and others, and that it should be a part of education to fit men not only for the proper pursuit of business, but also for the becoming enjoyment of leisure. One might recall, in connection with this, a saying of Pericles, in the remarkable funeral oration. He accounts it one of the peculiar glories of Athens that their laws provide for such frequent intermissions of care, by means of numerous and elegant recreations, whose daily delight charms melancholy away. Another point of the philosopher's argument is that rhythm and harmony tend to regulate and refine the mind, while the graphic arts lead us up to the contemplation of beauty, as letters to the contemplation of truth. The example of the Greeks, it may be remarked, will go very far to show that the study and practice of music, which among ourselves is so commonly neglected and so often despised, is not incompatible, to say the least, with profound wisdom or with practical fitness for the business of life.

We see, then, that however limited in comparison with the attainments of modern times, the field of acquired knowledge was really of great extent. With a considerable amount of Mathematics and Astronomy, and an active interest in the investigation of these and numerous kindred subjects, with Philosophy in all its divisions and Art in all its branches, and with an already valuable Literature,—there was material for a course of instruction protracted through many years. If, now, we combine with this result the conclusion previously reached as to the abundant supply of instructors, I think it will sufficiently appear that the Athenians of the age in question possessed such facilities for enlarged and thorough education as may account for the extraordinary degree, not only of mental power, but of mental discipline, which is so manifest in their history and remaining works. It would hardly be extravagant to assert, that in real training of mind, in mastery of principles and knowledge of men, in capacity for every form of mental effort, from the most refined speculation to the conduct of affairs, they were as highly educated a people as the world has yet seen.

The subject I have endeavored thus summarily to present might suggest a variety of reflections bearing upon our own educational interests. To a few of these I shall now allude.

Instruction among the Athenians was chiefly oral.

Books they had, but they were rare and costly. Much of their reading was with the peculiar disadvantages as well as peculiar benefits of using borrowed books. It was a matter of necessity that they should occupy themselves mainly with oral discussion. The multiplication of books and their cheapness has perhaps been the chief cause of that entirely opposite practice which now so largely prevails. Of course it is not necessary to discuss the merits of the two methods in this presence. The prominence of lecturing, in every department of the University, has beyond question contributed not a little to its success, stimulating to that sharpened attention in the lecture-room which intelligent visitors have so often remarked, and leading to a thorough comprehension of general principles on the part of students, while it almost necessitates laborious personal study, year after year, on the part of those who teach. One is surprised to find it said, by persons elsewhere who still hold to the opposite course, that this method proposes to throw away text-books altogether, when a judicious combination of the two is constantly advocated and attempted, a combination varying in the relative proportion of its elements according to the nature of the particular subject. Nor is it less strange to hear it urged, that the method is appropriate only for those who have decided maturity of mind, since a brief experiment would suffice to show that nowhere more than in elementary schools is oral instruction profitable and necessary. One might be inclined at times to suspect that a latent dread of the labor it requires is the true ground of opposition, did not the high character for ability and faithfulness of some who oppose, render the supposition inadmissible.—Moreover, the Athenians derived much of their knowledge from free conversation, not only between an instructor and his pupils, but in the social intercourse of cultivated men in general. Every one has observed the lack of this at the present day, particularly in our own country. Between the Professor and his class, it is, perhaps, mainly impracticable, and the great advantages of our modern institutions must make compensation. In general society the growing infrequency of intercourse for conversation upon elevated topics appears to result from several causes. We live in an age of feverish activity and incessant toil, when all leisure is apt to be reckoned loss. New and attractive books and periodicals constantly accumulate upon the table and engross every moment that can be snatched from pressing duties. Mingling little together, and with an ever-widening literature in the several professions and in the various departments of knowledge, our better reading is less and less in the same direction. Already there is often little common ground save politics and general news. The whole tendency is to a diminution of that intellectual sympathy which ought to subsist among men of cultivation, however diverse their callings. Even if we looked to nothing beyond obtaining valuable information, surely there is more to be learned from conversation with intelligent friends than from the hurried reading of every ephemeral publication which obtrudes itself upon our notice. Another cause is, that a higher morality forbids the excesses which have so commonly been connected with the intercourse of literary men. Certainly we had better isolate ourselves completely than revive the scenes of the Greek symposion or the English club; but it would be humiliating to acknowledge that excessive animal indulgence is indispensable to elevated intellectual communion. It may be said that the whole matter will regulate itself aright; but I may at least solicit your reflection, whether some remedy cannot be found for what does appear to be an evil.

The educational history we have been surveying suggests also the important fact that true education is not necessarily associated with vast acquirements. The famous saying of Macaulay that a modern school-girl knows more of Geography than Strabo, is in one sense true, but in another and higher sense it hides a dangerous error; for he who would measure education must not forget that it has three dimensions, and be sure to take account of its depth. There is hardly any lesson which our age needs to impress upon itself more constantly than that thoroughness is not to be sacrificed to extensive attainment. We remember, gentlemen, those of us particularly who were deficient in early advantages, the delusive hope of boyhood, that there would come a time when we should have read all books, and become masters of all knowledge. We learned long ago that this can never be; yet often one re-awakes to fresh disappointment, and finds that he has been dreaming that sweet dream of childhood still. It is painful to think that we must live on and die, and leave many a wide field of human knowledge untraversed and unknown. This longing to learn everything is in itself a noble element of our nature, and leads to noble results; but it requires to be checked by the stern voice of duty. It is this feeling, combined with an indolent preference of that which is comparatively easy, that induces some persons to spend their lives in skimming the surface of every science and all literature, nowhere pausing for thorough examination. It is this that produces the popular admiration of men who have the reputation of omnivorous reading, while they may not be, in any just sense of the term, scholars. And in no respect are its effects more likely to be injurious than upon the interests of the higher education. Students, where there is liberty of choice, are constantly disposed to attempt more than within the time assigned they can properly accomplish; professors have to struggle continually against a desire to make their course unduly extensive; while cultivated and enthusiastic spectators, who have forgotten their experience in the one capacity and are perhaps destitute of experience in the other, impressed with the value of some branch of a subject which is not included, call, and call with forcible argument and eloquent appeal, for enlargement. Now, when it is urged that additional studies shall be pursued in additional time, no lover of knowledge can fail to give a hearty approbation. When it is proposed to crowd other subjects into the same already crowded space, the project is very questionable. When it is desired that we shall seek some vague general benefit, in such a condition of things as to involve, whether that be the intention or not, a sacrifice of thorough study, any such scheme deserves to be resisted, firmly and forever.

In endeavoring to give a valuable course of instruction in any department of knowledge, the instructor must always keep in view three objects; and where the subject is unprofessional, and he is confined within such narrow limits as the present spirit and customs of our people impose, they ought to be held, if I correctly judge, in the following order of relative importance: first, to secure mental training; second, to awaken a love for the subject, which may lead the student to prosecute it hereafter; last and least, to furnish information. In teaching, for instance, one of the ancient languages, to those who cannot yet be induced to give to it more than a limited time, to make the student acquainted with whatever valuable truths the literature of that language contains, though very desirable in itself, must certainly be reckoned of inferior importance. If this were the principal object, there would be much force in the argument often urged against all study of those languages, that translations would suffice. The question then is,—Which will accomplish most in the way of mental culture and in awakening a relish for the classics, to spend the time which can be commanded in reading as widely as possible, though with a very imperfect knowledge of the language itself, or to make an accurate and philosophical acquaintance with the language the primary object—it being remembered that in order to this no small amount of reading is necessary, and that so much at least of the literature is read with a tolerably thorough comprehension and just appreciation? As to intellectual training, no one will question that the latter method is more useful. I think it can easily be shown that the same thing is true where some do question it, as to the cultivation of taste. If you should go with some young friend to a gallery of art, having but a comparatively short time at your disposal, and desiring to procure him the largest amount of benefit and enjoyment, your course, if unreflecting as the mass of men, would probably be to carry him through a rapid survey of numerous works, telling him the names of the great artists, and pointing out their most celebrated productions, and giving him all the critical common-places of would-be connoisseurs. Your friend would go away little inclined to come again, and with scarcely anything of real benefit, but marvellously prepared to shine in a certain kind of society by a display of his remarkable familiarity with matters of art. But if you select a considerable number of the finest works and fix his attention upon these till he shall, to some extent, drink in their deep inner significance and beauty, he will turn away, not imagining that he knows much, but with some true culture of taste, with a heightened love of the beautiful, and probably with a strong desire to visit again the spot where he found so much of genuine improvement and serene delight. Even so, if we desire nothing more than the ability to make large talk concerning even the most unfamiliar classic authors, and to ornament our pages with a plentiful sprinkling of classic allusion and quotation, then it will suffice to run rapidly over many works and read treatises on Greek and Roman Literature. But if we desire that true cultivation of taste, the faculty of taste, which the classics are capable of affording, we must study at least some works with such a patient attention as shall at length issue in appreciative contemplation and in sympathy with their peculiar genius. And let it not be objected that in order to this appreciation there is no need of critical study, as the great scholars of two centuries ago entered most fully into the classical spirit, while they knew very little of what we call philology. The objector appears to forget that condition which I have repeatedly mentioned, and which, however deplorable, can be corrected only by very slow degrees,— the lack of time. Milton and the other great scholars of his age spent a large portion of their lives in reading Latin and Greek authors, becoming almost as familiar with those languages, particularly the former, as with English itself. Thus they were brought into sympathy with the genius of the classic languages, precisely as in the case of their native tongue, by the gradual effect of this exceeding familiarity. Very similar, though within narrower limits, seems to be the plan pursued in England now. By an almost exclusive devotion during many years, their classical scholars attain to an extremely accurate and familiar knowledge of the languages, learning to feel the force of their idiom, not by philosophical examination, but by an immense amount of practical drilling. It might appear presumptuous to say that, even for them, a larger infusion of philosophy would augment the benefit their system already confers. It is sufficient to say that, among us, such a course as that pursued by Milton or by the modern English scholars is at present utterly impracticable. If we would, with far less time at command, still attain to the privilege of communion with the very spirit of classical literature, our best, if not our only method, is by critical, philological study. For it must be remembered that philology includes not only the anatomy, but the physiology of language—not merely the study of etymological formations, to the beginner often so repulsive, to the proficient so interesting, but of the precise significance of peculiar modes of expression, with the exact meaning and force of particles, and the relations of these to the inner life and informing spirit of the language. Is it not obvious that this affords the best possible means of entering into the genius of a literature, and securing a genuine culture, not only of intellect, but of taste?* We are all agreed, gentlemen—let it be distinctly understood—that it is desirable our young men should read the classics far more widely than they have ever done, and that, in order to this, as well as on other accounts, they should come to the university later, and remain longer, than is their wont. For the attainment of such a result, let us exert our united influence of every kind and in every place. For the rest, the standard of graduation in this department has been slowly rising with almost every year; the amount of reading necessary to a degree is already great; we may expect that this standard will continue to be elevated, and the requisite reading to be widened, as rapidly as the time students can be induced to give will possibly permit. Thus may they secure

* The polemical position here assumed in defending Dr. Gessner Harrison's methods will be found to have been somewhat modified in the memorial which follows.

the largest intellectual and æsthetical cultivation now, and thus, precisely as fast as our people shall be prepared for it, the course of classical instruction, while never ceasing to be thorough, may be indefinitely extended. Shall not such a plan, with all its valuable results in the past and all its promise for the future, receive general approbation? Or shall we ask that our young men may spend the time they now devote to the classics in somewhat more extensive and far more imperfect reading, when, if there is force in the brief argument we have considered, the consequence will be a positive diminution, not only of intellectual improvement, but of that very æsthetical culture which all consider important, and which some reckon paramount? That is the practical question upon which alone, so far as I know, there is any difference of opinion; and to the many among us who have some tolerable acquaintance with the subject, the decision of that question may be cheerfully committed.

One or two other topics of remark suggest themselves, which I shall only indicate.

The Greeks were in many respects pioneers of knowledge. Many subjects, particularly of mathematical and physical science, which for us involve no difficulty because their nature has been fully explained, were for them problems calling forth the mightiest energies, and demanding the most protracted application. Is it not true that strength of mind is still best attained, not by confining ourselves to those regions in which all difficulties have been removed by others' toil, but by approaching the boundaries of knowledge, and striving to extend its domain? It is sometimes lamented as a deplorable fatality that men cannot be restrained from laboring still at questions which the experience of ages appears to prove to be insoluble. Yet even though the effort should continue to be fruitless, is not that struggling effort itself a gain, because producing such vigor of intellect as nothing but pioneering work could ever give. It would be a fact worth considering, if it is true, that the unconquerable tendency of which men complain is in reality singularly fortunate; that where we often find disappointment and despair, there too we find the largest real benefit.

The thorough education of the period we have been considering did not prepare the Greeks for producing an epic poetry which should rival the creations of a past age. The greatly improved educational resources of subsequent centuries could never re-animate the decaying spirit of Grecian literature. There are influences at work among men far mightier than what we call education. It is not in the power of systems of instruction to reproduce the literary types of a remote time or a distant people. Nor is this at all to be regretted, where, in place of extinct forms, there is something equally valuable. Why need the Athenians of the age of Pericles lament that there was no new Homer, when they had the immortal dramatists? Why complain, a few generations later, that no other Socrates or Pericles arose, when Aristotle and Demosthenes were there? So with our own country. If the condition and character of the nation have directed the attention of our ablest minds to politics, is it nothing that we have produced a political literature such as the world never witnessed before?—Why lament that the mighty governing forces of social progress have appointed our people no different work, if they have performed with unequalled success the task that was set them? Have we not reason here to be satisfied with what our fathers accomplished, and be hopeful for our own future? And let no man ever forget that it is the business of education merely to give a harmonious development and thorough discipline to the powers of the national mind, not so much attempting any particular bias, as leaving it for the irresistible tendencies of the age to determine in what direction those powers shall be exerted.

And now gentlemen, let us unite in the desire that on this, as on every occasion of our annual assembling, we may turn away profoundly impressed with the duties we personally owe to the cause of education and to this University. It is pleasant to see so many of our number in high places here, of instruction and of control. It is cheering to hope that zeal tempered with prudence, and the spirit of progress chastened by conservatism, are to render truly illustrious this dynasty of the Alumni. But it is in the power of us all so to cherish the spirit of letters, so to prove the value of the training here received, that this noble Institution, which made us proud and happy in younger years by the bestowal of her unrivalled honors, may, at least to some extent, receive honor in return from the achievements of our ripened manhood and our advancing age.

XVII.

MEMORIAL OF GESSNER HARRISON.*

HE fell amid the storm of war. Three years earlier and the death of Gessner Harrison would have stirred the whole South. The journals of every State would have contained tributes from many an admiring and grateful pupil. In Virginia especially we should have been told in eloquent terms how much he had done to raise the standard of education throughout the State, and the story of his laborious life would have been lovingly connected with the history of that great University which was the pride of all educated Virginians. But he died when the war tempest had long been raging, when the darkness was deepening, and many hearts were beginning to shudder lest all things we most loved should go down together; and he fell almost as unnoticed as falls a single drop into a stormy sea. To this day it is sometimes asked by intelligent men where the famous Professor is, and what he is doing. Already when he died the hearts of men were becoming filled with the love of our great military leaders, the love which afterwards grew into an absorbing passion. *Inter arma silent litteræ.* And so it is likely that the young of to-day can scarcely believe, the old cannot without difficulty recall, how widely known, how highly honored and admired, how warmly

* Before the Society of Alumni of the University of Va., July 2, 1873.

loved, was the mere civilian, the quiet and unpretending Professor of 1859. It is surely worth while, then, not only out of respect for his honored memory, but for our own sake, and for sweet learning's sake, that we should spend an hour here, so near to his old lecture-room, to his home, and to his grave, in reminding ourselves and telling to all whom our voices can reach, what a man he was, and what a work he performed.

Gessner Harrison was the son of Peachy Harrison, M.D., of the town of Harrisonburg, twenty-five miles north of Staunton. His mother's maiden name was Mary Stuart. The father was a member of the Senate of Virginia, and of the famous Convention of 1829-30. He took great interest in politics, and was accounted the leader of his political party in that region. But he abandoned public life through love of his profession. He was the leading physician of Rockingham, including in his practice most of the best families of the county, and patients frequently came to him from other counties. Not only in politics and in his profession, but in all the relations and duties of life, he showed himself a man of uncommon good sense and sound judgment. He was very fond of reading, and collected a considerable library. He greatly admired the German character, of which some excellent though humble specimens were among the early settlers of that region, and the German literature, so far as it then existed and was known to him; and his liking for the Swiss poet Gessner, particularly for a poem on the Death of Abel, led him to give the name Gessner to his second son. He was a deeply devout Christian and a decided Methodist.

There are few things so truly honorable as to be a really good physician—a man of strong sense, good general and professional cultivation, superior skill, ready sympathies and earnest piety. All this the elder Harrison was, in a high degree. His son Gessner also was not mistaken in the early feeling which drew him toward the same calling, for he was by nature singularly suited to its pursuit, though Providence had other work for him to do. A much younger son, Dr. Peachy Rush Harrison, showed the same specific talent, and entered upon practice in Harrisonburg with extraordinary success and the brightest prospects, but was cut off by an untimely death.* The father died in 1848; his excellent and estimable wife survived till 1857.

Gessner was born June 26, 1807, in the town of Harrisonburg; but his father soon afterward removed to an old family homestead a little way out, so that his children lived in the country, and yet were near the town. The older son, Edward, delighted in hunting, but Gessner became fond of farming. Through all his career he longed for country life and agriculture, and in his last year or two we shall find him entering upon this with great relish. He began to attend school at the age of four years, and at eight began the Latin Grammar. He is described by a surviving relative as a very small boy, with ruddy checks; a favorite with the girls of the school, and at the same time exceedingly fond of his studies and of general reading. At home he always carried a book in his pocket, and when occupied in cut-

* Two sons of Gessner Harrison are physicians, Dr. George Tucker Harrison and Dr. H. W. Harrison, both of New York City.

ting wood or such duties he would never sit down to rest but the book was at once taken out.

Among his early teachers were a Mr. Davis, who had been tutor in William and Mary College, and Rev. Daniel Baker, a Presbyterian minister, who afterward became quite famous all over the South as a revivalist. In the *Life of Dr. Baker* is a note from Dr. G. Harrison, stating that for some years of his boyhood he was a pupil of Dr. B., and that he had always regarded him as having displayed, in a very eminent degree, some of the best qualities of a teacher of youth. On his last visit to the University, when quite an old man, Dr. Baker greatly amused the Professor's younger children by telling of the circumstances of a whipping which he had on one single occasion found it necessary to administer. Two other Presbyterian divines, Messrs. Smith and Hendren, were among the growing boy's instructors. And the case is scarcely singular: a large proportion of the best school-teaching done in Virginia in those days was done by the Presbyterian ministers.

Professor Henry Tutwiler, of Alabama, who was Gessner Harrison's school-mate at Harrisonburg, his roommate at the University, and his most intimate friend through life, states that there was in Harrisonburg a small town-library, of which Dr. Peachy Harrison was a stockholder, and the books of which his sons were accustomed to read, besides those they found at home. From this library Gessner obtained *Horne Tooke's Diversions of Purley*, which he read with great delight, and to which, Mr. Tutwiler thinks, his fondness for Philological studies is largely due. With all its blunders, and even absurdities, as they may now be considered, the *Diversions of Purley* was an epoch-making book, opening the period of philological study of the English language, of which we are now beginning to reap some good fruits; and it exhibits such kindling enthusiasm for the subject as could not fail to awaken any native appetency for the study of language.

Such were the advantages, domestic and educational, which Gessner Harrison had enjoyed, when, at the age of nearly eighteen, he came, with his older brother, Edward, to enter the University, whose first session then began, March 1, 1825. His father did not share in the fears which led many devout men in the Commonwealth to keep their sons away from the University, because there was no provision made in its Constitution for religious instruction or religious worship. Perhaps his intense political sympathy with Mr. Jefferson made some amends for the lack of sympathy as to evangelical Christianity. And, no doubt, he relied much on the religious education he had given his sons, on their fixed religious principles (the elder being, in fact, already a professed Christian), and on the influence which, even at a distance, would be maintained by their home and their parents. After all, these are a youth's best safe-guards as he goes to meet the temptations which, in one way or another, he must encounter; the armor in which he will best fight the battles that may not be escaped. The fears which have been mentioned as entertained by many were, no doubt, exaggerated. They had never heard or dreamed of a college without religious worship and compulsory attendance upon it, as, even to the present day, such compulsory attendance is regarded as necessary in most American colleges; and the idea of a University in which there would be no prayers nor preaching was to them in the highest degree alarming. But Mr. Jefferson's determination at all hazards to maintain religious liberty, as an indispensable element of freedom in general, if it led to an extreme in this case, certainly led to that extreme which lay in the right direction. He was confident that whatever was really necessary in the way of religious instruction and worship would, in one way or another, be voluntarily introduced here by the various denominations of Christians. And, although the void left was at first an evil, we all know how, in the course of a few years and in the ordering of Providence, it was filled; how, as nothing in this respect had been instituted, something grew, in a form perfectly free and generally satisfactory, attended by a thousand blessed results, and capable of being altered without difficulty, if the circumstances of the future should demand it.

There was nothing very striking in the appearance of young Gessner Harrison when he came to the University. He was somewhat below the middle height, with a low forehead, and a head whose general shape was an exception to the rules of Phrenology; his face, though quite engaging, was rather homely, with one remarkable exception. His dark eyes were singularly beautiful and expressive. One of the few sensible things which Miss Fredrika Bremer contrived to say in the extended account she gave of her visit, many years after this, to the University, was her laudatory reference to the Chairman of the Faculty's "beautiful, meditative eye." In truth, that eye would express, all unconsciously to him, not only meditation, but every phase of feeling; and, as the years went on, it seemed to a close observer to hide, in its quiet depths, all he had thought, all he had suffered, all he had become—the whole world of his inner life. These fine eyes, which were, no doubt, a little downcast when he first diffidently met the Professors, with the ruddy cheeks which had pleased the school-girls, and a voice most of whose tones were quite pleasing and some of them exceedingly sweet, made no small amends for his general homeliness.

Mr. George Long, who had come over from England to be Professor of Ancient Languages, and who is still living in the south of England, writes as follows: "I well remember Dr. Harrison bringing in his two boys, and my examining them. Gessner Harrison was then a good scholar, considering the opportunities that he had. He was very diligent, he possessed a good understanding, and was, in all respects, an excellent young man." Mr. Long states that, besides attending some of his classes during all the three years that he remained at the University, the young student also read with him privately sometimes in several Greek authors. Mr. Tutwiler mentions that he had brought with him to the University some knowledge of German, and that he studied German as well as French with Dr. Blättermann, the remarkable linguist who was Professor of Modern Languages. Intending to be a physician, and loving language, Harrison confined himself to ancient and modern languages, chemistry and medicine. But, in Mr. Tutwiler's opinion, he would have distinguished himself in mathematics, had he attended that school. The opinion common among the students in late years was very different. A story had great currency that, some years after Dr. Harrison became Professor, he and Mr. Bonnycastle, the celebrated Professor of Mathematics, undertook to teach each other in Geometry and Latin. This was true, but the story went on to say that before they had gone far Mr. Bonnycastle one day railed out, "Is it possible that you cannot demonstrate as simple a proposition as that?" The other replied testily, "Humph! you haven't sense enough to decline a Latin noun of the first declension." Mr. Tutwiler refers to this story, and remarks that it doubtless "had as little foundation as such stories usually have." So intimate with Harrison, at school and at the University, and himself afterwards eminent in Mathematics, Mr. Tutwiler can well judge as to his friend's capacities in this respect. Dr. Harrison himself was once asked about the famous story, and said, in his quiet way, that he was not aware that either Mr. Bonnycastle or himself gave up their proposed studies together for any other reason than the fact that they were both extremely busy. So much has been said upon this point for a reason. There is nothing more common among students than the notion that that rather nondescript thing they delight to call genius is best manifested by remarkable success in the study of some one subject, attended by remarkable stupidity as to others. Some bright enough, but slightly idle young fellow, who got badly started in Greek or in Algebra, and is now too proud or too indolent to go back and, in sheer school-boy fashion, work over the elements of the neglected subject, will readily abandon it altogether, with the persuasion that he has "no talent" for languages, or for mathematics; and this he states to his friends without shame, from a secret feeling that the fact only sets in bright contrast his greater talent for something else. And the fashion used to be to clinch the whole thing by telling the apocryphal story of Dr. Harrison and Mr. Bonnycastle. It is very certain that Dr. Harrison did not think lightly of Mathematics and Physical Science as one great department of our means of culture; though he had little patience with the notion, sometimes unwisely put forward, that the study of these subjects alone will constitute a complete education.

Of the little that is now remembered concerning his quiet and uneventful student life, it will suffice to mention one incident. It was noticed as a peculiarity of the young Harrisons that they would never study on Sunday. With their decided character and convictions, they would find no great difficulty in standing comparatively alone in this respect. But there came a severer test. The venerable Father of the University, who survived during the first and part of the second session, desired to become personally acquainted with the students. The desire was, no doubt, due partly to that affectionate and truly paternal interest in them which he manifested in every way, and partly also to the hope of gaining personal influence over them through the power of social intercourse—a power which the great statesman had fully recognized and constantly wielded in all his political career. Accordingly, he invited the students to dine with him at Monticello. As Sunday had always been a favorite day with him and many of his neighbors for dinner parties, and as the students had more leisure on that day, he invited them, by groups, in alphabetical order, to dine with him on successive Sundays. When the two Harrisons were reached they wrote him a note, stating that their father, who was a member of the Methodist Church, had trained them to observe the Sabbath with great strictness; that not even their having had the honor and pleasure of dining with Mr. Jefferson would console him for their having committed a violation, as he would conceive, of the Sabbath; and that, therefore, out of respect for their father's convictions—to say nothing of their own—they felt constrained to deny themselves the happiness, etc. Mr. Jefferson sent them, in reply, one of those exquisitely felicitous notes for which he was famous. He said it gave him the highest gratification, it was a consolation to his old age, to meet with such an instance of filial piety; to find young men showing such respect for their father's opinions, at a time when too many of the young were inclined to disregard the counsels of age and the wishes of parents. And he ended by particularly requesting that on a certain day of the next week they would dine with him, and he could take no denial. They went, were received with singular courtesy, and spent hours of great enjoyment, being, as the Faculty, in a tribute to Mr. Jefferson's memory the following year, said had often been true of themselves, "instructed and delighted by the rare and versatile powers of that intellect which time had enriched with facts without detracting from its lustre, and charmed with those irresistible manners which were dictated by delicacy and benevolence."

In July, 1828, at the close of the third session, the first graduates of the University were declared, viz.: three in Greek, three in Mathematics, one in Chemistry, and three in Medicine. The graduates in Greek were Gessner Harrison, Henry Tutwiler, and Robert M. T. Hunter; and Gessner Harrison was also one of the three graduates in Medicine, with the title of Doctor of Medicine.

Expecting soon to enter upon the practice of his profession, the young physician little imagined what awaited him. The London University had just been established, and Mr. Long, the Professor of Ancient Languages, and Mr. Key, the Professor of Mathematics, in the University of Virginia, both being Masters of Arts, and the former a Fellow, of Trinity College, Cambridge, were induced to return to England, and take the Chairs of Greek and Latin in the new institution. Mr. Jefferson had drawn the first professors nearly all from abroad, because his University was to be widely different from anything existing in America, and he wanted men new to the country. This plan worked well as to the instruction, though possibly the effect was not so good upon the discipline. Mr. Long states: "When I was leaving, I was consulted by some one or more of the visitors about the choice of my successor. My advice was not to get another professor from England, for various reasons, but particularly because I thought that they had a young man who was fit for the place, a Virginian, and I recommend Harrison." The proposition was somewhat startling. Mr. Long himself had become professor here at the age of twenty-four, but young Harrison was barely twenty-one, and had never been outside of Virginia. The visitors gave him the appointment temporarily for one year, and the next year made it permanent. It was truly an honor; for the visitors who consulted Mr. Long were, as he thinks, Chapman Johnson and Joseph C. Cabell, and the Rector at the time was James Madison. But the young appointee had scarcely time to think of the high compliment, for he was oppressed by a sense of responsibility, and by an almost painful self-distrust, which, even several years later, in his private letters, is still expressed.

It was a high privilege for the youthful professor to come into familiar association with such men as his early colleagues. He himself has left brief sketches of some of them in a valuable article on the University, which he contributed to *Duyckinck's Cyclopedia of American Literature*, and from which a few sentences may be extracted. Of his predecessor, Mr. Long, he says: "A man of marked ability and attainments, thoroughly trained in the system of his college, and having a mind far more than most men's demanding accuracy in the results of inquiry, and scouting mere pretension, he aimed, and was fitted, to introduce something better than what then passed current as classical learning." Dr. Blättermann, Professor of Modern Languages until 1840, a German, at the time of his appointment residing in London, "gave proof of extensive acquirements, and of a mind of uncommon natural vigor and penetration.

In connection more especially with the lessons on German and Anglo-Saxon, he gave to his students much that was interesting and valuable in Comparative Philology also, a subject in which he found peculiar pleasure." Mr. Bonnycastle, Professor at first of Natural Philosophy, but of Mathematics from 1828 to his death, in 1841, was an Englishman, educated at Woolwich, and "was distinguished by the force and originality of his mind, no less than by his profound knowledge of Mathematics. His fine taste, cultivated by much reading, his general knowledge, and his abundant store of anecdote, made him a most agreeable and instructive companion to all; and this, though his really kind feelings were partly hidden by a cold exterior." Dr. Emmet, Professor of Chemistry and Materia Medica till his death, in 1842, was a native of Dublin, but brought over in childhood by his father, one of the famous Irish patriots, and educated in New York. "His striking native genius, his varied science, his brilliant wit, his eloquence, his cultivated and refined taste for art, his modesty, his warm-hearted and cheerful social virtues, won for him the admiration and lasting regard of his colleagues and of his pupils." Dr. Dunglison, of England, Professor of Medicine till 1833, then removed to Philadelphia. He was "a man of learning, in his profession and generally, as well as of ability," and "gained a wide celebrity by his distinguished ability as a lecturer, and by his varied and valuable contributions to medical literature." Mr. George Tucker, Professor of Moral Philosophy till he resigned, in 1845, was a native of Bermuda, but educated at William and Mary College, Virginia. "He was, for many years, a member of the legal profession, and, for some time, a member of Congress from Virginia," where he took an active part in the discussions on the famous Missouri Compromise. "Before his appointment to the chair by Mr. Jefferson, he had published, among other writings, a volume of essays, characterized by the purity and elegance of style, and by the force and clearness of thought, which mark his writings." While Professor, he published the *Life of Jefferson*, and several valuable works on his favorite subject of political economy. After his retirement, when past eighty years of age, he issued a *History of the United States*, which, though not attractive in style, is believed to be unequalled as a reliable and instructive account of the formation and early working of the Government of the United States. Mr. Tucker "brought to the discharge of his duties a mind remarkable for clearness and accuracy, great industry and thoroughness of research, and an extensive knowledge of men and of books in almost every department of learning; and he allowed no topic to pass under review without investing it with the interest of original and searching investigation." In private, he was a singularly agreeable companion, ready in all subjects of conversation, abounding in wit and anecdote and felicitous literary allusion. John Tayloe Lomax, Professor of Law from 1826 to 1830, and afterwards a distinguished judge in this State, was a man of signal ability, of the highest purity and integrity, and enjoyed throughout his long career the unbounded respect and veneration of the bench, the bar, and the people of the Commonwealth. He published, after leaving the University, a

Digest of the Law of Real Property, three volumes, two editions, and a *Treatise on the Law of Executors and Administrators*, two volumes, two editions. On his retirement, in 1830, he was immediately succeeded by Professor John A. G. Davis, whose lamented and tragic death, ten years later, only rendered more illustrious his abilities and virtues.

Such were the men whose admirable gifts, attainments and exertions gave to the University a powerful and lasting impetus. Our young professor, who had read and thought much, but had not seen the world, derived great pleasure and profit from his early intercourse with these men of various accomplishments. From the English gentlemen he derived much as to the nicer points of English usage in language, in which he became critically exact. It must have been often noticed, by those who knew Dr. Harrison in middle life, how broad were his views, how catholic his sympathies. In politics, in religion, in science and literature, in daily life, he had decided opinions, which he would state frankly and positively; and yet he had a freedom from narrowness, and a kindly feeling towards those with whom he widely differed, such as seemed strange in one who had scarcely traveled at all, nor ever mingled in the activities of the world. This was due partly to his own naturally well-balanced mind, partly to intercourse with the early colleagues just mentioned, and most of all, it is likely, to the liberalizing, broadening influence of profound classical studies. It is one principal element in the benefit derived from such studies that we are drawn to take a lively interest in people far remote and widely different from ourselves, and who yet command our admiration and call forth our sympathies. Truly and lovingly to study their history, institutions and life, their noble languages and charming literature, is to travel, in the highest and best sense, far more profitably than when men "do" Constantinople or St. Petersburg, or wander, half instructed, among ruins they do not comprehend and inspirations they cannot feel, in Athens or in Rome. The materialist in education asks, Why study *dead* languages and *ancient* history? On the same principle, why travel, abroad or at home, except as a commercial traveler? why listen to the aged? why ever talk to your neighbor, unless it be in driving a bargain? Such people—and the world is full of them now—do not know the difference between getting an education and learning a trade.

Let it be added that Dr. Harrison often deplores in his earlier letters, as he is remembered to have done in his later years, the fact of his going comparatively so little into society. In a university where the schools are independent, and each professor pushes the subject in his own way, there is, perhaps, an aggravation of the tendency felt everywhere in our hard-driven modern life, by which every man is led to confine himself too exclusively to his own specialty; and the daily newspaper, valuable though it be, is but a poor substitute for social intercourse, where men revive and broaden and sweeten their general culture by free and varied conversation upon the thousand topics of literature and news and sentiment in which all alike take interest. When, and by whom, shall the evil be corrected?

In December, 1830, the young professor was married to Miss Eliza Lewis Carter Tucker, daughter of Mr. George Tucker, the Professor of Moral Philosophy. This honored lady still survives, and nothing more is proper to say than the remark, that one who has known her well does not wonder when he finds the husband and father, in letters to his bosom friend Tutwiler, constantly referring to the happiness he found, amid all toils and trials, in the society of his wife and children.

Dr. Harrison must have seen at the outset, and he felt it more and more with the advancing years, that the professors of the University must bear heavy burdens, and struggle against sore difficulties, in seeking to raise the standard of scholarship, through lack of good preparatory schools; and from the nature of his subject, and from his own longer term of service, this struggle proved more severe for him than for any other person. Education must work from above downward. The better education must begin in the higher institutions, by preparing teachers, so well trained, and filled with such a spirit, that they will afterwards send up pupils much better grounded in the elements than they themselves were. Then the toiling professor can step up to a somewhat higher level. Every few years he may, in this way, take a step a little higher, until, by slow degrees, he lifts the whole mass into some manifest and conscious, though still comparatively slight, elevation above its original position. But the process is greatly complicated and retarded by the fact that only a certain slowly increasing proportion of the students of later sessions have been prepared by his graduates. Others, and for a long time the great majority, have received their school-boy training after the old sluggish and unscientific fashion, and, for their sakes, the professor must still return to the elements. If he now hurries more rapidly over these elements than formerly, in order to gain time for carrying the course higher, he has the pain of seeing many worthy fellows soon left hopelessly behind, and some men of fine talents and high ambition struggling in desperate and sometimes vain efforts to supply, with the requisite promptness, the defects of their early training. With these he must deeply sympathize; and, to lighten the struggle for them, he must confine the progress in his course to slow, inch by inch movement, and must unsparingly give his own time and energies to the work of aiding and stimulating their revision of elementary studies. Misunderstood by many, bitterly complained of by some, and suffering through painful sympathy with good men who fail, he must work on through the weary years. There is something sublime in the spectacle of an unpretending, quiet, but deeply earnest and conscientious man, with the classical education of a great commonwealth, or of whole States, resting upon him, and slowly, slowly lifting up himself and his burden towards what they are capable of reaching. It was thus that Gessner Harrison toiled and suffered in this University for thirty-one years. And not in vain. During the later years of this period he was accustomed to say that pupils were coming to him from the leading preparatory schools with a better knowledge of Latin and Greek than twenty years or so before was carried away by his graduates. It is marvellous to our older men, when they remember how generally and in how high a degree the standard of education was raised in Virginia, and in the South, between 1830 and 1860. Let it never be forgotten that the University of Virginia did this; and there is no invidious comparison in saying that, far beyond any other man, it was done by the University Professor of Ancient Languages. The two able scholars and admirable teachers who are his successors to-day have had, since the war, some little experience in the way of repeating the process which he carried on so long; and each of them has repeatedly volunteered the remark, "I hardly know how we could get on at all if it were not for what Dr. Harrison did before us." He once said to a friend, who was about to become professor in a new and peculiar institution, "I suspect you will have about such a lot as mine; you will spend your life in clearing the ground and laying foundations, mostly out of sight, on which more fortunate men may afterwards build." It is pleasant to recall this saying in connection with the fact that his magnanimous and justly honored successors delight to recognize their obligation.

But it is proper to notice more particularly the progress of his studies and teaching in the leading departments of his subject.

Dr. Harrison promptly turned away from the existing English methods of classical instruction—viz., teaching the mere facts of Latin or Greek usage as facts, and strove after the rational explanation and philosophical systematization of these facts. Hence, he turned with lively interest to what the Germans were beginning to do—using it as materials and encouragement for his own laborious studies. He had already been several years at work when the modern Science of Language had its birth. It is so common to confine the term "science" to our knowledge of the physical world, so common to represent the study of language and literature as distinct from science, and even opposed to it, that many persons are scarcely yet aware that there exists a Science of Language. Yet it does exist, has achieved the most important results, is making rapid progress every year, and unquestionably deserves the full dignity of the name of Science.

The science of language first took definite shape in the first part of *Bopp's Comparative Grammar*, which was published in 1833, the sixth and concluding part not appearing till 1852. Sir William Jones, and other Englishmen residents in India, had made a knowledge of the Sanskrit language accessible to the scholars of Europe. All who paid any attention to it were struck with the resemblance of this dead language of India to the Greek and Latin. The great German, Bopp, made a laborious comparison of it, not only with the classic tongues, but with the other principal families of languages in Europe. This comparison, as is now well known, furnished the means of shedding a flood of light upon the inflections, the word-formation, and the word-history, of Latin and Greek. A copy of the earlier portions of Bopp's work was sent by Mr. Long to his successor, Dr. Harrison, and by him was seized upon with the greatest avidity. Quite independently, though gladly comparing the similar work which after some time began to be done in Germany, he applied Bopp's materials to the elucidation of the classic languages. His native fondness for such inquiries, sharpened by the studies and the teaching of several years, caused him to take intense delight in these applications of Comparative Etymology to Latin and Greek. All this is now universal among respectable professors. But for years and years it was done in this University alone of American institutions. In fact, he was pushing these applications when they were still unknown in the teaching of English Universities, and existed at only a very few points in Germany. The present distinguished Professor of Greek in this University* was in Germany from 1850 to 1852, studying at Bonn, Göttingen and Berlin. Classical Philologians and "comparative philologians" were then still arrayed in two hostile camps, and the great teachers whose lectures he attended were, in the main, unfriendly to the new science. Some of them ridiculed the idea of a man's having to learn Sanskrit in order to understand and explain the classic languages. George Curtius, the mediator of the two schools, was then a young man, having been born in 1820, and in 1852, as Professor in Prague, was beginning to publish works in which Greek Grammar was reconstructed on the basis of Comparative Philology. Upon entering the faculty of the University of Virginia (1856), our accomplished Professor found that his colleague, Dr. Harrison, had long been making free use of comparative philology, at a time when in the leading Universities of Germany it was scarcely at all

* Professor Gildersleeve, who subsequently removed to Johns Hopkins University.

applied to the explanation of Latin and Greek. It may be added that Dr. Harrison's medical studies prepared him to elucidate, with special interest and success, the physiological element of Language—to explain its relations to the human organs of speech, as well as to the faculties of the human mind.

These topics of instruction, which are a matter of course now, seemed far otherwise to most of the Doctor's students in 1835–45. To see the Professor exemplifying with his own organs the mode of formation of palatals, linguals and labials was a standing amusement. To hear every day the uncouth names of Bopp and Pott was odd to ears not so familiar as all students now are with German names, and provocative of that species of school-boy wit which some students find it hard to outgrow. And to be gravely asked for the case of *unde* or *quum* was the height of absurdity. The careful explanation of case-endings, tense-signs and mood-vowels seemed to them a great waste of their extremely precious time. And "Old Gess's humbuggery" was one of the mildest phrases with which free-spoken young gentlemen described these favorite teachings of the not yet famous Professor. There is a stage of many youthful minds when *omne ignotum pro magnifico* must be changed into *omne ignotum pro ridiculo*. And as we look back now we must not be too hard upon the boys, even as we remember in a kindly way the lad who amused himself at a crazy old gentleman blowing soap bubbles from a pipe, and watching them intently as they floated and burst, not knowing that Sir Isaac was studying Optics.

Had Dr. Harrison's life been less burdened with the overwhelming drudgery of elementary instruction, and had he been more favorably situated for publishing, it is believed that he would have taken an active and prominent part in the advancement of Comparative Etymology. He would have increased his slender knowledge of Sanskrit and Arabic, would have mastered the Turkish and Polish, into which he dipped with so much relish, and would have no longer been dependent for materials upon Bopp and Pott and the rest. But there was little time, no sympathy in all the wide land, and no possibility that writings of this sort could find sale outside of Germany. So he confined himself, as we have seen, to the application of Comparative Etymology to Latin and Greek. Most of the etymology, as well as the syntax, in his work on Latin Grammar was the result of his own studies. He himself distinctly says this, in a letter to Mr. Tutwiler, at the time of its appearance. Three or four years ago the book was shown by an American student to Professor Curtius, who is now at Leipzig, and stands at the head of all living scholars in Comparative Etymology. In returning it afterward he said, "This is a good book, an excellent book for the time at which it appeared; though, of course, we have got a good way beyond it by this time." The time at which it appeared was 1852. Had Curtius known that nearly all of the etymological portion, to which alone his attention was directed, had appeared in the earlier volume which Dr. Harrison printed for his class in 1839, only six years after Bopp's first part was published, and at least six years before Curtius himself made his first publication, he would, doubtless, have used still stronger language.

Dr. Harrison did not live to publish anything on Greek Grammar in general; but it is hardly necessary to say that he had made as careful application of Comparative Etymology to Greek as to Latin.

In the study of Syntax he was still more completely original. Here the material was at hand, for him as well as for others. His views of the subject were all thoroughly his own, were in some cases absolutely as well as relatively original, and were always of great practical value to the student who mastered them. The English and American Grammars existing during the greater part of his thirty years' work gave only empirical rules of syntax. The tendency of the German works on syntax, as most notably exemplified by Kühner, whose complete Greek Grammar appeared in 1834–35, was to construct *a priori* theories of syntax, and then ingeniously explain the facts of the language to suit the theory. Of late years, the English works have tended to be more philosophical, and the German to be more practical, than was then the case. Dr. Harrison constructed his system of syntax upon the true inductive method: he collected and compared the facts, analyzed and arranged them, and gradually worked his way back to such fundamental principles as seemed to comprehend them; then returning, he sought, by the help of these principles, to explain the facts as they occur, and so the process was complete. To his better pupils it was often delightful to see how completely he would explain the exact meaning of some obscure or uncommon expression by the application of the great and simple principles he had taught, and how satisfactorily these principles would guide them, when once really understood, through the task of composing in the languages studied.

Syntax is a high and difficult branch of metaphysics. In all metaphysical inquiries there is room for difference of opinion. It is not necessary to maintain that Hamilton is everywhere correct, in order to hold that his system is, in a high degree, able and instructive. And so here. Independent inquirers will, of course, differ as to various theories of syntax. Other views may seem to some of us better on this point or that, or even in general, and yet it may remain true that the system before us is eminently instructive and practically useful.

Besides the work on Latin Grammar, in Dr. Harrison's later treatise *On the Greek Prepositions and the Cases of Nouns with which they are used* (published in 1858), his truly philosophical, thoroughly inductive method of inquiry is, if possible, still more strikingly exhibited. It was a task of immense labor. Besides gathering from all existing collections, he often spent many days in hunting up, from Greek writers of every period, better examples, or new uses, of a certain preposition. Every particular use of it was carefully analyzed. Nothing was considered as settled by previous inquiry. Then, by gradual generalization, a theory was sought which, in the language often employed as to physical science, would "account for the phenomena." He was full of enthusiasm for his inquiries. A friend, who had some special sympathy with them, dropped in to dinner one day, and, when the doctor entered, he could scarce take time to say grace, before, in a voice tremulous and eager, he said: "I think I have found it, sir; I am almost sure I have got the true explanation of *meta* with the accusative in the sense of 'after.'" Beautiful enthusiasm! The would-be wise, the boastfully practical world will sneer. But there is hardly anything so much needed in America to-day, save honesty and the fear of God, as this very enthusiasm for pure science, as the spirit that will toil, no matter how long, to find out something, and will then break forth into its joyous *Eureka*, in the dear delight of added knowledge, not yet stopping to ask how far the discovery will be of practical utility. Heaven send us more of such men—not visionary dreamers, but sagacious, patient and enthusiastic inquirers after truth.

Dr. Harrison's books were both of them too difficult, and *The Greek Prepositions*, particularly, was too high above the ordinary range of classical studies in this country to become popular. They both paid expenses, the latter only because it was published by subscription. It was his purpose to publish elementary works, and refer the teachers and more advanced pupils who used them to these higher treatises. Many other plans he had—*e. g.*, to discuss the Greek Conjunctions as thoroughly as he had done the prepositions. Meantime, the two works have not been without gratifying recognition of their value. The Latin Grammar is still used in the University and some other institutions. *The Greek Prepositions* has been much employed by various students of

Biblical Philology. Bishop Ellicott, the foremost grammatical commentator in England, has spoken of it in high terms. Mr. George Long was deriving much practical help from it last year in the translation of a difficult Greek author. Dr. Addison Alexander, perhaps the leading scholar in Biblical learning that this country has yet produced, wrote to the author that he had read every word of both his works with unfailing interest and much profit; and this, though at the time he was not teaching either Latin or Greek. Dr. Alexander criticised the Latin Grammar as too condensed in style, too difficult for the ordinary student, and when the *Greek Prepositions* appeared, he said its style showed great improvement in this respect. Both statements were, no doubt, correct. Dr. Harrison's style of writing can scarcely be considered felicitous. In all his earlier publications, including the *Latin Grammar*, he aimed too much at compression, partly from the extreme desire to keep down the number of pages, through the well-grounded fear that books suited only to the higher class of students, and from a Southern author, would find but little sale. In the *Greek Prepositions* he indulged more in expansion and variety of statement; but here the nature of the subject, the very idea of five hundred octavo pages about Greek cases and prepositions, has restricted the volume to an extremely narrow circle of readers. Yet it may be questioned whether any book has ever appeared in America, if indeed any has appeared in Great Britain, that belongs to so elevated a plane of philological study, that so surely stamps its author as having been, in the department of philology, a great man. Would that the work might be so brought to the notice of true scholars in America and England as yet to find "fit audience, though few."

It may be added that as a lecturer Dr. Harrison's style, though peculiar and having obvious faults, was much better than in writing. He had not a ready command of expression; and his first statements of an idea were often partial, involved and obscure. But he perfectly knew—a thing not very common—when he had, and when he had not, made himself clear. He would try variety of expression, searching for the right word or phrase, would approach the thought from different directions, gradually closing in till he seized it; and when he reached his final expression it was vigorous, clear, complete. Then he would watch his audience with lively interest, and if he saw many clouded faces, would repeat his process, with all manner of illustration and iteration, till at last, the greater part of them could see clearly. This close observation of the class, this sympathy with their efforts to understand, and unwearied pains in helping them through difficulties, is one of the surest marks of the true teacher. He made constant use of the blackboard, often drawing quaint diagrams to assist the comprehension of the abstractions of syntax, and he enlivened attention by frequent and apparently spontaneous gushes of a homely humor, as racy as it was peculiar.

There is space for only brief mention of his work in other departments of the school. In his early years he devoted much study to Greek and Roman Geography and History, there being no text-books on those subjects that were at all satisfactory. In 1831 he was already laboriously rewriting his lectures on the Geography, constantly going to the original sources and finding Cramer, and even Mannert, to be full of blunders. In 1834, six years after he began, he printed in pamphlet form a condensed treatise on the *Geography of Ancient Italy and Southern Greece*, with outlines of the History, to be used as a text for his prelections. It had cost him great labor, and was full of valuable matter, but having designed it to be a mere syllabus, and expecting to lose money on the printing, he condensed too much, and it was, doubtless, hard work to pull the classes through it. This is the old story as to all higher instruction in history and geography. Without the details, one has difficulty in making it interesting, and for the details there is no time. To overcome these difficulties requires a specific talent, which Dr. Harrison did not in a high degree possess. In later years he spent less time in teaching Ancient Geography, but he always insisted much on the importance of Geography to the study of History, and took pains to point out those physical peculiarities of Italy and Greece which manifestly contributed to form the character of the people and to shape their history—a view comparatively unfamiliar at that time, and which, to some of his pupils, was full of interest and inspiration. In History he seized at the outset upon the ideas of Niebuhr, and even in the first half of his career made a great impression upon at least a few minds, though greatly hindered by the lack of a text-book. In the latter half he was cheered and assisted by the appearance of *Arnold's Rome* and *Grote's Greece*, followed by manuals not ill-suited to the wants of his classes. There was then in the University no Professor of History in general, and many remember as an epoch in their lives the views of history and the enthusiasm for its study which they derived from Dr. Harrison.

As to the æsthetic appreciation and enjoyment of classic literature, he felt an exceeding desire that his students should attain to this in the highest possible degree. Though not himself a literary artist, he had an intense love of the beautiful, in nature, in art and in literature. When he paused to remark upon the beauty of a passage, it was with a contagious enjoyment; and he would sometimes read a choral ode with rare felicity of tone and expression. Yet there was comparatively little of this, for several reasons. He regarded the cultivation of the intellectual powers which is derived from the philosophical study of language as more important than the cultivation of taste; and, embarrassed by lack of time and the deficient preparation of his pupils, he did mainly that which he thought most needful, and which best accorded with his own predominant tendencies of mind. He thought that for the student to gain for himself, through his own comprehension of the original, some glimpses of the charms of classic literature, was more suggestive and inspiring than to hear or read much eloquent description and eulogy of those charms from others; and he probably underrated the value of mere information concerning the classic writers and writings as tending to awaken interest. Besides, he was working for the future. He once said to a Greek class, "Gentlemen, I have no doubt the time will come in the University when some happy professor will ask his class, as a preparation for his next lecture, to read over a certain book of Herodotus, or oration of Demosthenes, or play of Sophocles, and they will readily do it." That was his notion of what would prepare students for hearing lectures on the literature.

One thing remains to this account of Dr. Harrison's University career, viz.: to speak of the part which he took in the discipline and general management. Mr. Jefferson's policy had proposed the largest liberty to the students, and most of his English professors, in accordance with the usage at the English universities, were inclined to take little account of the student's private life, caring only for his lessons and examinations. This soon led to license and riot, even during the first session; and the tendency then arose to react toward the opposite and familiar extreme of strict control and constant interference. The result was that for a number of years the University passed through sore trials. Very few of the young men were at that time controlled by religious principle, not a few were vicious and violent, parental influence and example were often injudicious, if not positively bad, while the discipline kept varying, according to the conflicting or changing opinions of chairman, faculty and board, between the extremes of laxity and severity. Dr. Harrison was, in his second session, violently assailed by a student who had formerly been his fellow-student, and would not tolerate rebuke from him. Ten years later a dismissed student attacked him with brutal violence, and another young man, who had been a student the previous session, entered his study with weapons displayed, and with the most abusive language threatened his life. By degrees there was a change; the character of the students improved, and the views of the authorities became modified. The general tone of society was rising. Christian influences became active in the University, and gradually strengthened. In 1833 a chaplain was appointed, an eloquent Methodist preacher, chiefly through the influence and exertions of Dr. Harrison, who had joined the Methodist Church a year before, and was the only professor of religion in the Faculty. Slowly things grew better, varying much according to the personal character of the chairman. Mr. Jefferson's scheme had been that each of the professors should be chairman for one year in regular rotation. This was soon altered into the plan of selecting, according to supposed fitness and willingness to serve, for one or two years, but never more than two without interruption. In this way Dr. Harrison was chairman from 1837 to 1839, and then, passing over a year, from 1840 to 1842, with what special results it is not known. In the next few years there were great disturbances. In 1845–46 that singularly good and judicious man, Mr. Courtney, was chairman. It is believed by the present senior professor that to Mr. Courtney is especially due the honor of clearly perceiving that the discipline had been passing from one extreme to the other and that a different course must be adopted, not exactly seeking the golden mean, but seeking the combination of liberty and law. On this subject Mr. Courtney often anxiously conferred with Dr. Cabell and Dr. Harrison. Whoever it may have been that first clearly perceived all this, it was Dr. Harrison who carried it into execution, and gradually established as the policy of the university that method of discipline which need not be here particularly described, because it still exists, and in judicious hands, together with the growing improvement in the average character of our homes and our youth, is attended now by such admirable results. Of course, it was the Faculty as a whole that made the change, and the Chairman could have done nothing save as sustained by at least a majority of his colleagues. But the Chairman bore the brunt, worked out the ideas, proved a different kind of discipline to be practicable. Dr. Harrison was made Chairman in 1847, with no thought of serving more than one or two years; but again and again it was urged upon him, pressed upon him, almost forced upon him, and toward the last sorely against his will. The venerable Rector, Mr. Joseph C. Cabell, and other eminent visitors, would personally entreat him to continue in the office. And so he served seven years, a thing then quite without precedent, and was at last most unwillingly allowed by the Board to resign. Though he doubtless made mistakes in opinion and in action, yet his general course as Chairman cannot be described otherwise than as eminently wise and successful; and it gained for him a very general and high admiration, both within and without the University. But when the number of students had reached three, four and five hundred, the duties of Chairman, added to those of Professor of both Latin and Greek, became excessively burdensome, especially for a man extremely accommodating and self-sacrificing, and full of kind feeling toward all youths who were not radically bad, a man who worked slowly through details and never slighted anything if he could help it, and a man who believed that it was far better to dispose of difficulties without formal action of the Faculty whenever that was possible.

This brings us to speak of the circumstances which finally led Dr. Harrison to withdraw from the University. Through all his career he had groaned under the burden of what he felt to be excessive and often unsatisfying labor. As has just been said, he naturally worked slowly. He had, too, an extreme desire to do things with thoroughness, to examine for himself every part of every subject with which he dealt. Receiving students in general very ill prepared, he could not raise the standard of classical scholarship save by submitting to much grievous drudgery in the correction of written exercises, and to the loss of time in reading with extra classes, etc. When the number of students rose to several hundred, and his own school, from having been one of the smallest for the first few years, became one of the largest in the University, the burden of correcting exercises became intolerable. In 1851 an assistant instructor was given him, especially to aid in the exercises, and a similar arrangement made for Mathematics and Modern Languages. In 1855 his school was divided and he chose the chair of Latin; but now without an assistant, it being, in fact, peculiarly difficult to make the plan of assistants work well in the ancient languages.

Another difficulty which pressed upon him was that of inadequate support. It had been thought necessary to limit the salaries of the professors to $3,000; and, with the diminished value of money through the influx of California gold and other causes, Dr. Harrison found this insufficient for the maintenance of a very large and necessarily expensive family. Most of his children were still to be educated, many of them quite young. He could not teach them himself, could make no satisfactory and permanent arrangement for having them taught at home, and had not the means of sending them to boarding-schools. He was oppressed to find that, while working so hard, he could not lay by a dollar, and could not secure the education of his younger children. His life-long friend and correspondent in Alabama had long before left the professor's chair to take charge of a boarding-school for boys, and had found it very profitable and not excessively unpleasant. Dr. Harrison thought of taking the same course, that he might educate his younger children himself, and might make some pecuniary provision for the future. He also thought that, in connection with the conduct of such a school, he could prepare elementary works in Latin and Greek, which would bring his elaborate treatises into greater demand, and pave the way for executing his yet higher schemes of authorship. Accordingly, in 1856, he arranged for the purchase of a plantation beyond Monticello, and proposed to resign his professorship. The idea excited universal regret and consternation among the friends of the University, for he was now widely famous and greatly admired. Finding that his great concern was for his family, the Board of Visitors proposed to remove, in his case, the limit upon salary, and give him the whole proceeds of his school. He shrank from such a discrimination as on many accounts undesirable, but urged to it by members of the Board and generous colleagues, who insisted that his long-continued and eminently useful services to the University entitled him to the distinction, he consented to remain, to the great joy of the students and the country. Some of the Visitors, however, were dissatisfied with what had been done, and procured, in 1857, the passage of a resolution that the arrangement which had been made with Dr. Harrison was not of the nature of a contract. He considered that it was, as the Board had themselves proposed it, had thereby induced him to withdraw his resignation, and had made no reserve or limitation at the time. The consequence was that unpleasant feelings arose between him and certain prominent members of the Board, and some efforts to remove the difficulty only increased it. The question who was right and who was wrong is not a proper one to be here discussed. The University has need of the united support of all her sons, and those who think they have something to forgive in the past ought, for her sake, to be forgiving. In 1859 Dr. Harrison thought himself compelled, in self-respect, to resign, having been professor in the University for thirty-one years.

Though not now wholly unexpected, his resignation caused the greatest grief. The students of the session presented him, on the Public Day, a service of plate, and no one who was present can forget his reply—so simple and sincere, with so much of tender regard for them and for the University, and of unaffected humility and delicacy.

The rest of the story may be briefly told. His school for boys for the first year, in the upper part of this county, was very successful and profitable, though the conduct and profits of the boarding department pertained to another. In 1860 he purchased a plantation in Nelson County, and made extensive arrangements, beginning with one hundred scholars, and with very bright prospects in almost every respect. His old pupils in Virginia and the Gulf States were eager to put their sons under his charge. But for the war, he could hardly have failed of signal success. He was only fifty-three years old, and apparently in very firm health. He was full of enthusiasm for his new undertaking, was relieved by at least a change of burdens, his early love of country life was gratified, and he had many proofs of such wide-spread esteem and appreciation throughout the South as has seldom fallen to the lot of an American professor. But for the war-cloud which was rising in the horizon, he would have enjoyed, in that autumn of 1860, no ordinary measure of happiness. But before the session ended the war had begun. Half his pupils had left, the rest found it very difficult to pursue their daily tasks, and the collections for the session could not be made. Having incurred heavy pecuniary liabilities for the plantation and the buildings, he could not but feel grave perplexity and apprehension. His greatest trouble was, as he wrote to his bosom friend, Tutwiler, that he could not make a contribution of money to the government at Richmond, as he had hoped to do. But he was thankful that he had three or four sons who would enter the army. He was intensely interested in the struggle. Having opposed separate secession as impolitic, he yet fully believed in the justice of the Southern cause in general. And while wise enough to foresee, as so many among us did not, that the conflict would be protracted and terrible, he declares, in strong terms, that it must be fought through.

In the autumn of 1861 he opened a third session, and pupils were not wanting. But pecuniary difficulties, deep concern for the country, and yearning anxiety as to the welfare, in body and soul, of his sons who were in the army, together with the labor of teaching, told upon his health. He did not seem to be sick, but his appetite became capricious, and he appeared to be depressed. Late in the autumn one of his sons was brought home very ill with camp-fever, and continued ill for several months. The father insisted on nursing him. He was a singularly good nurse for the sick, a thing rare among *men*, and a not unimportant indication of character. In the trying spring season, toiling all day as a teacher and oppressed with many cares, he would spend the night in watching beside the sick-bed. He had never known what it was to spare himself when there was a demand for toil and sacrifice, and, notwithstanding remonstrances, he continued this course. The youth was very ill, and it is believed that his life was saved by this faithful, tender and skilful nursing. But in so doing, alas! the father laid down his own life. He became sick with a disease obscure at the time, but, no doubt, a modification of the fever from which his son was beginning to recover. He would not stay in bed, but would lie, with a weary yet patient look, on the lounge, and the family had no idea how ill he was. One morning there came suddenly a violent chill, and he lay unable to speak. He looked longingly at his wife and children, strove vainly to speak, then turned his gazing eyes straight up to heaven, and in a little while he was gone. This was the 7th of April, 1862, when he was not yet fifty-five years old.

Some traits of Dr. Harrison's character have appeared in the course of this narrative, but it will be proper, in conclusion, to speak of his character in general.

For nothing was he more remarkable than his robust common sense. He applied this not merely to common things, but to his philological studies. The inductive method of inquiry means common sense, as opposed to mere speculative theorizing. A person who had a right to speak so familiarly once asked Dr. Harrison how he had gained his original views of syntax. He answered that he knew of nothing peculiar in his methods, unless it were that he tried to study language in a plain, common-sense way. Along with this, or rather as a part of it, he had a very sound judgment. When he thoroughly understood a question and had patiently considered it, his judgment was exceedingly apt to be correct. Of course he had his prejudices, of course he sometimes erred, but those who knew him best learned to have the greatest confidence in his judgment. His examination of all questions, in study or in practical life, was marked by patient thinking, that sublimest of intellectual virtues; and his studies were all conducted with the steady industry which ought to be so common, but is so rare, which is the condition of accurate scholarship, of all substantial and symmetrical knowledge. It is true that, in apparent contrast with these qualities, he appeared given to procrastination. But for this there were causes not implying a lack of industry or perseverance. From the beginning, as we have seen, he was overworked. The tendency of the University system, with its independent schools, is to stimulate every professor to do his utmost. The great lack of preparation in ancient languages, and the professor's extreme desire to raise the standard, had led him to excessive labor. Though careful of his health in many respects, he almost constantly denied himself the requisite sleep, and thus lived a little below par as to physical vigor—a state of things which always inclines one to postpone his more difficult tasks. But the chief cause was, that working slowly, and constitutionally incapable of doing anything superficially, he never felt himself to be fully ready, as for the composition of an important report, or the immediate preparation of a lecture, and, in the hope of more thoroughly mastering the subject, he would delay as long as possible. Meantime, this delaying tended to become habitual, and interruptions from without multiplied upon him, until, in his later years, his report as chairman was rarely written and his examination papers hardly ever read till the last moment. This habit of postponement—it was not exactly what we call procrastination—was the subject with him of much regret and self-condemnation. Whether the explanations which have been offered be correct or not, it is certain that, notwithstanding the habit in question, he exhibited a very high degree of patient industry.

Dr. Harrison was a man of great courage, both physical and moral. The present senior professor says he has seen no man with a larger measure of moral courage; that he was as unflinching as a rock. He had an unutterable contempt for sham and pretentiousness, and himself never failed to speak and act with sincerity and candor. His generosity of nature was conspicuous, not merely in the ordinary sense of that term, but in the broadest sense. He once remarked, in speaking confidentially of another person, that a man is not fitted to be a professor unless he has a generous soul; that however plausible his exterior, he will not long continue to win the confidence and affection of the best young men if there is any meanness in his make. That beautiful delicacy which we so much admire in women—delicate consideration for the feelings of others, and delicate tact in sparing their feelings, even when something difficult or painful has to be said—was constantly seen in Dr. Harrison's conversation and actions. In his family relations it was simply charming. In dealing with students who had misbehaved, he often showed true delicacy by perfect directness of speech. His first assistant instructor was a member of his family and occupied a study adjoining his own, with the door between them left open. It thus happened that he frequently heard the Chairman talking to some fellow who had been summoned before him for misconduct. It was really beautiful to see the straightforward, downright, and yet perfectly kind fashion, in which he talked. It constantly reminded one of a skilful physician probing a wound —prompt, steady, effectual, and thus most truly kind.

For warmth of affection to kindred and many cherished friends, for singular unselfishness and the readiest self-sacrifice, Dr. Harrison was also very remarkable. To give his life for that of his son was but to act out the character he had always exhibited. His daughters—and that is one test of a man's character—regarded him not with mere ordinary filial admiration and affection, but with an unutterable reverence, and, at the same time, a passionate fondness. He was their oracle, and yet approached with perfect freedom and familiarity. His sympathies were as prompt and tender as a woman's, and it was natural and became habitual for all his kindred and friends to go to him when in trouble, seeking sympathy and counsel, and never seeking in vain. Nor did he wait to be sought. If a family just arrived felt awkward and uncomfortable in their new circumstances, he would comprehend their situation and relieve their constraint by delicate attentions and pleasantries of conversation. If a foreigner without introduction was slighted and suspected, and yet seemed to have good in him, Dr. Harrison would take pains to give him countenance. When wounded United States soldiers were brought to the University after the first battle of Manassas, and some people in the first flush of indignation were inclined to shrink from them, Dr. Harrison, who happened to be on a visit here at the time, and who was intensely Southern, went promptly and repeatedly to their dormitories, caring for their wounds and reading to them from the Bible.

He had a deep and quiet love of nature. He would say that it "rested him" to look upon the beautiful landscape around us—a landscape which they who have travelled most widely will most warmly admire, which is really a means of education to susceptible students, and which the alumni ought long ago to have invested with the charms of poetry and romance. He was especially fond of flowers, long cultivating the flower-garden with his own hands; not inclined to talk largely about flowers, but just quietly enjoying them. He was the first person who purchased rare roses at a distance and brought them here. And with equal interest, while taking his occasional long walks in the mountains around, he would dig up wild flowers and bring them home to plant. One of these wild flowers is still standing in the garden he loved to till. Akin to this was his fondness for pictures. Unable, of course, to gather paintings, he greatly delighted in choice engravings, and the purchase of costly illustrated books was perhaps his only extravagance. His older children remember what a happiness it was to stand by his side and look at Kaulbach's striking pictures to Goethe's Reineke Fuchs, or at Retzsch's Outlines of Shakespeare, or of Schiller's Bell, while he told the stories with enthusiasm and joyous abandon. Music, too, he dearly loved. Some of his children had rare musical talent, and he spared no expense upon their training; and in those musical evenings which they and their neighbors or visitors would unite to brighten, he would listen with rapt attention and delicious enjoyment. As a matter of Christian duty, but also from the pleasure he found in music of every kind, he was always ready, however busy, to attend the choir meetings in preparation for the chapel worship. And in those dear

Sunday evenings after service, which can never be forgotten, if he could sometimes be induced to read a favorite hymn, there was a rhythmical charm about the reading which came from a familiarity with the Odes of Sophocles, and a devotional sweetness and simplicity born of deep Christian experience.

For Gessner Harrison was a fervently devout Christian. His early letters to his friend and Christian brother show many struggles; but he had taken his position, was resolved to persevere, and gradually made progress. In later life, with no loud professions, he was always outspoken as a Christian, ready for every good word and work, and making the impression upon all, and most deeply upon those who knew him best, that religion was the strength of his life.

With such abilities and attainments, and such a character, it is not strange that Dr. Harrison so powerfully impressed himself upon his pupils. Not only the hundreds of those who are now professors or other teachers, but many who are occupied with matters widely remote from Latin and Greek, are still constantly recalling his favorite ideas and characteristic expressions, and, what is of more consequence, their minds have taken shape and their characters borrowed tone from his influence. In every grade of teaching it is perhaps even more important to consider what your teacher is than what he knows.

Two years more and it will be fifty years since the University of Virginia was opened. In this checkered half-century it has achieved results which, considering all the difficulties of the situation, form a just occasion for wonder and rejoicing. A truly great institution of learning cannot be created in a short time. It must grow: must gradually form its atmosphere, gather its associations, hand down its honored names and inspiring traditions. The life we have been considering is, perhaps, more closely connected than any other with the history of this University and the constitution of its prestige. But Gessner Harrison is only one of many noble men who have spent their strength in advancing its usefulness and building up its reputation. The noblest legacy they have left us is this—that the very genius of the place is *work*. No professor nor student of susceptible soul can establish himself here without feeling that there breathes through all the air this spirit of work—a noble rage for knowing and for teaching. This is the glory and the power of the institution which boasts so many illustrious names among its Visitors, its Faculty and its Alumni. And let it be the last word spoken to-day concerning Gessner Harrison, spoken, as it were, in his name to the professors and the students of the University he loved so well—Sirs, brothers, FEAR GOD AND WORK.

XVIII.

SCIENCE AND CHRISTIANITY.*

AN eminent man of science who is a church-member and a decided and outspoken Christian presents by no means the unusual spectacle that some persons suppose. A certain class of writers and speakers seem really to have persuaded themselves that a new "irrepressible conflict" has arisen between science and Christianity, and that he who is a friend to the one must be an enemy to the other. The ground of this persuasion is not far to seek. Some men have thought they saw in the real or supposed results of scientific research a new means of attacking Christianity, to which they were commonly opposed on other accounts, and have very naturally been anxious to associate with their inferences and speculations the dignity and prestige which so justly belong to science. And then certain unwise defenders of Christianity have rushed to the rescue, and instead of attacking the unwarranted applications and assumptions of their opponents, have committed the

---

* Dr. J. Lawrence Smith, of Louisville, after receiving a great variety of scientific honors in Europe and at home, was in 1879 made a corresponding member of the French Institute, Academy of Science, the highest scientific distinction in the world, and one which few Americans have attained. On his return home, many eminent citizens of Louisville made a banquet in his honor; and, in response to a toast, "The Church," the following address was delivered. Dr. Smith had long been an active and useful member of the Walnut Street Baptist Church, and so continued until his lamented death in 1883.

stupendous blunder of attacking science itself. Amid the din of their conflict it is hardly strange if some have supposed that there must be war to the knife between all Christians and all men of science.

But meantime most of us are entirely peaceful. Certainly a very distinguished representative of physical science and a very humble representative of Christianity have sat side by side this evening in all peace and amity. A large proportion of the foremost scientific men of the age, in Europe and America, are known believers in Christianity, and not a few are, like our honored guest, ready on all suitable occasions to advocate its claims. And, on the other hand, the great mass of really intelligent Christians everywhere are warm friends of science, whether physical or metaphysical, linguistic or historical, social, political or religious science. Why should it not be so? The very essence of Christianity is light; its very life-blood is truth; error and ignorance are among its greatest foes; and all true knowledge, however misconceived and misapplied for a time, is in reality its friend and helper, and sooner or later will be so acknowledged.

Let all cultivated men try to repress this mistaken notion of antagonism. Physical science has its own great field, its grand achievements and a possible future which no man can now imagine; but there are facts of existence which its processes cannot explain or even detect. Men devoted to experiment and demonstration sometimes grow one-sided, as we are all prone to do, and deny all that does not come within their range. But physical science necessarily fails to account for our sense of right and wrong, our quenchless longings after immortality, our invincible belief in the Almighty, All-wise and All-loving. Our loftiest thought remains always a fragment till it finds completeness in the thought of Him; and our hearts—strange hearts, so strong and yet so weak, with joys so sweet and griefs so bitter—our hearts can know no rest save as they rest in Him.

Mr. Chairman and gentlemen, you have meant to show respect for the Church, the aggregate of avowed Christians. There are two things which I think that Christians ought, in our day and country, especially to propose to themselves and to urge on all around them. One is that we must all strive to combine the highest, broadest Christian charity with firm attachment to truth and fidelity to honest convictions. It is one of the practical problems of our age to combine these, not sacrificing either to the other. And the second thing: At a time when political and social evils spread so wide and strike so deep, when some men who are not foolish despair of the republic, and some despair of society, and some ask whether life is worth living, it becomes us indeed fearlessly to point out the faults of our current Christianity, that they may be mended; but it becomes us also to conserve and maintain the legitimate influence of Christianity over all classes of our population. Let all men beware how they speak the word that is to lessen that influence. Things are bad enough with us as it is; they would be far worse if that influence were destroyed. But let us hope that amid the mutations and reactions of human affairs, and under the control of that Divine Providence at the thought of which we all bow in reverence, there may be an increase of living Christian faith and genuine Christian morality, of real education and enlightened patriotism, that will bring better and brighter days for us and for our children.

XIX.

FUNERAL SERMON FOR GEORGE W. RIGGAN, D.D.,

Assistant Professor in the Southern Baptist Theological Seminary, Louisville, Ky. April 20, 1885.

For none of us liveth to himself, and none dieth to himself. For whether we live, we live unto the Lord; or whether we die, we die unto the Lord: whether we live, therefore, or die, we are the Lord's.—Romans xiv. 7-8.

SO then, both in living and in dying, we are the Lord's. We gladly regard ourselves as belonging to the Lord. (1) Because he made us, and made all that environment which renders life pleasant to us. (2) Because he redeemed us, and ever liveth to intercede for us—" that they which live should no longer live unto themselves, but unto him who for their sakes died and rose again." (3) Because he will judge us—" for we must all be made manifest before the judgment seat of Christ."

And we joyfully yield ourselves to his service. (1) Because he has use for us. It seems a wonderful thing, men and brethren, that the divine almightiness should have use for our poor human weakness, that the divine holiness should condescend to use us who are sinful; but he does have use for us, we can be of service to the Lord. (2) Because he helps us to be useful. Here lies the consolation—a consolation greatly needed by the strongest and best of men, a consolation all-sufficing when we most deeply feel our weakness. (3) Because he can determine better than we, in what ways we shall be most useful. He knows whether it is best for us to labor in one part of his vineyard or another, in one or another sphere and method of Christian exertion. Two weeks ago, when our beloved one last preached, his morning subject was the parable of the talents. And the Master knows whether we can best serve him with five talents, or two, or one—yea, whether by a long life, crowded with efforts to do good, or by what will seem to men a too early death.

There are two ways to regard the question of living or dying. From the human side, from the standpoint of personal choice and responsibility, we naturally and rightly wish and strive to live. The Bible does not at all teach the contrary, but emphasizes the joy of living, when we live unto the Lord; helps us to see clearly the real duties of life; and offers us divine assistance in performing them. But considered from the providential side, the Bible teaches us to regard life and death alike with submission and contentment. When it becomes clearly the will of Providence that we shall not have a prolonged life, then we may calmly accept an early death, because in either case we are the Lord's, he is dealing with us according to his own wisdom, and we leave it for him to determine how we shall glorify him best.

When a Christian who has become conscious of unusual native powers, who has seen Providence favor his earnest exertions to develop those powers, has rejoiced in beginning to use them, with vigor, energy, enthusiasm, for the benefit of mankind and for the glory of Christ, has sometimes felt great leaps of heart at the thought of becoming widely and grandly useful—when such a Christian finds himself about to die early, he must naturally desire that his death, as well as his brief life, should prove of some benefit to those who outlive him. We know not whether amid the fancies of a disordered brain our brother had any consciousness that he was drawing near to death; but we know how it would have been with him if thus conscious; and we must earnestly strive, in reliance upon the Divine blessing, to make his early death, and the story of his life and character, an occasion of profitable reflection and wholesome impulse.

The life of Dr. Riggan would not be called eventful, though it involved great changes. He was born thirty years ago, the 22d of February, and, probably by reason of his birthday, was called George Washington. His early life was spent in Isle of Wight County, Va., not far from Norfolk, as the son of a poor widow. The very little that is known gives glimpses of a situation not unlike that which five years ago became matter of national interest. The family had not always been so poor. When the little boy was eight years old, the servants all ran away with the invading army. The father had died several years before, and the family were now apprehensive for the future. There were daughters, and one older son, who died when nearly grown. Sometimes as the child nestled in his mother's arms at night, she would say that if she lived to be old, there would be no one to care for her but him; and then he would make a child's passionate promises. He had already been attending a neighborhood school. After the war, when public schools were established, he went to them. God be thanked for these schools, at which the children of struggling poverty can find opportunity of education. At the age of thirteen he spent a year in a lonely country store, sleeping there without protection; and at fourteen he became a boatman, and continued to work for some three years, first on the oyster-ships and afterwards as regular seaman on a trading-vessel. He once mentioned to a friend that he had at that period associated with some of the rudest and vilest of mankind. There is reason to believe that he bore the moral trial better than the physical trial. It was a life of great exposure, and during winter, in bringing up and handling the objects of their industry amid wet and cold and storm, a life of great hardship and often of intense suffering. It seems likely that during this period his constitution received a shock, which told on his subsequent history. At the age of seventeen, after being drenched by stormy waves during a hot fever, the lad abandoned this manner of life, at his mother's earnest entreaty, and years afterwards once expressed gratitude for the providential affliction which had led to this decision.

We presently hear of him as spending ten months in the school of Rev. J. W. Ward, a Baptist minister of that vicinity, winning marked distinction as a student, and afterwards as teaching some months. He had become a Christian shortly before abandoning his boat-life, and the church at Smithfield afterwards testified that already at the age of sixteen he was an earnest member and gave promise of usefulness. When eighteen years old he went to Richmond, where one of his sisters was living, and sought employment. After being specially encouraged to expect appointment as upper teacher in the public schools, he suddenly found that it was not to be so. He had a year or two before determined to become a minister, and desired to teach in order to obtain means of going to college, and preparing himself for that work. The session at Richmond College was now just beginning, but he had almost no means. He sought advice from Dr. J. R. Garlick, whose ministry he had been attending at Leigh Street, and who probably saw the light in the youth's beautiful eyes, for he encouraged him to enter Richmond College and trust to Providence. The Education Board, which has nobly aided so many worthy young men, gave him its assistance, upon the recommendation of Mr. Ward and the Smithfield Church. The Leigh Street Church, of which he soon after became a member, helped him from time to time. Mr. Ward and others of his early friends sent some contributions; and his mother, from her straitened means and personal exertions, furnished money towards paying the entrance fees to the College. A Baptist merchant in Richmond who has recently died, told me with some pride a couple of years ago that he had given the youth employment in the late afternoon or evening, first as a messenger and afterwards in writing up his books—and added that he always believed George would come to something. After the first session he found some employment in colportage, and afterwards in preaching; and during his last sessions was supporting himself by regular preaching to churches in the vicinity of Richmond.

At Richmond College he spent five years. The elective method of education, which is there consistently pursued, presents great advantages to a student whose preparation has been incomplete and irregular. He could work up the elements of knowledge in various departments under the personal instruction of the able professors, and amid all the stimulus of college associations. But the liberty of choice proved a snare to him, as it sometimes does in our Seminary, by encouraging him to attempt too many subjects in a single session. Fond of study, ambitious, and quite destitute of means, he took twice as many classes as most students, and yet was resolutely bent on doing all the work well. A brief diary shows that already during the first and second sessions he was repeatedly ill, and conscious of overwork. But it is very easy for an ambitious youth under such circumstances to persuade himself that excessive exertion is justifiable. He early became conscious of possessing unusual power. There was always observable in him a curious blending of timidity and self-reliance, of modesty and pride. Certainly the professors soon began to notice that here was a youth of great promise. To observe and assist the development of promising youth is a teacher's greatest delight. Mr. Riggan was specially distinguished in Mathematics and Moral Philosophy, but his attainments in the Classics were also remarkably accurate and solid. At the end of five years he was declared Master of Arts, which in Richmond College is a degree rarely obtained, and a sure proof of broad and thorough education. He gained also about all the medals and other distinctions that the college offered.

And so in 1878, at the age of twenty-three, he came to our Theological Seminary, specially commended in a private letter from one of the Professors as a man of whom they had very high hopes. His Seminary course showed superior powers, laborious thoroughness, unflinching application. He was far above the thought that high talent and general excellence will make amends for occasional negligence and inaccuracy in details. I remember that there seemed to me but one mistake in his three years' work. He spent too much time in preaching, often at a great distance, and involving absence from Saturday morning to Monday night. Meantime his work as a student must be thoroughly done, and he preached with consuming earnestness; and so his health suffered, and during the second session he was sometimes taken ill, and began to look worn. I remonstrated with him, and he simply replied that he was sure it was his duty. Years afterwards I learned incidentally that these desperate exertions were made from a desire to aid his now aged mother. He was young and felt strong, he remembered the passionate promises of his childhood to care for her in old age, and he would arouse himself when jaded and feeble by asking his conscience whether those promises had been fulfilled.

Before Mr. Riggan became a "full graduate" of the Seminary, in 1881, it was decided to make him assistant instructor in Hebrew, Greek and Homiletics. After two years of good work he was appointed assistant professor.

During nearly five years he has served as pastor of the Forks of Elkhorn Church, in Woodford County, some miles beyond Frankfort, preaching two Sundays in the month, and spending a good part of every vacation in that pleasant neighborhood.

Let us turn now to consider our brother's character. He had an acute and powerful intellect. A highly intelligent gentleman in the church of which he was pastor has said that he thought Dr. Riggan possessed the finest intellect he had ever known. It was a mind that always strove to reach the bottom of things, to discern principles and causes. His sermons often seemed too metaphysical for popular acceptance; and they would have been regarded by many as "dry," but for other qualities to be presently mentioned. His thinking was studiously clear, and he patiently sought clear and adequate expression. He had great argumentative power, and loved to exercise it in conversation as well as in public discourse. A year ago he published two long articles in the *Religious Herald* upon a current question of Old Testament criticism, in which was shown quite extraordinary power of seizing available points for defense and refutation, and of driving the argument home by a quick succession of vigorous blows. These articles were widely read with great satisfaction, and declared by some persons to be about the best newspaper articles they had ever seen. It was probably these that specially stirred the Trustees of Richmond College to recall his early promise and his rapid development and unusual distinction, and to signalize their appreciation by conferring upon him at the age of twenty-nine the honorary degree of Doctor of Divinity. It may be added that while fully in sympathy with the spirit of progress, and eagerly examining all living questions, Dr. Riggan was unwaveringly convinced of the truth of those opinions which are established among Baptists concerning the authority of Scripture and the Theology which Scripture exhibits.

He was a man of intense earnestness, readily blazing into enthusiasm. This contagious earnestness made people listen to his most metaphysical discussions. This blazing enthusiasm kindled a glowing sympathy in his congregations and his classes. I have often passed his lecture-room near the close of the hour and heard him speaking of the form or meaning of some Hebrew word with a vehemence of tone, an impassioned effort to explain and convince, which to many thoughtless persons would have seemed almost ludicrous, but which to his classes invested the driest details with lively interest, and stirred susceptible students to some corresponding zeal and endeavor. Whatever is worth teaching at all is worth teaching well; and there is no really good teaching without an enthusiastic interest in the subject, and a passionate desire to give the pupil all possible assistance.

Both in literature and life he exhibited a just taste. His College and Seminary course had rendered his literary taste decidedly severe, so that he inclined to despise the ornamental in style. This extreme tendency was yielding to further literary knowledge and experience. He highly appreciated the benefits of literary culture. Last fall he delivered to the class in Homiletics, during the Professor's absence, a couple of lectures upon Tennyson's "In Memoriam," the finest religious poem of our century. He had been reading the life of Frederick Denison Maurice, and undertook to depict those religious tendencies and longings with which Tennyson has dealt in the poem, as well as to awaken admiration for its literary art. The lectures kindled quite an enthusiasm in the class, and upon subsequently reading the rough notes one was not surprised at the effect. His preliminary criticism of the student's sermons, afterwards reviewed by the Professor, were from the beginning vigorous and helpful, and showed every year more of sympathetic insight, and of sound judgment and taste.

He was deeply conscientious. The fragments of diary kept while a college student show that he made conscience of all his daily life. His self-reproach at what many would consider trifling failures in duty reveals that sensitiveness of conscience which sometimes blends in such beautiful harmony with lofty ambition and energetic will.

He was a man of unselfish and generous spirit, of a kindly and affectionate disposition. Singularly modest he was, while so strong in convictions and in will; very discreet, too, in all deportment, while so impulsive and excitable; always ready to sacrifice himself to others, though full of ambition to make the most of his own powers. Hence he was greatly beloved by the students, who showed a beautiful pride in their young professor, a marked interest in what he taught, and readiness to do the work he requested. His colleagues regarded him with warm personal friendship, and all their intercourse and co-operation has been in the highest degree harmonious and delightful. In the interesting country church of which he was pastor he had come to be well known by summer residence, and in his case to be well known was to be warmly loved. An eminent physician who is a member of the church, upon hearing of the young pastor's illness, left home and practice behind, and coming to his temporary abode, some miles from Louisville, spent night and day in unremitting attention to the end; while other gentlemen of the church left large agricultural interests at this busy season, and came seventy miles to see if they could give assistance. Several students also vied with each other in going out to watch at his bedside. In this Broadway church to which he belonged he was becoming every year more widely known, notwithstanding the somewhat timid reserve of his manner, and was recognized as a power for good, and a brother to be loved. Of his home life I may not venture to speak. But it may be stated that his wife's venerable mother, prostrate with sickness and grief, rose passionately on her couch to say, "Ah! you gentlemen did not know him as I did. You, sir, were warmly his friend, I know you were, but you did not know him as I did. Ah! what a good son he was to me, and what a good husband to my daughter!"

Let us reflect, before we close, upon some special lessons of this sad hour.

Here is encouragement to struggling youth. The son of a poor widow, the toiling and suffering lad on the oyster-boats, rose in a few years after opening manhood to be the companion of scholars, the admiration of pupils and a power in the pulpit and the press. Far and wide over the land to-day are children of poverty, capable of developing into great power for good, if only they can receive the necessary stimulus, encouragement and aid. Happy those who generously endow institutions of higher learning, where struggling youth may find the best teaching without cost. Happy those who discern early signs of promise in one and another of the youth whom they encounter, and are quick to give the cheering word and the helping hand. We cannot but regret that this bright and inspiring example of what ambitious youth may hope to achieve amid difficulties, should be dimmed by so early a death. Yet far better even thus than to have lived inglorious, undeveloped, inefficient, through many years. Better to blaze and flame and set things on fire through a little time, than to smoulder long without power to warm or illumine, and then die unnoticed and unknown.

Here is a lesson as to prudent care of bodily health. A man of ardent nature, impulsive, enthusiastic and resolute enough to become a notable force in the world, will always find it hard to control himself and keep within the conditions of physical health. A man who grew up in the country, amid active employments and bracing air, and comes to live in a city, is very apt to err as to the matter of bodily exercise. The great majority of our leading business men, as well as professional men, in all the cities have come from the country, and they are all in danger of making this mistake. In our country life bodily exercise came as the unsought result of ordinary labors and amusements; and in city life we often fail to perceive that it must be made a matter of wise planning and systematic attention. It is clear that our lamented brother could not fully see how he was overworking himself. For years he had borne up, amid incessant strain, without adequate bodily exercise or mental rest, until it had become difficult for him to enjoy either, through the goading of a passion to know and to do. He was conscientious about this as he was about everything; he meant to be prudent, and tried; but his judgment as to duty and possibility failed to direct him safely. It is one thing to censure, it is another to lament. But we ought to notice that with men of ardent temperament, unselfish devotion and delicate nervous organization, it often happens that the judgment becomes perverted, and there arises a sort of romantic and irresistible persuasion of duty to put forth great exertion, just at the time when there is greatest need of rest. Two or three months ago our dear friend was sorely tried in the sickness and death of an infant child and the subsequent illness of his wife. He was really ill himself at the time, but bore up with his customary silent and determined resolution, while the subtle something we call malaria was fastening its deadly grasp upon him more and more firmly. He removed some miles into the country, in hope of finding relief, but was greatly depressed at times by the occasional interruption of his regular duties. Two weeks ago, when really too ill for such an undertaking, he thought it his duty to preach at the Glenview Chapel, having been obliged to decline several previous invitations. The morning sermon, though impressive to his hearers, seemed to him tame and feeble. At night he preached again with extraordinary effort and consuming intensity, and in garments all wet from the fearful exertion rode home through the night air. The resulting illness took the form of cerebro-spinal meningitis. Alas! that none of us understood in time his need of ceasing from all mental exertion and going away for absolute repose. Alas! for poor human wisdom, which often sees things so plainly when it is all too late.

Here is a lesson as to the need of more ministers. There have been recently several conspicuous deaths in our American Baptist ministry. A venerable college president in Texas has passed away. A noble and greatly honored pastor and teacher in Mississippi has fallen suddenly at his post. An aged and celebrated minister in New York City, of ripe wisdom and of wider reading than probably any other minister of any denomination in America, has fallen asleep amid the grand collection of books which had formed the companions of his life. And now this fine young man, of such rare early achievement and such rich promise for the future, is likewise gone. What does it mean? It means no thought of despondency, no such word as fail. When soldiers are fighting with stern devotion the battles of their country, and beloved comrades fall by their side, they only press forward in more determined endeavor, and promptly write home for recruits to fill the ranks. What does this mean? It means renewed prayer to the Lord of the harvest that he will send forth laborers, and renewed effort in all who have undertaken the work of the ministry, from the oldest pastor or professor to the youngest student, to fill the full measure of possible usefulness.

Here is a lesson as to the importance of preparing beforehand for death and the entrance into eternity. That last sermon into which our brother poured so much of his life was upon the text, "Let me die the death of the righteous." How often this is with other men as well as Balaam a mere vain wish! In fact, who does not wish to die the righteous man's death? But what right has any one to expect this who is not earnestly living the righteous man's life? The hope of death-bed preparation for death is among the greatest of human delusions. In not a few cases, there is no consciousness of the approaching end. In many others, there is a settled despair, which nothing can change into trust and hope, or a fixed indifference, the fruit of life-long habit, which nothing can arouse into endeavor or concern. O that that last text, emphasized by the preacher's speedy departure, may sink into the hearts of all who heard then, and of all who hear to-day.

Finally, may God grant to us all at this hour the consolation and guidance we need. May he comfort this sorrowing church of which our brother was a member, and the distant church of which he was pastor. A great sorrow has fallen upon all that Blue-grass neighborhood; and into every home and heart among them, as well as into the hearts of those who have come so far to be present at this service, may there enter the blessed consolations which God only can give. May the Holy Spirit comfort the students who mourn with deep and bitter grief the loss of their noble young professor, and lead them in high consecration and devotion to imitate him as he imitated Christ. There is even greater need of special comfort to his colleagues. Eight years ago we buried with the deepest sense of loss our oldest professor, who had been with us from the beginning. What a shock that the next to pass away should be our youngest! We cannot but feel like parents grown gray when called to bury a son in all his youthful prime. It is a mournful experience. God help us. And can I more say? Three years ago the orange blossom, and now these flowers that vainly essay to smile upon a scene too full of sadness. O pitying heavens, drop down the dews of your consolation. O pitying angels, doubtless ye care, but ye know not, O angels, the sweet, sweet human love, the bitter, bitter human sorrow. O sympathizing Saviour, thou didst weep with sisters beside a brother's grave, and thou knowest, thou knowest, O Saviour, that here is a grief still harder to bear. O Holy Ghost the Comforter, come now and comfort. O God and Father of our Lord Jesus Christ, the Father of mercies and God of all comfort, the father of the fatherless and the widow's God, come guide and uphold one who strives to be brave and calm as she leads forth into life the tottering steps of her fatherless little boy.

XX.

THE CONFEDERATE DEAD.

Address at Cave Hill Cemetery, Louisville, May 22, 1886.

IT is a long time since the war—part of a thousand years. And many changes have come. We hear much as to the wonders of our age, but to me the greatest of them all is the rapid restoration of good feeling in this country. You young people cannot imagine how we felt twenty-five years ago. And I am heartily glad you cannot. But to-day we meet beside the graves of our heroic dead without one thought or feeling of bitterness toward those who sleep yonder. As Pitt and Fox, after their life-time of conflict, sleep in peace together in Westminster Abbey, so here the Confederate dead on the slope and the Union dead on the summit of the same hill, the men who twenty years ago were engaged in the vastest and most terrible civil conflict that ever occurred on earth. Thank God that now all is peace! It is due partly to the mobile character of our people; partly to the ample resources of our great country, giving to all employment and hope, and partly, notwithstanding all our imperfection and short-coming, to the influence of Christianity. The great religion of peace has healed the wounds and softened the asperities of the great civil war.

It is useless now to raise the question who was right.

Perhaps in some respects each side would now acknowledge that the other was nearest right; perhaps in some respects both sides were wrong. Whenever the "impartial historian" arises—he has not arisen yet; certainly he has not published anything in the *Century Magazine* or in the Personal Recollections of any statesman or soldier—and if he should speak out now, he would probably offend both sides, or else would be neglected as tame and dull—but when he arises he may possibly hold that one side was nearest right according to document and argument, and the other according to the slowly changing condition of our national affairs. Of one thing I feel certain, neither side can claim any monopoly of good intentions, of patriotic aims, nor even of wisdom.

The side that triumphs is not always thereby proven to have been superior in wisdom. We were concerned in one of those mighty movements in human affairs which transcend all the penetration and judgment of the greatest individual minds. We ordinary people can to-day see meanings in that struggle which the greatest statesmen did not perceive when it began. And, of course, the end is not yet; it will be better understood hereafter. But this much is plain—the war had to come. The necessity for it was written in the whole history of the republic and of the colonies—yea, in the history of England for centuries past. It was written in the configuration and climate, the soil and productions of different parts of our continent. It was written on the flag of the first ship that brought African slaves to the English Colonies of North America. It had to come. The splendid eloquence and noble patriotism of the world-famous statesman of Kentucky, aided by others of like mind, delayed it for a time. The madness of some men doubtless hastened it; but with human nature as it is, the war had to come sooner or later. And we can see now that there were two great questions which imperatively required to be settled.

A certain point as to the character of the Federal Government our fathers failed to define, apparently because they could not agree. That point the war has practically settled forever. A certain great social institution, grown into portentous and tremendous proportions, had fallen under the ban of the civilized world, and, sooner or later, somehow or other, it must cease to be. I verily believe that it is worth all our dreadful financial losses, all the sufferings of the long and frightful conflict, yea, and the blood of our precious dead, to have those two questions flung behind us forever.

Well, then, did our buried heroes die in vain? Their side of the conflict was the side appointed to fail, but it does not follow that they died in vain.

The great struggle has preserved the self-respect of the Southern people. At a time when we believed that our rights were sorely endangered we could not have tamely yielded merely to avoid suffering and loss, and continued to respect ourselves. 'Tis better to have loved and lost, than never to have loved at all. And it is better to have been brave and beaten than never to have been brave at all, at a time when every instinct and sentiment and principle of manhood clamored its demand that men should stand for what they honestly believed to be truth and right. The graves of our fallen soldiers make it possible that this generation and the coming generations of the Southern people should feel no shame in consequence of their defeat.

The war has established mutual respect, and opened the way for mutual good-will between the long hostile sections of our great country. The Northern and Southern people underestimated each other's manhood; despised each other. But they feel so no longer, especially those of them who actually met in the imminent and deadly breach. There is kinder feeling on both sides now than would have been possible had our difficulties been settled in any other way.

And this has enabled the defeated combatants to yield a cordial and faithful devotion to the National Government, such as could not have existed if things had taken any other course. I make bold to say, however an occasional unwise utterance may misrepresent us, that many of the most sincere and earnestly faithful supporters of this great Union to-day are among the men who once did their level best to break the Union in twain.

No, the dead have not lived or died in vain, if the survivors know aught of right thought and right feeling. They are a power among us to-day. "A living dog," the wise man hath said, "is better than a dead lion." Yes, but even a living lion is nothing in comparison with a dead man. In proportion as he lived and died with a true manhood, his memory is cherished and proves a blessing to those who survived and those who come after. There are fathers buried here whose children do not remember to have seen them; yet the glorified memory of the father, as often depicted by the widowed mother, has become to those children the very glass in which to dress themselves, the model of all that is noblest in human character and life.

I was thinking not long ago concerning that greatest of all the poems ever written in memory of the dead, in which Tennyson has so well depicted the mental struggles and responded to the religious longings of our troubled age. Did it ever occur to you that *two* wonderfully-gifted young men went to the production of that great poem,—one who died to be its subject, the other who lived to compose it? He who died must have been a man of extraordinary powers and promise, in order to make so profound an impression, and turn all the poet's deepest thought and feeling for so long a time into pathetic memories of him. And if our noble young men have died in vain, it must be our fault.

Let us teach ourselves and our children to draw inspiration from these graves. As on this bright evening the little ones scatter flowers on the mounds, let us all resolve afresh to live worthy of the men who are buried here.

> "Thus, though oft depressed and lonely,
>   All my fears are laid aside,
>   If I but remember only
>   Such as these have lived and died."

XXI.

MEMORIAL OF A. M. POINDEXTER.*

A NEW generation is arising that knew not Joseph. A large proportion of the persons present can hardly sympathize with the profound interest which those who are older feel in the life and character of this long-departed minister. But transport yourself in fancy to a meeting of the General Association twenty years ago. A debate is in progress, involving some vital doctrine of Scripture, or some question of church government, or some point connected with ministerial or general education or with the work of missions. Some brother is presenting arguments or plans which others might regard as of questionable propriety. Instantly you see a man arise from one of the front seats, and go quickly towards the speaker. He is a man of somewhat less than medium height, but of graceful figure. His face has a rather haggard look; but his blue eye is as bright and tender as a morning sky in spring-time. He seats himself just in front of the speaker, puts in position an enormous ear-trumpet, lifting it towards the speaker's face, and gazes up at him with a kindly, eager and curiously humble expression of countenance. As soon as the speech ends, he quickly lays down the ear-trumpet, and rises with elastic energy to his feet. He

* Before the Virginia Baptist Historical Society, Staunton, Va., Nov. 13, 1886. Some portions were omitted in reading, for lack of time.

begins to speak without the slightest touch of arrogance, and yet with the unmistakable air of a man who thoroughly understands the subject. He calls up, accurately and without apparent effort, any and every point made, in the course of the debate, that he has occasion to use. He has evidently thought through and through all the principles involved, and his arguments come trooping as they are wanted. Everything erroneous or questionable finds itself overwhelmingly refuted, and the truth on the subject, as prevailing among intelligent Baptists, is set forth in complete and luminous statement. Presently his mind warms to the subject; his emotions are kindled by the thought of some great Gospel truth or duty; his movements become impassioned; his face begins to glow, and the blue eyes flash lightning; his voice, though harsh and not well governed, swells into mighty power; he takes possession of the entire assembly, leading them where he will, filling their whole soul with some strong conviction or some enthusiastic purpose. As he sits down, exhausted and panting, and the high-wrought countenance subsides into gentleness and humility, you hardly think of admiring the man; your mind is all engrossed with the persuasion that his views are right, that no one need attempt to answer him, that we ought to do, must do, will do just what he has said. In turning away at the close of the session, you hear one member say to another: "Poindexter was almost up to his best to-day;" and the reply is made: "Oh, well, we have nobody else that can speak like that; but I have heard him do better far."

Vain are all attempts to describe consummate eloquence. Pray join us, without further ado, in surveying the history and character of one whom many of us regard with unutterable admiration and love.*

Abram Maer Poindexter was of a Huguenot family, which came from England early in the last century, and settled in Louisa County, Virginia. The name shows it to have been a French family of the better class, for *point dextre*, the "right-hand point," indicated one of the chief positions on an escutcheon, as may be seen in Webster's Dictionary;† and, however this name may have been gained, it suggests military distinction. Young Thomas Poindexter was sent away from England by his parents to prevent a marriage with an English girl; but, in the course of human events, the girl crossed the Atlantic also, and they met in a curious and romantic fashion, which you may find described in Taylor's "Lives of Virginia Baptist Ministers," in the sketch of John Poindexter. A son of this marriage,

---

* The materials are rich at some points; at others, quite scanty. Dr. J. B. Taylor has kindly furnished Dr. Poindexter's writings—those printed and such as remain in manuscript—and has spared no pains to give aid in various ways. Extracts from letters, oral communications and newspaper articles of numerous friends will be credited where they are inserted. Towards the close, the widow of Dr. A. B. Brown kindly made search among her husband's manuscripts, and sent the following: (a) A long letter to Dr. Brown from Rev. William Hill Jordan, half-brother of Dr. Poindexter, written the year following Poindexter's death, and giving facts as to their ancestors and Abram's boyhood; (b) The rough draft of two mainly identical addresses on the character of Poindexter, made by Dr. Brown shortly after his friend's death, and which will be freely quoted below; (c) The beginning of a memoir by Dr. Brown, which furnishes, from his own knowledge, two or three facts not otherwise within reach.

† The explanation was suggested by Dr. Brown.

also named Thomas, married a daughter of Colonel Gabriel Jones, of Culpeper, and two of their sons became ministers, John Poindexter and Richard Jones Poindexter, the father of him whom we commemorate. These two brothers married sisters in Bertie County, North Carolina, whose mother was quite a remarkable woman. Her maiden name was Prudence Jordan, and she married a German, named Abram Maer, of whom we have no information, but who seems to have been a man of interesting character; for his not very euphonious name was borne by several of his descendants. The wife was one of the early converts of Elder Jeremiah Dargan (a kinsman of our Petersburg pastor), who came from South Carolina to this north-eastern portion of North Carolina, where his life-long ministry was richly blessed. She was famous for intelligence and piety, a valued counsellor of her pastor, and most deeply concerned for the salvation of her numerous children. Her grandson, William Hill Jordan, has preserved interesting narratives of the conversion of her sons. Three of her daughters were married to Baptist ministers,—one to Aaron Spivey, another to John Poindexter, and the third, Fanny, after a first marriage to Mr. Jordan, formed a second marriage with Richard Jones Poindexter. We thus see that A. M. Poindexter was of mingled French, English and German extraction, and that his ancestors included persons of marked intelligence and character.

Besides the son of her first marriage, William Hill Jordan, who lived a long life of the highest ministerial usefulness and distinction, Mrs. Poindexter became the mother of eight children, of whom only two lived to be grown, and the elder of these died when just entering manhood. She was always feeble and suffering, though she long outlived her second husband. Dr. Brown says that the country on the lower Roanoke was then badly drained, and the inhabitants greatly subject to chills and fever. These circumstances explain for us the important fact that A. M. Poindexter inherited a very delicately organized constitution, easily exposed to several grave diseases, and requiring a very active life to ward off their assaults. He also inherited from his mother certain excellent traits of character. Mr. Jordan says: "She was of a guileless simplicity and integrity of character, faithful in her friendships and undisguised in her dislikes. She possessed a fortitude almost invincible, and a courage I never knew exceeded in woman or man. Her piety was a steady, rather than a brilliant flame. She was not addicted to much talk about either her religious joys or sorrows. Her faith was unwavering. Amid sickness and sorrow, her children dying in her arms, and dark and heavy billows of tribulation breaking over her head, I do not suppose that she ever, the first time, questioned the goodness of the Lord, or doubted for a moment her acceptance with the Redeemer. She uniformly said, when led to speak of the subject, that she felt ready to meet the Lord. . . . In beautiful consistency with her life, these were about her last words,—'I have no ecstasy, but a firm faith in Jesus Christ.'"

Abram was born September 22, 1809. His half-brother remembered him as a lively and sprightly child, early displaying a great love of argument. On one occasion, when he was not more than ten or twelve years old, his father, in the conclusion of a discussion between them, said to him, laughing, "Well, my son, you have cornered me." The father was, Mr. Jordan says, "a man of extraordinary talents;" and "from the part taken by him in the associations of his day, he must have been a very active man, if not a leader."* He was particularly fond of metaphysics, and had good store of books on that subject, which, in the opinion of Mr. Jordan, probably served to whet to an edge the boy's naturally intellectual and logical mind. "Ministers and others who visited our family, and engaged in the conversation, expressed their admiration at the abilities he displayed in argument, when but a boy." The father was also very well read in medicine, and Abram stated, in later life, to Dr. Brown, that he early read very freely in his father's medical books, as well as in metaphysics. This was a felicitous part of his environment, that his mind was developed and trained by physical as well as metaphysical science, both through the books and through conversation with his father. He also stated late in life, to Dr. Manly, that in boyhood he read the Bible much and very attentively, though not yet a Christian, and acted as superintendent of a Sunday-school in the neighborhood, because no one else would take hold. Mr. Jordan says that he "enjoyed such opportunities for early culture as existed in the schools of the country, in which were taught the common branches of an English education. Subsequently he was sent to a school of higher grade, in which he ac-

* President C. E. Taylor.

quired some knowledge of the Latin language." The deafness, which greatly hindered him through life, is understood to have been produced in some feat of boyish diving, through the sudden rush of water into his ears. It grew worse in middle age, probably through complication with disease of the throat.

Some time during his boyhood there were certain strange occurrences at the home of the family, which three years before his death Dr. Poindexter narrated to Dr. George B. Taylor, whose recollection of the narrative is as follows: "For a long time inexplicable and awe-inspiring things were constantly taking place at his father's home, of which all the family, including himself, were cognizant. There would be the unmistakable sound of some one moving in the room, when nothing was visible; objects would be visibly moved from their places without an apparent mover. Doors would be opened and shut, as by the hand of some one who was yet unseen. A door would be opened, though locked and the key not in the lock, and the lock rusty. The bolt would be seen and heard to go back with a grating sound, and the door would open, all without any visible agent." There were many other details which Dr. Taylor does not recall. He adds,—"Dr. Poindexter had no theory as to the cause and nature of these manifestations, showing thus the philosophical and conservative character of his mind. He mentioned, merely as a part of the *res gestæ*, that it was found out that the former owner of the farm had in some way suffered, if nothing more, a deep wrong and injustice. . . ." One naturally puts along with this story the strange experiences suffered by John Leland, when living in Orange County, Va.,* and the 'Wesley Ghost.'"

During Abram's boyhood the family was in comfortable circumstances. The stepson inherited a considerable fortune, went much to boarding-school, and obtained quite a good youthful education. But this was mainly denied to Abram. There came "a great pecuniary crash in the community," and we of the present day know too well how such a state of things might exist a few years after the war with Great Britain. At such times men of delicate health and sensitive nature are frequently unable to bear up under the burden of financial disaster and solicitude. The father died in 1826, when Abram was 17 years old. His sons sought employment. The elder began the study of medicine, but died shortly after. Abram vainly tried to get into a printing-office, and was presently invited by a kinsman to study law with him, but on arriving found that the lawyer kinsman had changed his mind. He would hardly have succeeded well in connection with the press, for he was through life curiously deficient in spelling, and never facile in written composition; but as a lawyer he could not have failed to become eminent. These disappointments made him very despondent, and, determined to do something, he indentured himself to a mechanic, to learn a trade. Here he was sorely tempted by wicked associates, but, as he said later in life, was restrained by respect for his mother, and "unwillingness by any evil course to add to her afflictions." These manual labors seem to have continued several years.

*Sprague's Annals,—Baptist, p. 180.

Then he was converted, and at once the Christian hope lifted him out of despondency and gave his soul a new elasticity. "As soon as he professed religion he manifested a desire for the ministry, and he soon began to speak to others of the Gospel, the power of which he had experienced in his own heart. He was a preacher born. These incipient efforts in preaching showed the same clear, strong, logical thought which has since so fully developed itself as one of his most prominent intellectual characteristics. He was born a man."*

Poindexter mentions afterwards in his diary that in May, 1831, he began earnestly to seek the Lord, and on the 4th Lord's day, in June, was enabled, as he trusts, "to embrace him as mine." He was baptized by elder R. Lawrence into the fellowship of Cashie Church, Bertie County, in July, 1831, and licensed to preach in February, 1832. He now greatly desired to improve his education, and was encouraged in this by his half-brother. From January to July of 1832 he resided with Mr. Jordan in Granville County, N. C., and was doubtless greatly benefited by intercourse with this gifted brother, who had already entered the ministry. Rev. William Hill Jordan is remembered with the highest admiration in both North and South Carolina. Dr. T. H. Pritchard says of him: "I do not think I have ever known a more devout man; one who spent more time in prayer, or who seemed to live in closer communion with God. Nor was he less eloquent than his more distinguished brother. He had far more imagination, and was more widely read. I should judge

*Rev. W. H. Jordan.

him to have been a better *belles-lettres* scholar, but he was not so remarkable for powers of reasoning, in which Dr. Poindexter excelled any man I have ever heard speak. The two most eloquent speeches I ever heard in all my life were made by these two brothers. In 1866 the State Convention met in Wilmington. Mr. Jordan had once been pastor there. He was called out on some report relating to the progress of the denomination, and delivered an impromptu address of twenty minutes, abounding in personal reminiscences—which in point of pure eloquence surpassed anything I ever heard from mortal lips. It was simply transcendent; and gave me a conception of the orator higher than any I ever entertained before." Mr. Jordan lived till 1883.

It was at this period, January 25, 1832, when at the age of twenty-two, that young Poindexter began to keep a diary, or "Remembrancer," which he continued for five years, and which is still preserved. The earliest entries lament his want of devotional feeling, and one of them mentions doubts as to his call to the ministry. But he is prayerful and determined, and sometimes full of faith and love.

In the summer of 1832, under the influence of his brother, the young preacher determined to go and study with Abner W. Clopton, in Charlotte Co., Virginia. Mr. Clopton had been a teacher for many years before he began to preach, and in his later years was fond of having one or two young ministers with him, whose studies he would direct and assist, and who aided him as pastor of country churches. He impressed himself profoundly upon such young men, and his influence upon young Poindexter's piety was excellent. He had many books, and the youth doubtless read widely, in a desultory fashion, but with much reflection and with fine powers of memory. He stated, at a later period, that he learned very little of theology from Mr. Clopton, and nothing of homiletics. Clopton was a preacher of great power; but, after the fashion of the time, his preparations were by no means methodical. Poindexter was fond of saying in later life that it would have been of the greatest advantage to him if in youth he could have had some such treatise on the Preparation and Delivery of Sermons as those which now abound. Dr. Brown thinks that Clopton probably awakened his pupil's zeal for the cause of Temperance, in regard to which he was the great Virginia leader at that time, and of which Poindexter became a life-long advocate, equally zealous and moderate; also that Clopton directed his attention to the teachings of Alexander Campbell, which in after years he studied with singular thoroughness. In the first number of "*The Commission*," July, 1856, Dr. Poindexter says the following was given him by his "venerated instructor in ministerial duty, the late Rev. A. W. Clopton," viz.: "Never suffer an opportunity to pass unimproved, when you can properly introduce religious conversation with the unconverted." Coming to us from two such eminent and useful ministers, this counsel ought to be read again and remembered well.

During this year, 1832, especially in the latter half, when he was living with Mr. Clopton, our young minister preached quite frequently. In September he preached in a four days' meeting at Ash Camp, and "Lord's Day was a melting time." In October he visited his relatives in North Carolina, and "tried to preach ten times." At an association, an old minister "blundered greatly in his sermon, and I thought it my duty to correct his errors. O Lord, if I was actuated by any improper motive, make me to see it. This matter has caused me much uneasiness, but I cannot feel that I acted wrong. I fear the brother is deeply hurt with me for it. May the Lord heal the breach, forgive us both all our sins, and save us with an everlasting salvation." Thus early began the practice of that free-spoken but loving criticism of his ministerial brethren, for which Poindexter was remarkable through life, and to which many hundreds of ministers now look back with profound gratitude.

On the 12th of February, 1833, A. M. Poindexter entered Columbian College (now Columbian University), Washington City, which had then been in operation for ten years. Several able professors had already been connected with the struggling institution, and some of its early students became eminent ministers. The president, when Poindexter entered, was Dr. Stephen Chapin, and among the professors were William Ruggles, Adiel Sherwood and J. Chaplin. Poindexter remained at the college less than twelve months, and for a considerable part of that time was seriously ill. His preparation for entering upon college studies was meagre and irregular, including little Latin, no Greek, and not much of mathematics. He was soon perceived to be a preacher of extraordinary powers, and was greatly in demand in the churches of Washington and Alexandria. He made careful preparation for these sermons, and amid the novel surroundings doubtless threw into them all the passionate ardor of his nature. Meantime he was studying eagerly, especially striving to get up Greek. On April 1st he learned from the *Religious Herald* the death of A. W. Clopton, which he notices in the diary with deep feeling; and a few days later was astonished by the receipt of a letter requesting him to go and become pastor of Clopton's churches. Upon this he wrote to his brother for advice, who had recently left the college and gone to the Newton Institution. The following Sunday, preaching a second time at the Navy Yard, the church requested him to preach regularly, " once a Sabbath. . . . and say they will remunerate me." For the first Sunday under this engagement he mentions that they gave him five dollars. He speaks of rooming with "Brother Herndon," probably the gifted and lovable Traverse D. Herndon, of Loudoun County. The week following the Navy Yard engagement, after unusual exercise one day he began to feel very weak, and to spit blood. He had to give up study on Saturday, but still preached on Sunday. He determined to take more exercise. With the close of April the college session ended, but Poindexter decided to remain and continue his studies during vacation. He had concluded not to go to the churches in Charlotte, through desire to improve his education. On the last Sunday of the session he preached in O. B Brown's church, which was the principal Baptist Church of the city, and this at the special request of President Chapin;

25

which shows how highly the young student's ministerial abilities were already appreciated. Before a week of the vacation study has ended he speaks of " an almost incessant cough, and great soreness of the throat and chest;" but though quite hoarse, he "made out to speak to-day at the Navy Yard." A week later comes an outburst of thanksgiving that "Brother C. and Cousin A. have sent me twenty dollars to procure a commentary." It is greatly to be feared that he bought Dr. Gill's Commentary, for what else could a young Baptist minister of that day be expected to procure? Some time in May he preached the dedication sermon for the Central Baptist Church at Washington, and either before or after preaching wrote out the discourse, which is still in existence. On June 2d he was quite prostrated by preaching twice, and thought he must "give up regular preaching," and he did abandon the Navy Yard engagement a few weeks later. One of these sermons on June 2d was upon the Training of Children, Proverbs 22 : 6, and is preserved. It shows some crudeness of style, as might have been expected, but is rich with just thoughts, expressed in terse and vigorous fashion, with occasional outbursts of impassioned exhortation. Two features are observable in this and the dedication sermon, that marked his preaching through life,—1. Everything was argued out ; 2. The treatment of the subject takes a very wide range. Both these and the early sermons of which we have only notes, insist much on the atonement, on religious earnestness and on obedience.

A new session of the college commenced July 3d.

But Poindexter had become seriously enfeebled, and was threatened with consumption; so from July 21st to November 8th he traveled to improve his health. There is no account of the journey, but he thought his recovery was perhaps retarded by preaching too much while traveling. We can well suppose that people were eager to hear him, and he was burning with zeal. After returning to college in November he speaks of "an ugly cough," and "health very precarious," and presently, for some weeks, "a severe attack of pleurisy." Henceforth he had always a strong tendency to bronchitis, and it was a violent attack of that disease, passing into pneumonia, that ended his life. Dr. Brown somewhere refers to "that terrible bronchitis which was again and again throttling him all the days of his mature life." In December he speaks of being impressed by reading an account of the "Darkness of Burmah," and by reports of "the truth taking hold in that dark land." We know that it was just then that Judson's work began to have large and encouraging results. On January 20, 1834, he records that after long consideration he perceives his health to be too frail for the student life, and has determined to leave for North Carolina.

We see from all this that Poindexter was deeply impressed with the desirableness of regular education, and made determined and almost desperate efforts to obtain it, giving up only when his very life was in peril. Such education would scarcely have made him a better speaker, save in furnishing a wider range of illustration; but it would have made him a much better writer. Dr. Chapin, in a written criticism on one of his early compositions, said, "If I could write as well as you *can*, I would write better than you *do*." Dr. T. W. Sydnor entered Columbian College two years after Poindexter left, and says: "He was spoken of as a young man of uncommon mental vigor and of studious habits, but a little restive under the routine and restraint of college life. He did not apply himself closely to the college text-books, preferring to arrange a course of study for himself. I think he was not fond of classical or mathematical studies or of *belles-lettres*, but preferred philosophical and scientific studies." The explanation of this account seems to be, that with very feeble health and extreme nervous sensitiveness, he would every day grow weary of attempts to master the elements of classics and mathematics, and in his prostrated condition would seek refreshment in his favorite lines of reading. Far from fancying himself superior to the regular drill of college study, he never ceased to lament that he had lacked that early advantage, and would not unfrequently allude to it when urging young men to put themselves through the most thorough possible training.

Leaving Washington, he tarried some time with relatives in Louisa County, his health rapidly improving, and afterwards stopped in Charlotte. Here, through fatigue and exposure in waiting on a sick friend, he had an attack of "bilious pleurisy," which brought him "to the gates of death." His physician and friends thought that he would not recover; and the celebrated Luther Rice, who was visiting the neighborhood at that time, told him afterwards that he had begun to prepare his obituary. Reaching his North Carolina home in

March, he speaks in his diary of his afflictions as a means of spiritual benefit; saying that during the sickness he had more full and elevated views than ever before of "the character of God, the glory of Christ, and the blessings of the Gospel."

As soon as he felt well enough he began to travel and preach. Through letters from his friends, Deacon Roach and Rev. Daniel Witt, he presently came to a protracted meeting at Catawba Church, Halifax County, Va. The result was a call to that church and to Clarksville, in the adjoining county of Mecklenburg. After due consideration he settled with these churches in July, 1834, having been ordained a month earlier at his home church in Bertie County, the Presbytery consisting of Elders James Ross, Reuben Lawrence and Andrew McCraig. He was now nearly twenty-five years of age. His health was still quite feeble, and he speaks of himself as "in danger of having a liver disease." This would, of course, aggravate the trouble of throat and chest, and would be itself increased by the immense excitement which attended his zealous preaching. We are not surprised to find him taken ill during a protracted meeting in Bertie County, just after his ordination.

Here, then, began Brother Poindexter's life as a pastor, when a little less than twenty-five years old. He soon enters upon systematic visiting in his church, endeavoring to "stir them up to active piety." He has "presented a plan which seems likely, from the satisfaction they express in it, to draw forth and unite the brethren in support of the benevolent enterprises of the Christian public." This is interesting, for it shows the young pastor as unconsciously preparing to become the great agent. At this time begins a new manuscript volume of sketches of sermons, and in September a funeral sermon is written out in full. In October he "heard some pleasant news from Wake Forest Institute—very flourishing—great revival, in which twenty students professed conversion. Bless the Lord, O my soul." He speaks of attending the Roanoke Association with great pleasure. Another passage may be quoted from the diary, as showing the beginnings of a life-work. "In view of the success that has attended several efforts lately made for the adjustment of difficulties between brethren, I feel encouraged never to consider any case as hopeless so long as prayer and effort can be made in it; and am determined to secure the promise to peacemakers." Far and wide over Virginia and the whole Southern country did the A. M. Poindexter of subsequent years carry his wise and loving efforts to make peace between individuals, and to restore harmony in churches and Associations. The diary, or Remembrancer, is full here, as often elsewhere, of devout lamentations, thanksgivings, supplications and solemn dedication of himself to God. We find him striking out to preach in various directions; among other places, a monthly appointment at an Episcopal church near Halifax Court-House. In December he receives a letter from James B. Taylor, inquiring, "How do you feel, my dear brother, respecting a mission to the heathen? Have you thought much about China and South America as interesting fields of labor?" This was a dozen years before Dr. Taylor became Foreign Mission Secretary. Busy as a Richmond pastor, toiling at a voluntary agency for the Virginia Baptist Seminary (afterward Richmond College), and anxiously corresponding and advising as to Baptist affairs in Baltimore, he still found time to address this inquiry to the gifted young pastor in Halifax, five years his junior. What they were consulting about was Foreign Mission work in connection with the Boston Board. How little could they suppose that twenty years later they two were to be Foreign Mission Secretaries together in Richmond. To the above mention of Taylor's letter Poindexter adds, " O Lord, I am thy servant. Send me whither thou wilt, only let thy presence be with me wherever I may be." A few weeks later he replies to Taylor, " I have for a long time been considerably exercised relative to becoming a missionary. But I do not now think it my duty." We know very well that his health would by no means have justified his going forth as a Foreign Missionary. In February, 1835, he mentions receiving a letter from Brother Luther Rice. Dr. Brown states that at this period Poindexter was much in company with Rice, who loved to visit Halifax, and sojourn at the hospitable home of Mrs. Wimbish, where the young pastor was living. In later life he declared Luther Rice to have been " in virtues among the first, and in talents the first of those whom he had intimately known." Dr. Jeter states, in an editorial after Poindexter's death : "We remember to have heard Luther Rice, who possessed a discriminating judgment and was widely acquainted with the rising ministry of the United States, say of Poindexter, soon after he commenced preaching, that he was the most promising young preacher whom he knew." This intercourse with Rice would deepen Poindexter's interest in missions and in ministerial education, the two great objects to which his life was to be mainly devoted. Luther Rice died the following year.

Some time in 1835 Mr. Poindexter planned seven lectures "On the Evidences of the Divine Authenticity of the Bible." The titles of the seven are given at the beginning of a note-book, and follow the usual method of lectures on evidences at that time. Two of the lectures are written out in the book. It is likely he concluded, after reflecting upon his experiments, and consulting with wise hearers, not to complete the course. A series of really useful lectures on the Evidences must always require mature wisdom, and intimate acquaintance with the kind of difficulties existing in the community addressed. Otherwise one may do more to awaken doubts than to allay them. He who thoroughly knows the underlying tendencies of his time, and can silently correct such as are evil by simply enforcing the corresponding truth, will always do great good. The outlines of sermons which remain from this period show diligent study of Scripture, thoughtful and sober interpretation, and a fairly good, but not remarkable, talent for the construction of discourses.

Thus passed the two years of this early pastorate in Halifax. In the spring of 1836 he mentions taking a trip to raise money for printing the Burman Bible. The results for this object are not stated. But during the journey he met with Elder Daniel Witt, who spoke of having just declined a call to Charlottesville, and expressed the opinion that his friend would be the man for the place. In June, Poindexter attended the General Association in Richmond, and there received a call to Charlottesville. He resigned the churches in Halifax and went to Charlottesville in August, to stay some months and see whether he would remain permanently. The village had then eight hundred to one thousand inhabitants. He was interested in the field and preached much in the country around. He established a Minister's meeting, and got on foot a plan, by which several months of voluntary missionary labor would be given to the churches of the Albemarle Association. But there were two difficulties in the way of his remaining at Charlottesville. His health " seemed to be sinking under the rigor of the climate and the severity of labor necessary to meet my engagements." This helps to explain his life-long course. He had a high standard of pulpit excellence and always preached with consuming earnestness and exhausting effort. He was inclined to take large subjects and expatiate in each discourse over an ample range of thought. To prepare two or three such discourses a week and at the same time look out for general improvement, to which he would be stimulated by proximity to a great institution of learning, soon proved too severe a task for the constitution which had utterly given out at college and whose restless and sensitive energies would again and again demand travelling as a necessary condition of health. The other difficulty was that he had formed, during the period of his sojourn at Charlottesville, an engagement of marriage with a lady in Halifax. The Charlottesville Church could not offer a sufficient salary to support their young pastor and a wife—and the affianced lady possessed a good country home in Halifax. Thus ended his brief stay in Charlottesville fifty years ago. Dr. Brown says: "His six months' pastorate in Charlottesville was for its length the most fruitful in good that I have known. The very best material in the church for the next fifteen or twenty years was brought in under his ministry."

After a visit to Raleigh, where his brother, Mr. Jordan, was now pastor, and their mother lived with him, Mr. Poindexter was married, in Halifax, May 25, 1837, to Mrs. Eliza J. Craddock, the widowed daughter of Mrs. Wimbish. They settled on his wife's plantation, which continued to be his place of residence for the next seventeen years or more. Here the Remembrancer ends, as promptly after the marriage as if it had been a novel. Henceforth we have few minute details concerning Brother Poindexter's life. He was pastor of various churches in Halifax and Charlotte Counties, viz.: Catawba, Hunting Creek, Millstone, Republican Grove, Beth Car and Charlotte C. H. He had charge of the plantation and negroes, and there were four children of his wife's former marriage. Dr. Jeter says: "The marriage proved to be one of great happiness and usefulness. Mrs. Poindexter was a lady of great excellence, the light of his house and his counsellor, and for many years shared his burdens and promoted his success."

For several years after his marriage we have no incidents in the life of the quiet country pastor. Dr. T.

W. Sydnor considers that he was "not successful as a pastor, either in adding to numbers, or in promoting efficiency;" but adds that he was all the time "exceedingly popular and regarded as incomparably the ablest minister of any denomination in all that region, and crowds attended upon his ministry." Dr. Brown, in one of his addresses, insists that Poindexter's preaching, at protracted meetings and in his own churches, while not productive of numerous conversions, brought in highly valuable material. To the remark already quoted concerning Charlottesville, he adds: "And at Hunting Creek and Millstone, till how recent a time were the best elements in each church the fruits of a preaching which combined the red-hot logic of Fox with the saintly fervor of Stephen."

In 1842 Mr. Poindexter published in the Baptist Preacher a sermon on "Piety the Chief Element of Ministerial Power," which had been delivered before the Virginia Baptist Education Society at its June meeting. This appears to have been his first published sermon, and is one of the best we have from his pen. We shall have occasion to point back to it hereafter, but must quote a few words at present: "Brethren of the Educational Society, let me entreat you not to overlook, in your anxiety to give the churches an educated ministry, the supreme importance of furnishing them at the same time with a pious ministry. Require decided evidence of a supreme devotion to the Saviour in all whom you receive as your beneficiaries. And always endeavor to impress upon them the importance of high attainments in the divine life." Preached with his overwhelming earnestness, this judicious and practical sermon doubtless made a great impression, and it may have had something to do with the fact that a year later, in 1843, Columbian College conferred on him the honorary degree of D.D. He was then at the age of thirty-six. In that year he published in the *Religious Herald* a series of articles on the connection between baptism and the remission of sins. These papers show his profound study of the controversies excited by Mr. Campbell and his followers. Dr. Sydnor states that they were written at his house during a visit of several days, and that as published they attracted much attention.

It was in 1845 that Dr. Poindexter was first induced to become an agent. The Columbian College, of which he had for a short time been a student, and which had recently honored him with its degree, desired to make a special effort for the increase of its endowment, being encouraged by a conditional offer of ten thousand dollars from John Withers, of Alexandria. This agency lasted three years, to 1848. It was followed by that of Dr. Wm. F. Broaddus, upon another offer from Mr. Withers. Professor A. J. Huntington finds in the archives of Columbian College Dr. Poindexter's final report, showing that he paid over to the treasurer more than twenty-five thousand dollars, besides Mr. Withers' subscription. His home was still in Halifax. His custom was, throughout all his agencies, whenever distance and other circumstances would admit, to spend one week of every month at home. In April, 1846, we find in the *Baptist Preacher* a funeral sermon which he had preached at Antioch, in Charlotte County.

In August, 1846, while pursuing this agency for Columbian College, he attended the Potomac Association— or was it not then called Salem Union?—at Upperville, Fauquier County, and preached two sermons, which are vividly remembered by at least one person who was present, and which may be referred to as illustrating the usefulness of many kinds which Dr. Poindexter always connected with agency-work. A youth, who had been teaching school in that vicinity two or three years, had just been released in order to enter the University of Virginia and study medicine. For three years a professed Christian, he had often thought about the question of becoming a minister, but considered himself to have finally decided that it was not his duty. On Sunday Dr. Poindexter preached upon Glorying in the Cross. The young man had often heard with enthusiasm and delight such truly eloquent and noble preachers as Barnett Grimsley, Cumberland George and Henry W. Dodge; but he thought, that Sunday at Upperville, that he had never before imagined what preaching might be, never before conceived the half of the grandeur and glory that gather sublime around the cross of Christ. One allusion is remembered across the forty years, showing how Dr. Poindexter, like all other highly effective preachers, would draw illustration from things just then going on. Dr. Judson had for some time been on a visit to America. The story of his early sufferings had become familiar to all intelligent Baptist people through the memoir of his first wife, true heroine that she was. The *Religious Herald* had acquainted us all with the career and character of that noble woman, the second Mrs.

Judson, who had been buried at Saint Helena. And now it had been only a few days since Dr. Judson and his third wife had sailed from Boston. It is perhaps impossible, after recalling all these circumstances, to appreciate the charm and transporting power of the preacher's allusion, when, in urging self-sacrificing devotion to the cause of Christ, he said—"Like her who is buried beneath the Hopia tree, or her who sleeps on the rock of ocean, or her who now gently ministers to declining age." The next morning Dr. Poindexter was requested to preach at 11 o'clock in the church, the Association adjourning to hear him. The sermon was one which he often preached in the journeyings of later years, on the Parable of the Talents. In pressing the duty of Christian beneficence, he adopted a plan which will be remembered by many as characteristic. He mastered the complete sympathy of many hearers, the prosperous Baptist farmers of that beautiful region, by arguing long and earnestly that it is right for the Christian to gather property, and right to provide well for his family. Excellent brethren were charmed. No preacher had ever before so fully justified the toil and sacrifices by which they had been steadily growing rich. They looked across the house into the faces of delighted friends; they smiled and winked and nodded at each other in every direction. But when the preacher had gained their full sympathy, the sudden appeal he made to consecrate their wealth to the highest ends of existence, to the good of mankind and the glory of Christ, was a torrent, a tornado, that swept everything before it. Presently he spoke of consecrating one's mental gifts and possible attainments to the work of the ministry. He seemed to clear up all difficulties pertaining to the subject; he swept away all the disguises of self-delusion, all the excuses of a fancied humility; he held up the thought that the greatest sacrifices and toils possible to a minister's lifetime would be a hundred-fold repaid if he should be the instrument of saving one soul. Doubtless the sermon had many more important results, which have not fallen in the way of being recorded; but when intermission came, the young man who has been mentioned sought out his pastor, and with a choking voice said, "Brother Grimsley, the question is decided; I must try to be a preacher." For the decision of that hour he is directly indebted, under God, to A. M. Poindexter; and amid a thousand imperfections and short-comings, that work of the ministry has been the joy of his life.

In August, 1848, Dr. Poindexter became corresponding secretary of the Southern Baptist Publication Society, Charleston, S. C., and held the office more than two years. His duty included the collection of funds, and the editing and publication of religious books and tracts. A depository was established in Charleston, and the report for 1849 gives as depository agent Rev. James P. Boyce, who was then editing *The Southern Baptist*. Dr. Poindexter did not take his family to Charleston, but boarded at a hotel. Dr. Boyce remembers his preaching at the First Church two sermons on Imputation, probably occasioned by theological discussions then going on in South Carolina; and in 1850 he published in *The Baptist Preacher* three sermons on Imputation: (1) "The Imputation of Adam's sin to his posterity;" (2) "The Imputation of sin to Christ;" (3) "The Imputation of the Righteousness of Christ to Believers." This was the first publication which revealed, what many had seen from his sermons and conversation, that he was a master in theological thinking. The young Charleston editor, and future theological professor, found great delight in the sympathetic comparison of views with one who had independently wrought out that same system of theological truth which we are wont to call Calvinism, but might better call Paulinism.

Besides meeting annual expenses, Dr. Poindexter collected a fund of twenty thousand dollars, to be spent in stereotyping books. Among the works published during his term of service as secretary was the "Baptist Psalmody," by B. Manly and B. Manly, Jr., issued in 1850, and one of the very best hymn-books in existence. Dr. Poindexter and B. Manly, Jr., spent several weeks in Charleston in the final revision of this collection, and Poindexter wrote for it the hymns numbered 22, 416, 840, 880, 893 and 950, all good hymns, though scarcely of remarkable excellence.

Dr. Poindexter's first agency for Richmond College extended from June, 1851, to June, 1854. This institution began in 1832, as the Virginia Baptist Seminary, in charge of the always beloved and now venerable Dr. Robert Ryland. In 1840 it obtained a college charter. Dr. Poindexter's agency was designed by the trustees to raise eighty-five thousand dollars for endowment. The resolution put on record at the close of his agency, viz.: "The trustees hereby express their high sense of the self-denial, industry and eminent success with which he has prosecuted his work for the past three years," would seem to indicate that he had obtained subscriptions for the whole amount proposed. He was aided by several brethren appointed for temporary effort in particular localities. How easily we seem thus to record the work of three years! But it must have been a season of much laborious journeying by every species of conveyance, of numerous elaborate and exhausting addresses to associations and churches, and of unnumbered vehement appeals to individuals, which would often kindle him to as glowing and consuming excitement as ordinary men feel in their most impassioned public discourse.

In June, 1854, began a new form of labor, which was to make A. M. Poindexter a great power for good throughout the Southern States. He was made assistant secretary to the Foreign Mission Board, to aid the laborious and overburdened secretary, James B. Taylor. The two men were curiously unlike. Both were remarkable for clear intelligence and sound judgment, both were eminently pious, and both had prodigious strength of will. But one was an extraordinary specimen of suavity and gentleness, while the other was excitable, impetuous, and to all appearance very likely to be impatient. People used sometimes to wonder whether it was possible for the two to live and work together without unpleasant collisions. But we have ample testimony that their mutual relations were uniformly pleasant and fraternal. So declares Dr. B. Manly, who was a particularly active member of the Foreign Mission

Board, knowing all that went on. Dr. George B. Taylor says: "They were almost as different as two such good men could be, but their mutual respect, love, confidence and forbearance was perfect. I speak what I know when I say that never was there a cloud as big as a man's hand between them." Add this from Dr. Charles E. Taylor: "For several years before the war he and my father sat side by side at their desks in the mission room. I, a half-grown boy, used to think of them as John and Paul, and I have never ceased to think that there was much in Brother Poindexter that was Paul-like. He was self-reliant, courageous, vigorous in thought and expression, wonderfully skilled in dialectics, and withal, transparent and tender-hearted as a child. The great public knew the deeper side of his life. My own memories now dwell more lovingly upon its surface as seen by me in those early days. A thousand little hints and suggestions of his I can never forget."

Each of the secretaries spent much time in long journeys throughout the South, speaking for Foreign Missions at State Conventions or General Associations, and very often at such particular churches as they could reach. The sweet and gracious influence of Dr. Taylor, in such visits, is well remembered by our older pastors, and its spirit is embalmed in that admirable memoir, which all our young ministers ought to read for generations to come. The impression made by Dr. Poindexter in those more distant States where he had not been known, was often phenomenal. He had, as we have seen, been deeply interested in Foreign Mission work from an early period. He had associated on the most intimate terms with Luther Rice himself. Cut off by ill-health from the possibility of becoming personally a Foreign Missionary, he felt all the more anxious to awaken prayerful interest and elicit generous contributions in behalf of those who had been able to go. And now that all his thoughts and toils were given to this great enterprise, we can dimly imagine how before his ardent gaze it must have risen high as heaven and spread wide as the universe. The powerful arguments and the transporting appeals in one of those grand addresses of his before some State Convention would make themselves felt by all the more susceptible minds throughout the State. Besides speaking in public and in private for his own special enterprise, he did great good in many other ways. There were growing in those years among Southern Baptists certain marked divergences of opinion, which at one time seriously threatened to produce utter alienation and denominational division. Not a few were driven by mutual antagonism to insist on extreme positions and to indulge unbrotherly feelings. The survivors of those conflicts would doubtless gladly agree to-day that there was much misunderstanding, and would heartily unite in thanking God that we now see no occasion for division upon any of the questions involved. But at that time Poindexter was a very important connecting link between the alienated extremes. He was anything else than a half-way man. He took a strong and bold denominational position. But it was such as enabled him to sympathize more or less with both sides in the existing controversies. Few might exactly agree with his views, but almost all inclined to claim him as substantially agreeing with themselves. And if the matter were now deemed worth discussion, it would probably appear that very many at the present time think almost exactly as he thought. At any rate, his influence in respect to those controversies was powerful and wholesome.

There probably never was an agent in all the world more completely free from all the narrowness of exclusive devotion to his own particular enterprise. Whenever occasion arose in his own State, or in any other that he was visiting, Poindexter would throw his whole soul into an appeal for any other denominational undertaking, especially if it were for Home or State Missions or for the Higher Education. He was broad and high enough in intellect to perceive that such a course was good policy. But he was so full of generosity and great-heartedness, so prompt in brotherly sympathy and interested in every department of Christian work, that he would engage in such advocacy from sheer love of the brethren and love of the cause. It was at this period, 1857, that he made the great speech at Raleigh, in behalf of Wake Forest College, to which we have already alluded, under the guidance of Dr. T. H. Pritchard. "The Baptist State Convention met in the State House, and the subject of Poindexter's address was Education and the endowment of Wake Forest College. Within half an hour after the speech was closed, about twenty-seven thousand dollars was subscribed to the endowment. During the delivery of the address I saw Governor Thomas Bragg on the floor of the body, and observed how deeply he was moved. He was, in his day, the first lawyer in North Carolina, and no mean master of oratory himself; and he pronounced that speech the most powerful he ever heard in his life." Cases have been mentioned, in which, at some State Convention or local Association, there would arise question as to precedence, in presenting Home or Foreign Missions; Poindexter would cheerfully concede the first opportunity to the Home or State work, and make a powerful appeal in behalf of it; and brethren would be so pleased with his generous spirit and won by his true eloquence, that when the hour came for Foreign Missions, they gave larger contributions than usual. We ought all to perceive that the very genius of Christianity is unselfishness; and that in any apparent conflict of really Christian enterprises, the unselfish course is supported by the whole logic of the situation and will command all the noblest sympathies.

Dr. Poindexter was at this period deeply interested in the plan of establishing a General Theological Seminary for Southern Baptists. This had been often thought of during previous years, but had never proven practicable. At the Virginia June meetings in 1854 a committee was appointed to suggest to the brethren attending the next Southern Baptist Convention the propriety of renewed efforts to secure a common Theological School for the South. To this statement Dr. Boyce adds: "A meeting was therefore held May, 1855, in a small room connected with the house of worship of the First Baptist Church of Montgomery, attended by not more than twenty-five persons."

Among the most zealous and influential of these was Poindexter. A special convention was next held in Augusta, May, 1856, which appointed a committee to receive propositions from different localities for the endowment of such an institution. In August of that year Professor James P. Boyce, of Furman University, delivered at Greenville, S. C., an inaugural address, entitled "Three Changes in Theological Institutions," which Dr. Poindexter heard with hearty approval and admiration, and which, when printed, he took much interest in circulating. The new and wise ideas of that address were laid at the foundation of the seminary soon actually established. Another special Educational Convention was held at Louisville, in 1857, in connection with, though organically distinct from, the Southern Baptist Convention. This Educational Convention, which was largely attended, decided to accept the offer brought by Professor Boyce from South Carolina, for locating the proposed General Seminary at Greenville, in that State. In these deliberations Dr. Poindexter took an eminently earnest and useful part, along with such revered and now departed fathers as Howell, the elder Manly, Jeter and others. In the final Convention which met at Greenville in 1858, to organize and establish the seminary, Dr. Poindexter was one of the leading spirits. Especially was he solicitous that the Articles of Belief which were appointed to be subscribed by the seminary professors, with the promise that they will teach in accordance with, and not contrary to them, should correctly and strongly state the established faith of the Baptist Churches. He could not become general agent of the seminary, as was earnestly desired, for the Foreign Mission Board declined to give him up; but the seminary continued to receive his loving and devoted support through life and feels his impress to this day.

Early in his term of service as Foreign Mission Secretary, Dr. Poindexter removed his residence from the plantation in Halifax to the city of Richmond, and there remained till the early part of the war. Besides enabling him to be more at home, this gave better opportunity for the education of his children. Dr. George B. Taylor remarks that Poindexter was a lover of hospitality. Surrounded by the spacious and eminently hospitable homes of the Thomases and the Worthams, he had less occasion for this than would otherwise have been the case, but many of us remember the privilege of being his guests, and the unaffectedly hearty reception given by him and his household. In like manner do many of us remember the great pleasure of having him as a guest in our own homes. His deafness made it natural for him to take the lead in conversation. Yet he never did this in the way of monologue, like Doctor Johnson or Coleridge, but introduced every new topic in the form of a question, desiring to compare views, and greatly delighting in conversational discussion. Many a young minister of that day can recall the wholesome thrill of excitement produced by measuring swords in debate with this knightly and doughty comrade. The young man might feel himself hopelessly inferior, and be tempted to yield the point at the outset; but Poindexter wanted nothing of that sort, and would redouble his questions with such kindly persistency and unfeigned good fellowship as would constrain the man to argue, and often arouse in him a lively spirit of debate and a heightened love of truth. Dr. Pritchard mentions an instance, which Poindexter must have exquisitely enjoyed: "In 1855 I spent several days at his home in Halifax, when A. B. Brown was there. They were kindred spirits, and kept up a discussion of some of the most abstruse and difficult questions of theology and metaphysics during the whole time. It was a battle of Titans, and I remember how it fairly made my poor head ache to try to keep up with their discussions—certainly the most intellectual I ever listened to." Dr. Manly recalls a similar experience, when Poindexter, Brown and himself, cut off by torrents of rain from going to an Association, spent a day at the house of Brother Bird L. Ferrell, in Southern Virginia. He says that Poindexter and Brown fairly revelled in the joy of debate. There was a trundle-bed in the room they occupied, and the two would just roll on the bed like school-boys, and discuss every question on which they had ever differed, fighting with fierce glee along every ramification of each succeeding topic. Now and then they would turn eagerly to Manly that he might act as arbiter of some dispute, while the kindly host looked on and listened by the hour with immense amusement.

In 1856 Dr. Poindexter published in the *Herald* an excellent funeral sermon on "The Future State of the Righteous." In July, 1856, the Foreign Mission Board began publishing a monthly missionary magazine called

The Commission, which lasted four years, until stopped by the war, and was a publication of great interest and value. This was chiefly under Dr. Poindexter's editorial management, though sometimes, in his absence, an entire number was edited by Dr. Taylor. The four volumes of this periodical contain many practical articles from Poindexter's pen upon missionary topics, with several impassioned appeals, that remind one of his great oral appeals. There are careful discussions to vindicate the scriptural propriety of Foreign Mission Boards and other machinery. In two elaborate papers on "The Lord's Day—a Neglected Ordinance," he urges that apostolical example shows it to be the duty of every church to meet every Lord's Day for united worship and mutual edification, and strikingly connects this view with the Sunday-school work. Another article insists on the duty of personally reading the Bible every day, and frequently conversing with others about its teachings. In the number for December, 1859, he describes the desirable qualifications for Foreign Missionary work—such as a good constitution, without any tendency to nervous depression, an ingenuous and confiding disposition (necessary to co-operation with other missionaries and with the Board), and yet great decision of character, a well-trained mind and an acquaintance with the laws of Biblical interpretation, and with the system of doctrine and polity taught in the New Testament, and earnest, self-denying, self-sacrificing piety. He especially advises young men who contemplate Foreign Mission work to take a theological course, because a missionary will be so largely thrown upon his own resources, and because he will be doing foundation work, in which his errors will perpetuate themselves, with no counteracting influences. During 1860 there are elaborate and valuable articles on Faith and Repentance.

Through the blended and powerful influence of Secretaries Taylor and Poindexter, and the rapid growth of intelligence and diffusion of missionary knowledge among ministers and churches, the Foreign Mission work of Southern Baptists was by 1860 coming into a very healthy and promising condition, though only on the threshold of what was manifestly possible. Some wealthy individuals and some well-trained churches were beginning to give really considerable amounts; the Board was amply supplied with funds, and calling loudly for additional missionaries. Several of our most gifted and thoroughly trained young brethren about that time openly devoted themselves to the Foreign Mission work. The skies seemed bright and brightening.

And then came—the war. Very soon we were cut off from communication with our missionaries in foreign fields, and it became impossible to expect systematic contributions from churches in which all financial arrangements were uncertain, and the enormous expenses and unmeasured losses of the war were multiplying year by year. In the early summer of 1861, before the first battle of Manassas, the Poindexters returned from Richmond to their home in Halifax, and for the years of the war we hear very little of the family, save in the pathetic and mournful way that is common to so many family recollections of that dark and awful time. The marriage of Dr. and Mrs. Poindexter had been blessed with a daughter and two sons. Both the sons were killed during the war. The younger, William Jordan Poindexter, an impulsive and ardent youth of seventeen, volunteered at the beginning in a company of dragoons. There remains one letter to him from his mother, written in July. In November he rode out one morning to relieve picket-guard, and dismounting, took his pistol from the holster and put it in his bosom. Soon after, stooping to gather some fodder for his horse, his pistol fell and went off, the ball entering his forehead. He lingered some time, and for the most part was rational. The afflicted father ends the brief notice in the family register by saying: "We have hope that he was prepared for death." The older son, Abram Wimbish Poindexter, at the age of twenty-one, volunteered before his brother's death in an infantry company which he materially assisted in raising, and was elected first lieutenant. Afterwards, by the death of Captain Easley, he became captain; it was Company K, Forty-sixth Virginia. The young man had made a public profession of religion the previous year, was a graduate of Wake Forest College, and principal of Talladega Academy in Alabama. As teacher and as officer he showed superior talents, and great force and charm of character. He was exceedingly beloved by his men; some were converted through his recognized instrumentality, and his letters, for months previous to his death, showed deep and growing devotion. Obituaries which remain from different friends present discriminating and exalted eulogy. What a joy he must have been to father and mother and sister! Before Petersburg, July 30, 1864, the enemy exploded their now famous mine, and poured through the great gap in the works, enfilading with deadly fire the thin Confederate lines on either side. Captain Poindexter's company was especially exposed, and stood its ground amid heavy losses. Every officer but himself was borne away severely wounded. Addressing the little remnant of his company, the young captain said: "Boys, we must hold this position, or die in our places, for the salvation of the town depends upon the enemy's not carrying these works." Presently an officer rode by, and seeing the little handful of a company standing firm, he asked who was their commander. They replied, pointing to a dead body, "There's our captain; he told us we must hold these works, or die in their defense, and we mean to do it." And they did. Without an officer, the little fragment of a company obeyed their dead captain's command, and stood firm before the enfilading fire and the rush of the foe. The story was told to Dr. Poindexter by one of the men. Truly that was a captain! truly those were men!

The only written production of Dr. Poindexter's that remains from those trying years is a manuscript sermon "On the Kingdom of Peace." It was written after the death of Stonewall Jackson, May '63, for that event is mentioned, and apparently before the death of Captain Abram Poindexter, in July, 1864. Taking as text the inspiring passage in Micah and Isaiah which predicts that all nations shall flow together to the mountain of the Lord's house, and beat their swords into ploughshares, etc., he makes one of the most impressive sermons that remain from him in print or in manuscript. The opening sentence is this: "Now, while on every side is heard the roar of cannon, and our borders are deluged with blood, it is well to turn away from the violence and contention of earthly powers, and contemplate the progress and triumph of the Prince of Peace." It was a topic well-suited to comfort and cheer believing souls amid all the fierce outbursts of human passion, and the terrible conflict and frightful losses of war; and the preacher kindles as he depicts under the guidance of Scripture the future triumph of the Gospel and the peaceful reign of Christ.

We come now to the closing period of Dr. Poindexter's life, from the end of the war, in 1865, to his death, in 1872. We might easily describe life on that Halifax plantation for the year following the war, for the same thing was witnessed all over the wide Southern land. Our people, especially in the great planting regions, moved about as amid the wreck of a universal earthquake, considering whether it was possible to rebuild their prostrate fortunes, and ever live on earth again in comfort and happiness. Ten thousand families which had dwelt long in affluence and culture, in the gratification of all refined tastes, were reduced to struggling and painful poverty. How the Southern people did manage to pick themselves up and stand on their feet at all after that great earthquake, remains a wonder unto this day.

In December, 1865, the family had experience of the brightness with which youth and love know how to gild the darkest days. Dr. Poindexter's only daughter, Fanny, was married, December 13th, to Rev. James B.

Taylor, Junior. The previous relations of the fathers and the families, and the personal character of all concerned, must have made this marriage an occasion of great joy. But before the end of the same month, December 30th, after the fashion in which sorrow so often dogs the lightest footsteps of joy, there came a sad bereavement. The two sons of Mrs. Poindexter's first marriage had both been men of distinction and usefulness. Both were physicians with good estates, both highly esteemed by their fellow-citizens, and the elder honored with a seat in the Legislature; and best of all, they were earnest and useful Christians. But at the time we have mentioned the elder son, Dr. Charles J. Craddock, died, to the great grief of his parents as well as his wife and children. His daughters are now the wives of Dr. A. E. Dickinson and Judge W. R. Barksdale. Mrs. Poindexter's other son of her first marriage, Dr. John W. Craddock, lived until 1885, and left an interesting family. His two sisters also have both passed away.

In May, 1866, the Southern Baptist Convention at Russellville, Ky., advised the Foreign Mission Board to re-engage Dr. Poindexter as assistant secretary. The Board made the appointment; but it was declined, because a few weeks later, at the June meetings, he was asked to become agent a second time for Richmond College. This second agency continued from June, 1866, to June, 1870. The college had lost great part of its endowment by the war. Like many others of our struggling Southern institutions, it had to face the question of life or death. There is nothing nobler in American history than the spirit with which our Southern people stood up amid the wreck of their fortunes, and declared that their institutions of higher education should not perish. The history will never be adequately told of the sacrifices and overburdened toils by which professors in those institutions kept them in operation, and in many cases have gradually built them up into something of strength. But even more remarkable sacrifices were made by many contributors for endowment or for current support. Men with nothing left of former wealth but poor land and plenty of debts, numerous ministers and others who were living by the hardest upon some inadequate and sadly uncertain income, gave what they could not spare, gave not grudgingly, but with high enthusiasm, gave without the personal interest naturally felt by instructors themselves, and for pure love of education, love of country, love of Christ. The Board undertook to raise one hundred thousand dollars for the endowment of Richmond College, and this was the object of Dr. Poindexter's agency. He had a great reputation in this species of work, and he bore well the competition with a famous man's worst rival, the glorified recollection of his own past achievements. He was in hearty sympathy with those elevated and enthusiastic feelings by which the nobler part of the people were stirred. The memory of his great speeches during this canvass of Virginia will be handed down from father to son. Nor did he dream of contenting himself with public argument and appeal. He sought men at their homes. He could not be escaped nor repelled, and while courteous, it was passing hard to shake him off. The story has been lately told in the *Herald* of his following some brother to the field he was harrowing. The brother protested he could not give, and had not time to listen to any representations, for he must go on harrowing. What should the great orator do but take a seat on the harrow, where his weight would make the teeth strike deeper into the soil, and talk Richmond College to the farmer as he drove. Did he get a contribution at last? Probably not; in fact, it would spoil the story if he had. The story reveals his persistency, and also that hearty sense of humor which belongs to the character of almost every man who does much of the world's highest and hardest work. He had many odd experiences in these appeals to individuals. A gentleman somewhere, who had retained more than usual of his former wealth, and was naturally minded to retain it still, tried to put off the agent with a small contribution. The characteristic answer was,—"Pray, don't give me that; such a contribution from you would damage the cause. Give nothing at all, or else more than that." Then launching into a vehement appeal, he solemnly said: "My dear brother, we have thirty-one young men now studying in the College for the ministry." "What, Dr. Poindexter, you ain't going to turn all of them loose on us, are you?" He evidently thought they were all to be trained for agents, and of the Poindexter variety. Either during this or his former agency for Richmond College occurred an instance, as narrated by Rev. A. Bagby, of his unconquerable resolution. "One day, travelling in a buggy, we reached a stream of water much swollen by late rains. As we came up, he said: 'Can we cross?' I answered, that I did not know the creek well enough to say. 'Well,' said he, 'I'll soon find out.' Instanter we alighted and unhitched, when he sprang upon the harnessed horse, plunged through to the opposite bank, and, speedily returning, reported that the buggy could not be taken through; the current was too strong. We headed the stream, and gained our point before twilight."

It is probable that he did not secure subscriptions to the full amount which had been proposed. In resigning, June, 1870, though asked by the Board to continue, he gave as his reason, "the present difficulties of collecting funds on account of the depressed condition of the country." In fact, the people of Virginia were far less hopeful then than during the first year after the war. Many vague hopes fondly cherished at first in regard to possible recovery of fortune had been sadly disappointed. The process of political reconstruction was here peculiarly slow, and old indebtedness hung like a mill-stone around the necks of the people. Dr. Poindexter's success, under all the circumstances, was very great. His work, and the admirable teaching done by able and devoted professors, have made the college a permanency and a power. Those who wish to invest money for the highest good of humanity may be confident of building there upon enduring foundations.

During this period occurred a somewhat celebrated Conference between the Baptists and the Disciples of Virginia, to consider the possibility of union. Dr. George B. Taylor says: "I never saw him appear to so great an advantage as at this Conference. Undoubtedly he was the ruling spirit of the body and his speeches were masterly. While the ablest and most effective defender of distinctively Baptist principles, he almost provoked some of our brethren engaged in the discussion, by seeming at times well-nigh to go over to the other side, though he was really only recognizing and stating with clear-cut precision the truth which he admitted to be held by the Disciples." We have already observed that it was characteristic of Poindexter to state fully and strongly the opposing side of a disputed question. And sometimes he could reconcile parties much at variance by simply stating each side in its full force, so that they could see ground for respecting each other's positions and agreeing to disagree without strife. Dr. B. Manly remembers being with him at an Association, where a bitter division existed as to Temperance. Dr. Poindexter got the floor, stated the position of each side better than they could have done themselves, and then suggested action which satisfied all, and tended to far better results than any one-sided action could have produced. There was here no rhetorical trickery and no half-way position, but the power to combine antagonizing views and blend them in a higher unity, which is one of the noblest achievements of true philosophical thinking.

Dr. Manly remembers another Association, when, in a sermon, Poindexter assailed the inconsistencies of professing Christians, without allowing a single exception, in so fierce and trenchant a fashion as to arouse indignation. Perceiving signs of this, he repeated his accusations with redoubled strength, with terrific denunciation, till nearly all present seemed positively furious with anger at such unjust censure of their fellow-Christians, if not of themselves. Then he turned to speak of the mercy and grace of the gospel, the hope of forgiveness, and of deliverance from all sin and eternal safety from sinning, till the whole assembly was melted into loving tears. Such extraordinary feats must never be imitated by others, though they may be studied as revealing the principles of persuasion. And they cannot be safely repeated at will by the speaker himself. Let him once attempt to work himself up by calculated effort to such lofty passion, though it be with the best motives, with a sincere desire to do good thereby, and the result will be perhaps apparent success, but real failure, and with a very grievous reaction upon the genuineness of his own religious emotions. Public speakers of every kind, who frequently set fire to their audience, and at length become aware that they are expected to do so, must beware of trying to meet this expectation with the product of manufacture rather than of natural growth. It has been thought, by some judicious and most friendly observers, that Dr. Poindexter sometimes made this mistake of working himself up into passion. If so, it was one of those casual errors of judgment in a great and good man, which we must recognize with reverence and study with humility.

A year after this last agency for Richmond College began, viz.: September 14, 1867, Mrs. Poindexter died. The loss of husband or wife is the greatest of all bereavements, which seems to darken the whole horizon of the survivor's life. Dr. Poindexter's sensitive and passionate nature found this great loss almost intolerable.

For thirty years he had rested in her, finding the sympathy and solace which such a nature must have, or the burdens of life cannot be borne. Their religious sentiments had been much alike. They had grown assimilated by common joys and sorrows. In his long absences she had wisely managed the household and the estate. Together they had borne the loss of property, together the death of their soldier boys. How could he exist alone? It is said that he was thrown into literal convulsions. But soon the fervent Christian's habitual submission returned, and the mighty will regained control over the storm of passionate emotion. Shortly after her death Dr. Poindexter made his home with his son-in-law, Rev. J. B. Taylor, Jr., at Culpeper. After two or three years he gave up the agency in June, 1870, and doubtless expected much pleasure in the home of his daughter and his grandchildren, where he might carry out the cherished desire to write down the products of life-long thinking in philosophy and theology. But again came speedy sorrow. On the 7th of November, 1870, that singularly noble and lovely woman, Mrs. Fanny Poindexter Taylor, was taken away by death. Her fine intellect could enjoy the profound discussions so often held in her presence, while her vivacity and ever kindly wit gave a great charm to general conversation. Her delight in learning and teaching Christian truth, her unselfish generosity, delicate consideration for others and eager desire to be useful, were lovingly portrayed in obituaries that remain, and her memory is precious still in the beautiful village where she lived and died as a pastor's wife. Her two sons, Abram Poindexter

Taylor and James Boyce Taylor, now the only descendants of A. M. Poindexter, have a heritage that ought to awaken in them all worthy aspirations.

In the latter part of 1870 and the beginning of 1871 Dr. Poindexter spent some time in helping the Foreign Mission work, both at the rooms and by travelling. On June 27, 1871, he formed a second marriage with Miss Marcia P. Scott, of Orange County, Va., an esteemed lady who still survives. Dr. Jeter says: "All his friends congratulated him on the prospect of a calm, pleasant and useful close of his life." His home was henceforth on her farm, a few miles from Gordonsville. Happy in new ties and surroundings, he addressed himself vigorously to the preparation of essays and treatises for publication. Many elaborate articles and several extended series of articles appeared in the *Religious Herald*, his pen being far more active during the last year of his life than ever before. "He also accepted the pastoral care of the churches at Louisa C. H. and Lower Goldmine, each about fifteen miles from his home. They had been accustomed to meet only once a month and objected seriously to more frequent meetings, especially at the Court-House, where long usage had allotted the Sundays to the different denominations. But he insisted on preaching twice a month at each place and doing much pastoral work besides. His ministry drew large congregations, both churches gained somewhat in numbers and immensely in efficiency, and still cherish the memory of his brief pastorate as one of the most useful in all their history."[*] In October and November

[*] Dr. H. H. Harris.

he delivered before the young men at Louisa C. H. three lectures, which were written out and are still preserved, entitled "Pleasure," "Conscience," and "An Old Acquaintance."

Somewhat earlier he had published an article on "Valid Baptism," especially on the question of immersions performed by Pedobaptist or Campbellite ministers, which he did not think a Baptist church ought to accept as satisfactory. This probably suggested a series on "The Organization of the Primitive Churches." The principal topics are (1) The meaning of *ecclesia*; (2) The membership; (3) The ordinances; (4) The officers; (5) The government; (6) The objects of the Churches. He added discussions as to the administrator of baptism, a call to the ministry, ordination, and Pedobaptist Churches. He holds that "it cannot be certainly proved that the administration of baptism is an official function. But there are considerations which render it probable that it was thus regarded." And he concludes, "I incline to think the common opinion of the official relation of the act more probable, and certainly not contrary to any explicit scripture, and conducive to good order and a just guarding of the ordinance." As to evangelical Pedobaptist churches, he holds that we cannot properly recognize them as *scriptural* churches; but that we should gladly recognize the Christian character of all those in whom we see evidences of true piety, and that while protesting against what we regard as their erroneous teachings and practices, Scriptural churches and their members are bound to regard and treat evangelical Pedobaptist churches as helpers in the work of Christ—the salvation of souls. The closing paragraph on this point is as follows: "While, then, I conclude that there is nothing inconsistent or wrong in the occasional interchange of public labors with Pedobaptist ministers, yet it is my conviction that it is not expedient that such interchange be carried to any great extent."

He also published articles on the following metaphysical and theological topics: Cause and Effect, Uncaused Being, Creation, The Creator and Sovereign, Revelation, Miracles (three articles, including one on Miracles of Jesus and his Disciples), The Law of Progress in its Application to Theology, Conscience—this last appearing only a week or two before his death. The slips from the *Herald* which contain the above essays are followed in his Index Rerum by two similar essays in manuscript on The Creation of Man and The Fall of Man. These various essays present no novel teachings on the great topics involved,—a thing neither to be expected nor desired,—but they give the results of his lifetime thinking upon fundamental topics with clearness and vigor. They would not be widely read as newspaper articles, nor widely circulated in a volume, but they would be of real value to young ministers.

It was apparently at the same period that he began "The History of Jesus," which he carried as far as the beginning of our Lord's ministry. Dr. Brown states in one of his addresses that Poindexter had outlined and partly written a work on Systematic Theology, exhibiting "great originality of thought and great excellence of style." Dr. Brown hopes that this fragment may be published; but it is not now to be found in the collection of manuscripts. There remains a sermon written in full, and dated March 20, 1872, on The Importance of Regular Attendance on Public Worship.

Some controversy in the *Herald* with Dr. Caswell about Communion seems to have been the special occasion of Poindexter's preparing a treatise on "The Lord's Supper." This is complete, and he was endeavoring to arrange for its publication. A letter from Dr. J. L. M. Curry, after reading the manuscript, is dated 30th April, 1872, just a week before Poindexter's death. Dr. Curry says, "The argument, to my mind, is compact, lucid and unanswerable. Many of the positions are of course familiar, but they are often presented in a striking light." After some slight criticisms, he adds, "As a treatise on the general subject, I know nothing clearer." It may be well to give an analysis of this treatise: Chapter I. The nature of the rite. (1) The Supper, a positive Christian Institute. (2) The Supper a permanent Institute. (3) The Supper a social Institute, and as such a church ordinance. Chapter II. The design of the Supper. (1) It is intended to commemorate Christ's death. (2) It is a symbol of the sacrificial nature of Christ's death. Chapter III. Who may partake of the Supper. (1) They must be disciples of Christ or believers. (2) They must be members of a church of Christ. (3) None but those who have been baptized have a right to the Lord's Supper. Chapter IV. How often should the Supper be observed? Chapter V. By whom is the Supper to be administered? Chapter VI. Objections considered. The whole treatise would form a tract of less than a hundred pages, 18mo.

While busily engaged in these tasks and plans of useful authorship, Dr. Poindexter probably neglected the activity of life which his health had always imperatively required. He was taken sick on April 30th, with a chill and the accompanying pains. Though compelled to lie down much on the following days, he arose and dressed himself every morning. On the fourth of May he wrote to his son-in-law: "I have no idea that I can go to the Convention. If I were free from disease, I should be too weak for such a trip. Last May another was prevented by sickness from attending, and has since gone to a more glorious Convention." This affecting reference is to the death of James B. Taylor, a few months before. Dr. Poindexter's disease was an aggravation of that from which he had so long suffered, an exacerbated bronchitis, upon which supervened typhoid pneumonia. Early one morning he began to sink. His son-in-law states in the *Religious Herald* that "his sufferings were very great, as he lay gasping for breath and unable to cough up the phlegm. Seeing the agony of his wife, he begged her not to give way, adding, 'It is all right.' A short time before his death, when asked as to his hopes and feelings, he said in substance, 'I have given all that into the hands of God, and he will not deceive me.' His immediate dissolution was painless—he passed away without a struggle;" this was May 7, 1872. His remains were interred in Orange.

The Southern Baptist Convention met at Raleigh, North Carolina, two days after Dr. Poindexter's death. On reaching Raleigh, or upon the trains in going there, the delegates heard the news with the greatest surprise and distress. Nothing had been generally known of his sickness. No one thought of anything else than meeting him at Raleigh, and delighting again, as so often before, in his conversation and his inspiring addresses. Dr. Jeter remarks: " From the organization of the Convention to the close of his life he was one of the ruling spirits who shaped its measures and inspired it with zeal and vigor. In some sense Poindexter and Taylor were present at the meeting in Raleigh. Their names were often mentioned. Their piety and labors were frequently called to remembrance. Many eyes were moistened by the touching allusions made to their bright examples and their happy end. How much the kind feeling, harmony and devotion prevalent on the occasion were due to these melting and hallowed reminiscences it is not for us to know. Good men are a blessing while they live; and, dying, they bequeath their example, their reputation, and their influence, a precious legacy, to the world. Virginia Baptists are becoming rich in the memories and the renown of their departed worthies. Let us then, brethren, 'be not slothful, but followers of them who through faith and patience inherit the promises.'"

One of the allusions to Poindexter's recent death was made by Dr. Richard Fuller, in a missionary address on Saturday evening. It was in the form of an impassioned apostrophe, such as cannot be adequately reported. In fact, a report of true eloquence is at best only a pale photograph, where the lineaments may be correctly given, but the eye cannot flash, nor the cheeks glow and burn, nor the voice thrill with its more than magic power. Somewhat as follows Dr. Fuller spoke: " I almost think sometimes that I would not exchange places with an angel in heaven; if I did, it would not be with Gabriel, but rather with that angel whom John saw flying in the midst of heaven, carrying the everlasting gospel 'to every nation and kindred and tongue and people, saying with a loud voice, Fear God, and give glory to him.' Fly faster, O angel! on thy mission; sweet angel, fly faster; and, if thou canst not quicken thy flight, go turn over thy commission to Poindexter's mighty spirit, and he shall bear the message with more rapid wing and more glowing love than thou canst, O angel! He knows a love thou canst never know; he is now singing a song thou canst never learn,—the song of a redeemed soul bought by the precious blood of Christ."* There is an interesting and affecting coincidence between this apostrophe and a passage in Dr. Poindexter's sermon of thirty years before on Ministerial Power (*Baptist Preacher*, Vol. I., page 232), to which we have already referred: "Oh, it is a commission which angels might desire to share. To proclaim 'peace on earth, good-will to men, and glory to God in the highest,' through the redemption of lost man—to be sent forth on this errand of love might fire the heart of a seraph with greater ardor. Even the archangel before the throne is conscious of a higher joy and a greater honor when commissioned to fly through mid-heaven, 'having the everlasting gospel to preach unto them that dwell on the earth.' And may a poor mortal join in this blessed work? Then let me proclaim salvation! Yes, let me tell it to a world, that Jesus died to save them! Oh, that my

* Compare Cuthbert's Life of Richard Fuller, p. 191.

voice could pierce the ear of my most distant countrymen! Oh, that I had a tongue for the poor, wandering savage of our western wilds! Oh, that I had a voice for Burmah, and for China, and for the Islands of the Sea!

> 'Salvation, oh, salvation!
> The joyful sound proclaim,
> Till earth's remotest nation
> · Has learned Messiah's name.'"

Various characteristics of A. M. Poindexter have already been made the subject of passing remark. But it will be appropriate to attempt some general estimate of his character and powers. In this we shall be able to quote from several brethren who knew him well, and especially from the addresses delivered soon after his death by Dr. A. B. Brown, who, through striking similarity in certain respects, and through long and intimate association, was particularly qualified to speak of his character.

Dr. Poindexter was a strong and deep thinker. He perpetually strove to reach the bottom of every subject; to understand the very essence of things and their most intimate relations. Every branch of theological and of metaphysical thinking had for him a charm, and he never wearied of renewed effort to attain more just, comprehensive and discriminating views of truth. He had extraordinary power of recalling, at a moment's notice, long trains of thought. Dr. Brown asked him one day about a controversy which he had been conducting in one of the newspapers. Poindexter instantly stated, without the least appearance of effort, the line of thought in every article that had appeared on both sides. Many a time has he been known to rise in an association or convention, when some quite unexpected question had been sprung upon the body, and discuss the whole matter involved, with such complete understanding of its fundamental principles, such orderly arrangement and terse and vigorous statement, as to be simply amazing. You might ask him at any hour of the day or night for his views upon any topic of Bible interpretation, theological thinking, philosophical speculation or practical Christian duty, and he would at once reply with as full and exact statements as if for twenty-four hours he had been thinking of that subject alone. Dr. Manly accounts for this by the fact that Poindexter habitually associated every thought with other kindred thoughts, as a careful business man piles away papers in their proper pigeon-holes. We might say that he had a place for every thought, and every thought in its place. He loved to pursue trains of thought without writing, and, in his long journeyings for many years, he would spend much time in the most profound reflection upon the greatest questions. After giving the maturest consideration, and reaching what seemed satisfactory positions, he liked then to put it all down in writing, with a view to exactness and completeness of statement and to permanent preservation. Probably most men do better to aid themselves with the pen at earlier stages in their investigation of a subject. But every one should cultivate, as far as for him may be possible, the power of thinking consecutively without external aids. This power is not only helpful otherwise, but of inestimable value to a public speaker. William L. Yancey, that marvellous tribune of the people in Alabama, once said to Dr. Curry that "the great thing for a speaker is to be able to think on his legs."

Dr. Poindexter possessed, with a partial exception in one respect, all the faculties and the forces which make up a true orator. He had great argumentative power. He delighted not simply in logical analysis, but in logical construction. We have seen that high debate with vigorous antagonists, whether in public or in private, was with him a source of exquisite enjoyment. He fairly loved discussion, as fishes love to swim, and birds to course through upper air; it was his mind's very element. And he loved victory. Yet no man could ever accuse him of arguing for victory rather than for truth. On this point hear Dr. Jeter: "That Poindexter should resort to any trick or artifice to promote his ends was impossible. He scorned all demagoguism, and if he could not carry his points by truth and fair argument, he would suffer defeat rather than appeal to prejudice and passion for his support."

He was a man of strong and excitable feelings, which, when aroused by some great thought of Christian truth or duty, would swell, as he went on arguing and appealing, to the loftiest passion, till they threatened to carry him away into wild extravagance, till it seemed that only a little more and he would be a raving madman, even as was sometimes charged by enemies upon Demosthenes and upon Paul. Yet it was wonderful to see how completely these swelling, passionate feelings were controlled by his mighty will. In the very torrent, tempest and whirlwind of his passion he did not need to "acquire and beget a temperance;" he possessed it, by force of constitution and force of lifelong habit. Some years ago, in Munich, great attention was drawn to a picture which had been long hidden in a mountain castle. A horseman has been observing from a mountain's summit a vast plain below, on which great armies are engaged in a conflict. Eager to take part, he starts in furious gallop down the gentle slope. Suddenly the horse is on the brink of a precipice. The rider draws rein, and the powerful animal throws himself back, with strained intensity and mighty self-mastery, safe and strong, though within an inch of destruction. One could hardly fail to think, when gazing upon that powerful picture, It is like Poindexter in one of his great speeches. He was fond of addressing himself to some particular individual in the audience, especially to one who sat near him, with a pointed argument, or a sudden and vehement appeal. Occasionally he would rush up to one who stood near, throw his arms around the man's neck, in some paroxysm of passion, and while continuing to speak, would embrace him with ever tightening grasp, almost to the point of choking. On other rare occasions, after ranging widely about the floor in front of the pulpit, suddenly, in some grand outburst, he would spring up with one foot on the front seat, and stand poised like a winged Mercury, with arms all abroad and face on fire, upborne by the tempest of his passion. And from any such abnormal situation he could recover with perfect simplicity, because of his absolute self-possession. He used to say that physical power is immensely important to a preacher, and so is intellectual power, but most important of all is heart power.

Another characteristic of the orator is imagination. Dr. Brown thinks that Poindexter did not possess a high degree of imaginative power. Others have expressed a different opinion. We all notice how imagination and passion act and re-act upon each other. It may be that Dr. Poindexter's deeply passionate nature had to be first kindled before his imagination would take fire, while in some persons the imagination is kindled first. Certainly in his higher flights of impasioned appeal he used imagery that revealed imagination of a high order.

His language was excellent in point of clearness and careful discrimination, and, considering that he so often spoke without immediate preparation, its terseness and force was very remarkable. This, of course, connected itself with his habits of exact thinking and careful co-ordination of thoughts. Our thoughts become distinct to our own minds only by silently associating them with appropriate words, and so there is a very intimate relation between exact thinking and precise expression. One who really knows just what he wishes to say, can commonly say it in fit words and few.

The one great and marked defect in Poindexter's public speaking lay in his voice. It had considerable power, and did not lack some elements of native sweetness. But it was seriously damaged by the throat disease which began during his college life and clung to him through all the years. The harshness thus produced was aggravated by his serious deafness, which prevented delicate modulations of tone. And he early fell into a faulty vocal habit. We have seen how very feeble his health was during the first years of his ministerial life. Nervous weakness always makes it difficult for a man who speaks with great excitement to control his utterance. This surpassingly excitable young minister, speaking in a storm of passion to large audiences at some protracted meeting or association, perhaps in the open air, gradually fell into a sing-song, which grew upon him through life. Very many Baptist ministers of a hundred years ago had fallen into a kindred, but far worse habit, called the "holy whine," from preaching with intense excitement for a long time, so that the over-strained vocal organs instinctively relieved themselves by alternately raising and lowering the sound, just as one who is tired of standing will instinctively change position. Occasionally, even at the present time, one hears a great lawyer or political speaker who shows a similar tendency. All who greatly strain their voices in speaking, especially if they are very excitable, ought to know that they are exposed to this danger. In his later life Dr. Poindexter much regretted this blemish in his speaking, and would carefully guard against it in all the calmer parts of a discourse; but when he became greatly excited, the old habit of utterance re-asserted its sway.

The other externals of his public speaking were decidedly good. His face was rugged, but strong, and that is the only important point in one who seeks to exercise mental dominion over others. Dr. George B. Taylor remarks: "His eye told the tale; that pleading blue eye which Dr. Fuller declared to be irresistible, and which, with all its intelligence, often seemed to me to have something of the wistfulness of the most devoted of dumb creatures." His figure, as we have intimated at the outset, was graceful and pleasing, and his action was natural, varied and often extremely commanding.

In regard to his power as a public speaker, let us add at this point from a eulogy by Dr. Brown: " His sermons were characterized by great variety in the exhibition of a few fundamental doctrines. A talented man who felt at liberty to discuss everything might have displayed more variety. Few circumstanced as himself could have shown equal richness of resources in dealing with the cardinal points of the faith. The frequent recurrence of the same terms, atonement, redemption, substitution, etc., and his poverty of literary and scientific illustration, consequent on want of time to read, misled some persons in their judgment of his variety. Wide as his mind was in its range, when he selected his theme he was incisive and progressive rather than discursive in its treatment. As he moved majestically forward, making all luminous in the line of his progress, you would regret that the blaze was not thrown on many interesting collateral subjects; but he judged it best to reserve them for another line of exploration, and pressed on. He commenced dry, calm and perfectly self-possessed. His congregation might indicate some impatience with these drier beginnings, and demand by their manner a premature introduction of the luxury of more glowing thought and intenser passion. But the enthusiasm must grow out of the logic and the movement; and he would not be hurried. So he regularly increased in passion to the end. Logic was dominant even in the sometimes tempestuous conclusion. But it became more direct, and the individual thoughts more vivid, as he advanced; till, having been all through more convincing to the reason, he became in the end more moving to the deeper affections, and emphatically more constraining to the will, than any orator I have ever heard." Dr. Tyree says: "Under the sermons, and especially under the addresses, of Poindexter, I have witnessed greater effects than under the addresses of any other great preacher of the Old Dominion." Dr. Sydnor made a similar statement in his opening address as president of the General Association, at Staunton, a few weeks after Poindexter's death.

We have seen already that both in public speaking and in private life Dr. Poindexter exhibited prodigious strength of will. It may be added that he was a man of unsurpassed courage. On this point let Dr. Brown speak: "It was a theory of his that moral and physical courage were usually conjoined. They certainly were in his case. Uncommonly superior to the fear of danger and of death, he was still more an example of every phase of moral courage. Keenly alive to the ridiculous, and naturally very ambitious of honor, he seemed utterly destitute of all the weakly and weakening bashfulnesses and timidities. He defied opposition, obloquy, scorn, and would have parted from his warmest friend, though his affections were the deepest, rather than surrender his honest conviction. All the courages, active and passive, were his. He could have defied priests and devils with Luther; he could have quaffed the hemlock with the undisturbed serenity of Socrates; he could have mounted the block with the unfaltering step of Russell; he could have led the fight for civil and religious liberty with a brain all keenly alert and a heart all on fire like the brave Zwingle." As an instance of his moral courage, it may be mentioned that in his earliest pastoral life he unintentionally gave offence to some persons by a remark in the pulpit, and shortly afterwards a young man, blind with misunderstanding and furious anger, led the young preacher some steps away for a conversation, and there commenced a personal and ignominious assault. Here was a conflict between the two forms of courage. Poindexter in his private "Remembrancer" quietly says: "At first I felt irritated, and had like to have struck him. I only, however, caught at his whip, which I did several times, when this passage came with sweetness and force to my mind, 'Blessed are they that are persecuted for righteousness' sake.' I let my hand drop, and committing myself unto God, felt inexpressibly happy." That was courage indeed. The matters involved were afterwards explained, with due acknowledgments, and the parties became friends.

Dr. Brown adds on a related point: "His temper was naturally rather quick, of immense force, and now and then of tremendous violence. An outburst or two in boyhood greatly alarmed him. His strong affection for friends and his conscience warmly recommended, and his vigorous will enforced, its almost entire suppression. I have seen him in keen and sudden encounters. I have seen him strongly indignant, but I never saw from him a decided outburst of anger." Some have supposed that there was such an outburst at an educational convention held in Richmond in 1871, and composed of delegates from all parts of the country. Dr. Poindexter thought he had been misunderstood in a political allusion, and wished to correct the impression. As soon as he took up the subject, the presiding officer pronounced it out of order, but he continued speaking. The President went on rapping, louder and louder, but Poindexter elevated his voice till he had said his say. Some thought that this was unseemly anger. But he went immediately to the President, who was Dr. Boyce, and said, "You were right about the point of order, but I was determined not to let these brethren go away without explaining my position. I was bound to be heard." Dr. Boyce says that "there was not the slightest unpleasant feeling on either side."

He was remarkable for tender and warm affections. Several have testified, in print or in writing, and many of us retain cherished personal memories, as to the ardor and fidelity of his friendship. His half-brother, Mr. Jordan, gives this closing paragraph: "It falls not within my province to undertake any general description of Dr. Poindexter's character. But I may be permitted to speak of him in the relation we sustained to each other, and to drop a tear upon his grave, as from my full heart I exclaim, He was a good and noble-hearted brother! He measured not his kindness to me by the rule of a cold and cautious reciprocation, but when, from negligence, I failed to return his visits or reply to his letters, he still, with a manly dignity, an amiable magnanimity, an unabating kindness, as if all the offices of affection were due from him, continued to me his visits and his correspondence. Oh, my brother, truly thou wast a good man. Stern in the integrity of principle—inflexible as adamant in his opposition to error—neither concealing nor trying to conceal his intense disdain for all duplicity or tergiversation—abhorring whatever involved the sacrifice of principle, and whoever was involved in such a sacrifice, his heart was full of sympathy and kindness; and the hand which mercilessly crushed the unprincipled recusant, lifted with the very gentleness of a mother the child of sorrow, misfortune or penitence. No wonder that such a man was loved."

One way in which he showed affection was by candid and outspoken criticism and even rebuke. Many a young minister remembers the benefit to himself of some kindly criticism upon his preaching or his life which Poindexter made. Take the statement of Dr. George B. Taylor: "He was not only a sharp critic, but extremely outspoken; nevertheless, so far as my experience and observation go, his censorship did not rasp the feelings or offend self-love, as does that of some well-meaning persons. His criticisms seemed to imply that he thought the subject worth mending, and so they had an encouraging and tonic effect. Indeed, while he frankly pointed out defects and faults in me and my work, no man ever encouraged me more to hope that I might make something of myself. A more affectionate heart than his never beat in any breast. His love for his own dear ones was tender, his friends were bound to him with hooks of steel, and his highest joy was to be in the midst of the brethren, even though they were plain and uneducated." Add a deeply pathetic passage from Dr. Brown: " Personally I have long thought him, all in all, the best friend I had on earth. Other friends I have who would equally rejoice with me in prosperity, sympathize as deeply with me in adversity, and deal even more tenderly with me in the hour of humiliation. Very few friends have I remaining so judicious in counsel, so active and untiring in their efforts; not one, not one so sternly and yet so tenderly faithful. O his place can never, never be supplied. Brethren, you have not the nerve to do it. Hereafter—it is a sad thought—I must look to my enemies, if I have them, to do the work which had been so much better done by this incomparable friend."

Nothing in A. M. Poindexter was more remarkable than his whole-souled piety. All his great faculties and strong proclivities seemed to be pervaded by the spirit of the gospel, consecrated to the service of Christ. We find, upon this point, some characteristically discriminating and strong expressions of Dr. Jeter: "Brother Poindexter was quite as notable for his piety as for his talents. He was a man of deep convictions; and of nothing was his conviction more profound than of the truth and importance of Christianity. His feelings were intense; but most intense on religious subjects. Naturally his temper was impulsive, rugged and overbearing; but grace made it gentle, kind and conciliating. His impetuosity might lead him astray; but his honesty of purpose would bring him to the right point. As much as any man, if not more than any man we have ever known, his words were an index of his heart. Frankness was his distinctive attribute. When he spoke you might be sure, not only that he expressed his honest convictions, but that he kept back nothing through fear or affection. So strong was his inclination to speak with faithfulness that it was not always restrained by the dictates of prudence. He had his faults—such as are inseparable from ardent, strong and resolute natures. He was sometimes indiscreet, rash, overbearing and even obstinate; but he was a Christian of strong faith, warm heart, generous hand and disinterested toil." Dr. Sydnor writes: " He was a deeply pious man. I had abundant opportunity to learn his devotional habits." Dr. Brown gives the following account: " I never heard from him a doubt about his personal salvation. I have heard enough indeed to be sure that he was scarcely to any extent troubled with doubts. He and his first wife, who had great influence over each other, were alike in this. He exhibited as deep a sense of unworthiness as any Christian I ever conversed with; he lamented as profoundly that his life had been so unprofitable; yet neither of them expressed any doubts. They knew that God promised salvation to the believer. They were conscious of some faith, as every one who believes at all must be. From an accurate examination of the whole Gospel, and a careful survey of their own attitude to that Gospel, they reached the assurance of having cordially accepted the soul-saving truth, and the inevitable result was a personal appropriation of the promise. Brother J. B. Taylor and myself well remember a conversation we had with him a few months before his death. Something was said by one of us about reaching heaven, as if it were a thing still doubtful. Our hearts were thrilled with his emphatic tone and gesture when he said, with mingled remonstrance and tenderness, 'Oh, we shall get to Heaven. Those who love Christ will all get to Heaven.'"

It is not often that a man of Poindexter's oratorical gifts has also great practical wisdom and power. Every minister of the gospel has indeed an urgent need for this combination, to be at once an impressive preacher and a wise and energetic pastor. The most wonderful thing about Mr. Spurgeon is, that while he holds the world as an audience for his preaching, he shows also administrative talent like that of a great railway president or the commander of an army. Dr. Poindexter's judgment in practical affairs was highly valued by his friends. Dr. Jeter makes no exception, but says, "There was no man whose counsel we so much prized, and whose commendation we were so anxious to merit." And among many similar statements, add this from Dr. George B. Taylor: "Poindexter was a capital adviser, willing to study carefully a question presented to him, and then give frankly his views. I remember once, when two courses were open to me and I was much perplexed, I submitted the case to him. His opinion was given with such strong reasons in its favor as at once to relieve and decide me." His powerful influence over men was often shown, as we have seen, in healing estrangement between individuals or factions. It appeared also in his agency work. In fact, he used to be sometimes accused of extorting the last dollar, through his great personal influence and his vehement appeals in public and in private. Dr. Brown was very anxious to correct this impression, and remarks: "Some would seem to have thought him an artful and a merciless magician, that would charm them out of their money, or extort from them whether they would or not. This is a great mistake. If I should name that one agent of all whom I have known that was most scrupulous in awakening and addressing right motives for giving money, it would be A. M. Poindexter. As to getting the last dollar he could, hear a single fact. I was with him once when a revered brother now no more, after hearing his representations, promptly and cheerfully gave him his bond to Richmond College for a hundred dollars. In a walk which we took soon afterwards he remarked, 'I could have gotten three hundred dollars from this friend, but I wouldn't do it. He might have felt sore on reflection, and his benevolence would have been chilled. He will be glad that he has given this amount, and his benevolence will be cultivated rather than checked—a result at which I constantly aim.'" So wise and good a man as Dr. Poindexter would of course discern the principles involved in this matter, and aim at what was most judicious. If it be supposed that his ardent temperament and absorbed devotion to the object then in hand sometimes led him by overwhelming appeals to draw from persons more than they would be willing to give the next year for Foreign Missions, or a larger subscription for the College than they could be afterwards induced to pay up, this is only to say that he was human, and may have sometimes erred—not to dwell on the fact that the contributors were human likewise. In sooth, to obtain pledges which could not afterwards be collected, or repeated in a subsequent year, has been the fortune of others among us, who have never been successfully accused of overwhelming eloquence. Remember also that most of Dr. Poindexter's work as an agent was of a kind which he did not expect to repeat, and was performed in a state of things somewhat different from the present situation. There is no doubt that all agents should aim not simply at present results, but still more at such cultivation and seed-sowing as will promise a yet richer harvest in coming years.

As to attainments, Dr. Poindexter would hardly be considered a man widely read. His manner of life, as required both by temperament, health and the earnest wishes of his brethren, was unfavorable to extensive and varied reading; and he loved better to think profoundly upon great themes, than to range over the fields of literature. Yet he was well acquainted with leading writers in metaphysical and ethical philosophy, as well as with systematic theology, and was a thoughtful student of the Scriptures themselves. He once told Dr. Boyce that he had earnestly tried to decide for himself, as far as was possible, the exact meaning of every sentence in the Bible. He did not excel in verbal or exact exegesis, but had great power of putting himself in sympathy with the sacred writer's thought and tracing out the general connection of a passage. He had a good acquaintance with general history and particularly with the state of the world in our own time. He also read in rhetoric and in general literature. Whatever he knew he was apt to know accurately and permanently, and to make it the subject of fruitful reflection.

The Baptists of Virginia have had many great and noble leaders. We are tempted to sore depression at the thought that their places cannot be supplied. But in truth every great man is *sui generis*. This was emphatically true of A. M. Poindexter—he stood out in distinct outline as markedly different from all other men. And it was true of his chief associates in ministerial labor and denominational leadership. How curiously unlike were Poindexter and Jeter! Any attempt at comparison between them would run perpetually into contrasts. And how unlike to either was Taylor, or Howell, or William F. Broaddus! Yet they were all highly endowed, all deeply pious and all eminently useful. It is then idle to think of supplying such a man's place, by the substitution of another man. But the broad and busy field of human endeavor may be equally filled by successive generations, though no two individuals successively occupy the same space. Every one must strive, in simplicity and humility, and by the help of God's grace, to develop his individuality, to make the most of his inherited possibilities and providential opportunities. It may be true, in the sphere of religious or of political activity, that the present workers comprise no man equal to the great leaders of a former time. But let every man simply and faithfully do his best, and by God's blessing the world's work will still go on. Take care, O brother, if ever you begin to speak of discouragement, or hint at failure in any department of our dear Lord and Redeemer's service, take care—lest Poindexter should spring out of his grave to chide you. O, with what burning words would he tell of the work that now presses to be done; of the Master that is the same, while his servants go and come; of the grace of God that is sufficient to help, and the promises of God that are sure to be fulfilled! "Remember your leaders, who spake unto you the word of God; and considering the issue of their life, imitate their faith. Jesus Christ is the same yesterday and to-day, yea, and forever."

"STORY OF THE BAPTISTS."

Seventh Edition, Thirty-third Thousand.

BY R. B. COOK D. D.

416 pp., 16mo. Illustrated.

NOTICES OF THE PRESS.

" Dr. Cook has a direct and unaffected style, and puts on every page the glow of his earnest soul. We need popular works on this line, and we are sure that this book of Dr. Cook's will furnish helpful reading to many who are eager to know more of the Baptists. We warmly recommend it to the kindly consideration of the public."—*Religious Herald.*

"It should find a place in every Sunday-school library, and in the family libraries of our people. It will certainly be read with both interest and profit, even by those who have long been familiar with the wonderful story."—*The National Baptist, Phila., Pa.*

"It is a valuable addition to Baptist History."—*American Baptist Flag, St. Louis.*

"It is replete with interesting and valuable information."—*Tenn. Baptist.*

"A great amount of information of interest to every Baptist."—*Christian Herald, Detroit.*

"The story compasses the entire field."—*Journal and Messenger, Cincinnati.*

"It indicates great industry and wide research."—*Baptist Weekly, N. Y.*

"The book is admirably suited to enrich the Sunday-school library."—*Christian Index.*

"It is destined to meet with an immense sale, on account of its cheapness, convenience and general worth."—*Texas Baptist, Dallas, Texas.*

"We are sincerely happy to give it our warm endorsement. It is the best book of the kind that we know."—*Standard, Chicago.*

"As a popular history it has some decided merits, and supplies a large fund of information that will be most useful to any intelligent reader. We welcome any attempt to write the history of the Baptists, for comparatively few of our members know anything about it."—*Examiner, N. Y.*

"Three copies should have a place in every Baptist family, one to keep at home, and two to lend out to the neighbors. 'The Story' will be found full of interest and information, and interspersed with facts and arguments that must make a strong impression for truth and purity wherever read."—*Texas Baptist Herald.*

"The author presents an amount of exceedingly valuable information concerning Baptists, both in ancient and modern times, which is contained within no other volume within our knowledge. We believe that every Baptist parent would do well to put this book into the hands of his children. Such is the pressure brought upon the children of Baptist parents from outside influences that it is exceedingly important that they should be familiar with Baptist history and Baptist principles. We trust that the book may have a wide circulation; certainly it deserves it."—*Central Baptist, St. Louis, Mo.*

"Many facts are given that Baptists ought to know, and are not likely to learn outside the volume before us. It deserves, and is having a wide circulation."—*Western Recorder.*

"Ought to be in the hands of all young Baptists. Gives a plain, clear and concise history of the Baptists."—*Kind Words.*

"It contains a large amount of valuable information in an interesting form. It would be a good text-book for ministerial students in the schools for the colored people."—*Home Mission Monthly, New York.*

"We find this volume exceedingly interesting. The facts and incidents here collected cover a wide area of time and space, and are many of them intense and thrilling to a great degree"—*Christian Secretary, Hartford, Conn.*

SOLD BY SUBSCRIPTION ONLY.

AGENTS WANTED in every part of the United States and Canada.

OPINIONS OF PROMINENT MEN.

"A fine volume. You did well to be generous in the use of pictures in a book intended to go into all homes. They will interest old as well as young, and give such a varied view of men, institutions, churches, etc., connected with our denominational life, as will be instructive and inspiring."—*G. D. B. Pepper, D. D., LL. D., Prest. Colby University, Me.*

"I very heartily commend the work of Dr. Cook, 'The Story of the Baptists,' as worthy of a wide circulation."—*Henry G. Weston, D. D., President Crozer Theological Seminary.*

"Every Baptist family ought to have it."—*J. B. Hawthorne, D. D., Atlanta, Ga.*

"I very much hope that every member of the church and congregation, who possibly can, will have possession of this book. It is very necessary to have it."—*Wayland Hoyt, D. D.*

"It is the best book for general information ever offered the denomination."—*M. B. Wharton, D. D., Montgomery, Alabama.*

"I would like to put it in the hands of every Baptist in the land."—*F. H. Kerfoot, D. D., Brooklyn, N. Y.*

"Its perusal will give to all a clear and thorough view of our principles."—*Hon. Horatio Gates Jones, D. C. L., Vice-President Pennsylvania Historical Society.*

"I have read 'The Story'—every word of it. It is good, interesting and edifying. You have done the work well, condensed grandly. You have given us a large library in one small volume. Pastors and Superintendents would do a good thing to have several copies of The Story' in the Sunday-school and church libraries, and urge upon their people to read it."—*Rev. J. W. M. Williams, D. D., Baltimore.*

"It contains a vast amount of useful information."—*Robert Lowry, D. D., Plainfield, N. J.*

"I heartily congratulate you on the success of your book. It meets a felt want."—*Rev. T. T. Eaton, D. D., Louisville, Ky.*

"I have been much pleased with the perusal of this book."—*Rev. Wm. Henry Strickland, D. D., Nashville, Tenn.*

"I take great pleasure in adding my hearty commendation. I have read the book with great interest. It ought to have a place in every Sunday-school library and in the homes of our people. Parents could not do better than to put it in the hands of their children after they have read it themselves."—*A. J. Rowland, D. D., Baltimore.*

"You have attempted the *Multum in parvo*, and so far as I can judge from a mere glance, you have had remarkable success."—*W. S. McKenzie, D. D., Boston.*

"Very attractive volume. Real addition to my library, and helpful in my studies."—*Rev. Geo. E. Horr, Jr., Charlestown, Mass.*

"Contains a vast number of most interesting facts bearing upon the history of the denomination, and is worthy of a wide circulation. The book will do good."—*Prof. S. M. Shute, D. D., Columbian University, Washington, D. C.*

"You have done your work well, and I am glad it is appreciated by the public."—*Rev. J. M. Pendleton, D. D.*

"I have read 'The Story of the Baptists' with much interest. I am not surprised at its rapid and remarkable success. It should be in the hands of every Baptist, young and old."—*Wm. Cathcart, D. D., Author of the Baptist Encyclopædia.*

"It deserves to be called the 'Hand Book of Baptist History.' No book contains such accumulations of knowledge which every Baptist ought to know, and not knowing, should feel deeply ashamed of his ignorance. We sincerely trust that it may have as wide a sale as did Time and Ernest, and that it may serve its historical purpose as fully as did the latter book its appointed design."—*J. W. T. Boothe, D. D., Phila.*

"It is a valuable compendium of Baptist history and warrants me in endorsing all the good things said of it in the 'notices.' I congratulate you on your success."—*President James C. Clark, LL. D., William Jewell College, Liberty, Mo.*

LIFE AND WRITINGS OF
A. B. BROWN, D. D., LL. D.

By DR. and MRS. WM. E. HATCHER.

12mo., 352 pp., Cloth, $1.00.

WHAT THE CRITICS SAY.

"We have read with great interest this work; we went through the book in one afternoon, omitting but few of the 351 pages.—*Richmond Dispatch.*

"Have read the Memoir of Dr. A. B. Brown with thrilling interest and profit. Wonderful genius. Had no idea we had such a man among us."
—*J. W. M. Williams, D. D.*

"This volume is a worthy tribute of a loving heart and a graceful pen to the memory of a man of rare talents and of still rarer virtues. If any person can read the biography of Dr. Brown without at least desiring to attain higher intellectual and spiritual life, such a person must be insensible to the influence of example."
—*A. Broaddus, D. D., Sparta, Va.*

"Some of us remember well the intellectual face and head represented in the frontispiece to this volume. The book itself is a tribute of admiring Christian friendship, and supplies a most interesting record of a noble and beautiful career. The addresses of Dr. Brown are a valuable feature of the book."—*Standard.*

"This is a collection of loving sketches of a noble, remarkable and learned metaphysician, mathematician and linguist. His diffidence alone prevented such publicity as would have insured fame and rank among the scholarly and pious of the land. The book is full of deserved tributes to one of the best endowed men of mind, heart and piety. The memory of Dr. Brown deserves the perpetuity which his influence is sure to have. He was among the great and good who never die."—*National Baptist.*

"We knew Dr. Brown personally and loved him tenderly, and in view of this fact are all the better prepared to appreciate this memoir. The 'Sketch' is carefully prepared, well written and candid."—*Central Baptist, St. Louis, Mo.*

"The work is well done by editors and publishers, and deserves to be read by every Virginia Baptist and thousands in other States."—*Religious Herald.*

"I have been deeply interested in the clear and striking portraiture given us of one of the purest and best of men, and one of the noblest and most thoughtful of our scholars and teachers."—*Thos. Hume, Jr., D. D.*

"The life of Dr. Brown is intensely interesting."—*T. W. Sydnor, D. D.*

"This is a loving tribute to the memory of a noble man. Dr. Brown was an ardent, thorough scholar. In metaphysics, he stood without a peer among his brethren, and he was hardly less distinguished as a linguist. His memory in his native State is fondly cherished, and this memorial volume will be a treasured possession in many homes in Virginia, and especially where those are to be found who have shared in his ministry or his instruction."—*Zion's Advocate.*

"This is an affectionate tribute of friends, well and fitly rendered. We are glad to help perpetuate the memory of such a man, and to place him before the young as an example, and hence trust that the book will have a large sale."—*Journal and Messenger.*

"The publishers have gotten up the book in really excellent style, and have produced a fine specimen of bookmaker's art. In a word, this is a worthy tribute to one of the grandest intellects and noblest men who ever adorned the pulpit or the professor's chair, and should have a wide sale.
—*J. Wm. Jones, D. D.*

"The book sets forth clearly Dr. A. B. Brown. It is not a eulogy of him; indeed, there are some things mentioned which some of his admirers would prefer were omitted, but they are put in because needful to complete the picture and to show the man as he actually was. The editors must have got their methods of treatment from the Bible, since they deal with Dr. B. on the same principle on which the sacred writers deal with Abraham, Jacob, David, Elijah, Paul and the rest. And that is the only right way to do it."—*Western Recorder, Louisville, Ky.*

"I thank you very sincerely for the copy of the biography of Dr. Brown. I have not had a chance yet to read it, as one member of the family after another has been devouring it. They are delighted, and some of them are better judges than your correspondent, but he claims the privilege of reading and judging for himself, and thinks perhaps the half has not been told him. I doubt not, that the authors have risen to the height of the subject, and if so, they have done grandly.—*H. A. Tupper, D. D.*

www.ingramcontent.com/pod-product-compliance
Lightning Source LLC
Chambersburg PA
CBHW032006300426
44117CB00008B/920